LED ZEPPELIN

Heaven and Hell

LED ZEPPELIN

Heaven and Hell

AN ILLUSTRATED HISTORY
BY CHARLES R. CROSS
AND ERIK FLANNIGAN
WITH PHOTOGRAPHS BY NEAL PRESTON
PHOTO EDITING BY CHARLES R. CROSS AND NEAL PRESTON

WITH CONTRIBUTIONS BY JIMMY GUTERMAN,
DAVE SCHULPS, AND ROBERT GODWIN

RESEARCH ASSISTANCE BY BILL BRATTON AND HUGH JONES

ADDITIONAL PHOTOGRAPHS BY CHUCK BOYD, CHRIS DREJA,
ROBERT ELLIS, CLAUDE GASSIAN, HERB GREENE, SUSAN HEDRICK
COLLECTION, HUGH JONES COLLECTION, LONDON FEATURES LTD.,
JIM MARSHALL, HOWARD MYLETT COLLECTION, B. WENTZELL,
MICHAEL ZAGARIS

DESIGN BY CARRIE LEEB
PRODUCTION BY DAVID DAY

HARMONY BOOKS
NEW YORK

Published by Harmony Books, a division of Crown Publishers, Inc.,
201 East 50th Street, NewYork, New York 10022.
Member of the Crown Publishing Group.

HARMONY and colophon are trademarks of Crown Publishers, Inc.

Manufactured in the United States of America

Library of Congress Cataloging-in-Publication Data

Cross, Charles R.
Led Zeppelin: heaven and hell / Charles R. Cross and Erik Flannigan
with photography by Neal Preston.–1st ed.
p.   cm.
1. Led Zeppelin (Musical Group) 2. Rock Musicians–England
Biography. I. Flannigan, Erik. II. Title.
ML421.L4C76 1991
782.42166'092'2–dc20
[B]   91-3435

ISBN 0-517-583089

10 9 8 7 6 5 4 3 2 1
First Edition

CONTENTS

Part One

SHADOWS TALLER THAN OUR SOUL

SHADOWS TALLER THAN OUR SOUL

From Heaven to Hell with Led Zeppelin

Robert Plant, you've got great hair!" A kid is screaming this at the top of his lungs in the sort of impassioned cry you might expect to hear from a courtier who knows he has but one sentence in which to win his lover's heart. On the tape I am listening to the scream stands out from a field of screams, both because of its volume and because it is such a foreign thing to hear from the crowd at a rock 'n' roll concert. At any rock 'n' roll show you're bound to hear certain things shouted from the audience—"rock 'n' roll," "fuckin' great," and "Stairway to Heaven," are the top three from the audience at most Led Zeppelin shows—but most fans do not yell niceties about the sheen of the lead singer's hair.

The kid making the observation on Robert Plant's locks was in Tampa Stadium in Tampa, Florida, packed in with 56,800 other frenzied Led Zeppelin fans. The time was 40 minutes after eight in the evening of June 3, 1977. The moment was captured on audiotape by an enterprising young fan, presumably not the dude doing the screaming since you'd be crazy to yell into your own tape. The fellow who made this tape frequently recorded rock concerts in the Tampa area in the 1970s and he had one signature habit that identified concerts he taped: he would start his tape recorder a full five to ten minutes before the band came onstage. Consequently, all the recordings made by this taper start off with the crowd noise which builds as the band walks onstage and the concert begins.

The taper in Tampa has only recently begun to trade his recordings, so his tapes are newly in circulation among collectors. Recently, this taper sent a friend a six-hour tape that includes a 1981 Rolling Stones concert, a 1982 appearance by the Who, and the entire brief performance of Led Zeppelin from their Tampa Stadium gig in 1977. (The Zeppelin show is infamous because it was canceled after only 20 minutes due to rain and a makeup show was never arranged.) This tape affords the unique chance to compare the audience chatter and the excitement that precedes these legendary concerts by the three biggest acts in rock 'n' roll playing coliseum-sized venues in the seventies.

The Stones' 1981 tour was one of their most ambitious, with Mick Jagger parading around with a giant inflatable penis and playing from a stage that stretched like a football field. The band was touring for the first time in three years and promoting their hit album *Tattoo You*. Critics were again describing the Stones as the biggest act in rock 'n' roll, and the concert was called the tour of the year. It was such a looming event in the rock history of the eighties that some fans talked about the show for years after; it would be eight more years before the Stones would go back on the road again.

In 1982 the Who also came to Florida pushing a successful album, *It's Hard*.

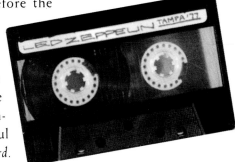

Though the band suffered from rifts between its members, they were still playing to the largest crowds of their long career, and fans had lined up in advance for what some thought might be the last chance to see one of the history-making superstar bands of the era.

These recordings of the Stones and the Who capture the excitement of the crowds before these sold-out concerts. Just listening to the tape you get the feeling something momentous is about to happen. The anticipation is apparent and when the bands are finally introduced, both are greeted with thunderous applause from their adoring fans.

But when my tape switches over to the Led Zeppelin portion of the recording, something entirely different is happening. As the tape begins, the crowd noise is so loud I imagined that for this particular show, the Tampa taper might have broken his rule and saved tape, like most bootleggers do, by only recording the actual music performed at the show rather than the preconcert chatter. The tape begins with screams, and yells, and primeval chants that are so loud you wonder just what in the hell has happened onstage. Has the band come on and begun tuning their instruments? Is this an encore? Is Robert Plant doing a striptease? Has there been a human sacrifice onstage?

But the band has not even come onstage yet. The tape continues, and the cheers go on and on, for another full five minutes and the band still doesn't arrive. People talk about being able to hear a pin drop in a crowd full of anticipation; at the Zeppelin Tampa show, the crowd was so loud and so excited you could not have heard a chainsaw start. When the band finally does arrive, the cheering sounds like an explosion. As Led Zeppelin are introduced, and begin, you might think the world has ended. Here is the loudest band in the history of rock, playing behind a monolithic sound system with stacks of Marshall amps looking like some Aztec monument to the Gods (none of this meek stuff like the Beatles had at Shea Stadium when they were drowned out by pubescent girls—this was equipment that could make your ears *bleed*), and you can't hear them over the applause. The fans are virtually foaming at the mouth with excite-

ment. Which is where our friend comes in and screams, "Robert Plant, you've got great hair." Even listening to the event on tape, almost 15 years later, you can't help but come away thinking, "This . . . *this* is a rock concert."

This is Led Zeppelin.

As I write this I am sitting in room 342 in the Edgewater Hotel in Seattle, Washington, and I am fishing out my window. This particular room was the one Jimmy Page usually stayed in when Led Zeppelin came to Seattle and I am here because it is the place most shrouded in Zeppelin history in my hometown. Once this was the nicest hotel in town; all the celebrities stayed here. Now it's considered merely very good, but it still sits right on Puget Sound and you wake up to the sound of ferry boats. The hotel used to loan rod and reel to the guests so they could "fish out your window," as a big sign on the side of the building boasted, but that little amenity was abandoned a few years ago. I've brought my own rod and tackle, hooked up some frozen herring, and tossed my hook out the window into the murky depths below. The water stinks and just having the window open is gross—I have no idea what I'll do if I catch anything.

Fishing from the Edgewater seems like the place to be, since this hotel looms large in the mythology surrounding Zeppelin: this was the place the group is rumored to have caught a shark and stuffed it up a poor groupie's private parts in some strange, sadistic act. The so-called mud shark incident is the single most famous sex act in rock history. It's the kind of story that makes hot copy whenever the Oprah show does something on groupies, and one day it may rate as a question in Trivial Pursuit or on *Jeopardy* (the *Jeopardy* answer: A mud shark. The *Jeopardy* question: What form of sea life was used as a dildo by the English rock group Led Zeppelin?). In the annals of "groupiedom" it ranks as the ultimate act of rock star degradation. The story's longevity probably owes more to Frank Zappa (who wrote a song about the incident) than to Zeppelin, though it is surprising how many peo-

JIMMY PAGE,
ROBERT PLANT,
DETROIT, MICH.,
APRIL 30, 1977

ple have heard about this incident. The Edgewater ought to install a brass plaque.

The sheer staying power of the story owes more to the fact that people *want* to believe it than it does to the truth. It confirms what everyone hoped was the case anyway, that these crazed English lads were so weird, they couldn't even cheat on their wives in the way normal folks do. It sounds exactly like the sort of act that sicko satanist Jimmy Page and hot cock Robert Plant would do, at least that's what most people thought. Sick again, indeed!

So if walls could talk, maybe Jimmy Page's room can provide the answer. I've already looked in the closet to see if a pile of mud sharks has been left (the band was also fond of leaving any fish they caught in the closets to surprise the maids). I have yet to find any aquatic animals or occult paraphernalia, and there are no groupies in sight. Even the vibes are decidedly mellow.

Just what are the facts of the mud shark inci-

dent? Well, first off, it wasn't a mud shark, it was a red snapper. And secondly, and perhaps most importantly, no member of Led Zeppelin had anything to do with the act. The band's former road manager, Richard Cole, proudly admits that he was the perpetrator and that the only member of the band even in the room was drummer John Bonham, who watched from the corner. Mark Stein of Vanilla Fudge filmed the whole scene, though no home video has yet been released. (Zeppelin were on the road with Vanilla Fudge at the time.) This all took place in Richard Cole's room and even Cole says the young woman was drunk, as was he, and she was willing. Cole caught the snapper from his window. Strange young woman, strange road manager, strange story, poor fish.

John Bonham was 20 years old at the time and he already had a bad habit of drinking too much, a habit that later would cause his untimely death. Two days later Led Zeppelin would get stranded in a snowstorm and most of the band would take refuge in a bar, with the exception of Bonham and

Plant who had to wait outside in the cold since they were too young to legally drink in America.

At the time of what has become known as "the mud shark incident," Led Zeppelin were on their first tour of America and they were the opening act. They barely had any groupies yet. With the exception of Page, who had toured the United States before with the Yardbirds, and Cole, a veteran of numerous shenanigans, they were mere kids who found themselves suddenly stars in a rock band in a country they knew nothing about. On the first tour they suffered from homesickness more than horniness, and Plant and Bonham were so lonesome they usually slept in the same room together. They were boys, not lechers.

If the incident can be thought to have proven anything, it was that Led Zeppelin had a rather perverse road manager. Cole would later go on to ride motorcycles down hotel hallways, insult Elvis Presley by swearing in front of him, and, when he was desperate for money, provide most of the dirty details that would make up Stephen Davis's book *The Hammer of the Gods*, the sensationalistic report of the band's offstage antics. What most fans who read *Hammer of the Gods*, or who passed along stories like the mud shark scenario, failed to note was that most of the stories seemed to revolve around Richard Cole himself rather than the members of Led Zeppelin. *Hammer of the Gods* is one of the best-selling books ever written on any rock band, and a surprising number of fans actually seem to believe that it is an authorized biography, done with the support of the band. Yet even while Cole dishes the dirt on his former bosses (who fired him in the late 1970s), he admits to having had a drug problem while working for Zeppelin. In *Hammer of the Gods*, Cole says he was "smacked out of my mind on heroin" by the time he was fired, so perhaps his perspective is not the one from which to judge Led Zeppelin from in the first place. The members of Zeppelin are very to the point whenever journalists have asked about *Hammer of the Gods*. Robert Plant says quickly, "That's true masochism. The whole humor of the band disappeared." The book, and many of the critics of the band, failed to take the suggestion Plant offered when he sang "Stairway to Heaven" in concert, putting great emphasis on the line "Does anyone remember laughter?"

The members of Led Zeppelin were no angels—they suffered with personal demons and over their lengthy career had their own bouts with heaven, and with hell. But ultimately what remains, more than a dozen years after the demise of the group, is a catalog of music that, as Jimmy Page was fond of saying in his best British accent, "speaks for itself, duden' it?" It also speaks as a powerful soundtrack for a generation, with a vibrancy and passion that seem even more obvious today. As for the band's offstage antics, surely many of the stories are true (even the band admits to suffering from "road fever" at times) and some of the tales of sex and drug use are substantiated. This sort of band behavior is not unique to Led Zeppelin, nor is it unique to their former road manager, but it is not the reason that more than a million people have paid in the vicinity of $50 for the Led Zeppelin remastered boxed set. At some point, the band seem to have given up on trying to defend themselves since there is ultimately no use telling the truth when so many people want to believe the myth. When asked about the wild stories revolving around the band by *Rolling Stone* in 1990, Jimmy Page again succinctly summed up the lack of perspective most fans had on the band: "It's only a myth to people who never heard us live, I suppose. I mean, if you heard us live, you'd know exactly where it was at."

The music of Led Zeppelin, as opposed to the myth, is what remains eleven years later, and it is the music that this book is all about. The popularity of the 1990 boxed set only proves what Zeppelin fans have known all along: that songs like "Tangerine," "Kashmir," and "Achilles Last Stand," exist as something separate and distinct from the band that created them. Listening to the boxed set today, the best of the music Zeppelin produced sounds better today than it ever did in the seventies (thanks in part to Page's remastering effort). I'm blasting a tape of it right now in the

FOLLOWING PAGES: THE FORUM, LOS ANGELES, CALIF., MARCH 24, 1975

Edgewater. Page and Plant always got into trouble in hotels like this for playing music too loud. The Zep boys preferred to crank up stuff like Little Feat and Joni Mitchell. Just imagine what my hotel neighbors think about hearing "Immigrant Song" at four in the morning.

Spread out in front of me are parts of the manuscript for what will become this book, along with the hundreds of photographs of the band that will be edited to provide the visuals. The pictures jump out at me in this dim light, and even in the two-dimensional form they accentuate the music coming from the boom box. Here's Jimmy Page at Bath in 1970 wearing that crusty old Giles hat and coat; here's Plant at Knebworth with his polka-dotted shirt tied at the waist; here's Jonesy trying to fade into a crowd backstage in Minneapolis; here's Bonzo drunk on the band's chartered plane. Most of the shots are from the book's photo editor, Neal Preston, whose extraordinary work stands above

the rest in capturing the true essence of Led Zeppelin. Queerly, it was Preston's work that provided the name for Stephen Davis's book on Zeppelin. Going through pictures with Page one day, Preston asked the guitarist what he was looking for in selecting the shots. "Power, mystery, and the hammer of the gods," Page replied. That considered, these shots represent the "real" hammer of the gods, and the true document of what Led Zeppelin was.

Preston began photographing the band when he was still a teenager, and at the time he was more a wide-eyed fan than a seasoned photographer. But perhaps because he loved the music of the band so, he had an eye for capturing their power and passion that few other photojournalists ever rivaled. Though many of Preston's shots have appeared on the band's album sleeves, on magazine covers worldwide, and in his own excellent book of black and white shots of the band, *Led Zeppelin Portraits*, most of the shots sitting in front of me have never been reproduced before, particularly some of the stunning full-color photographs. Additionally, Preston has collected some of the best work from other photographers, including such luminaries as Chris Dreja (from the Yardbirds), Jim Marshall, Herb Greene, among others who've shot the group over the years. The majority of this work has never seen the light of day before this publication.

The manuscripts in front of me are piled nearly to the ceiling. In words they document the music this band created on record and onstage. If Jimmy Page says the way to understand the myth of Led Zeppelin was to see them live, then the concert listings that appear here are the true legacy of the group on paper, and the next best thing to listening to the band. Other sources have attempted to record the band's performance history with marginal results, since like all aspects of Zeppelin's career what people want to believe the group did and what they *really did* are different matters entirely. Using tour itineraries, newspaper reviews, and the resources of several of the largest Led Zeppelin collectors worldwide, we have put together an annotated concert listing that relives many of the nights of magic this group created in the stadiums and concert halls they called "the houses of the holy."

Whereas other writings on Led Zeppelin have either been an attempt to ridicule the band (as much of the criticism in the rock music press did) or attempts by fans to pay homage to the group, this book attempts to present the sights and sounds of the group without either of those slants. If anything, I feel Led Zeppelin should be demystified—they are best understood when taken as musicians creating rock 'n' roll music, no more, no less. That music is what drew me to the band in the first place, and what drew the vast majority of Zeppelin fans, and it is what I listen to as I write this.

The photos and writings collected here are meant to tell the story of a four-piece rock 'n' roll combo and to shed new light on some of the critical illusions cast on Led Zeppelin over the years. Included is an analysis of where the roots of Zep-pelin's music really lay, as opposed to the popular theory that the group did nothing but rip-off old blues numbers (though of course they *did* rip-off a few). Many insights into the group's recording process are offered in the best interview Jimmy Page ever gave (and probably will ever give), where you can read in the words of the man who invented this group just what he had in mind when he took over the remnants of The Yardbirds and created Led Zeppelin. The phenomenon of Led Zeppelin collectibles is explored in detail, with an analysis of all the bootleg material from this group that has leaked out over the years. Until the release of the band's chronological live set (the dream project that Page mentions more and more frequently in interviews as the years go on), this material is the best representation of what this band was like in concert. And a song-by-song analysis, gives the details behind the writing and recording of every Led Zeppelin song released on record, from "Good Times Bad Times" off the first album through to "Travelling Riverside Blues" on the 1990 boxed set. Included are never-before-revealed details of how the band's music came together and how their seminal releases were recorded, planned, and executed. Ultimately, the best way for a reader to immerse him/herself in this work is to do what I'm doing at the moment: play the band's catalog as you read their story on paper. Just don't get the hotel manager after you.

I am still sitting in Jimmy Page's room but I am now doing something entirely un-Led-Zeppelin-like, which is watching MTV. I kind of doubt that Led Zeppelin ever sat around this room and watched Music Television, but you never know. Robert Plant was in Seattle recently, on his latest solo tour, and even Plant was back staying at the Edgewater again (he said it was for "old times sake"). Maybe Robert Plant sat around the room next door (he always stayed in 338) and watched the video to "Big Log."

The sound is off on the television and "In the Evening" is playing on the boom box while a video from a group called Warrant plays. I far prefer the Zeppelin soundtrack, but then I hate poser bands like Warrant. Who are these guys kidding? I know they sell a lot of records, but their music seems to appeal to the lowest common denominator. This particular song is really dull in places (especially on the vocal passages), very redundant, and certainly not worth the three and a half minutes Warrant gives it. It would seem that, if they're to help fill the void created by the demise of Zeppelin, they will have to find a producer (and editor) and some material worthy of their collective attention.

The last two sentences above are more than applicable to Warrant, but they were first written in 1969 to describe Led Zeppelin. The lines are from John Mendelsohn's review of *Led Zeppelin I* from the March 15, 1969 *Rolling Stone*. I've substituted Zeppelin's name for Cream, the group that in 1969 everyone was compared to, and Warrant's name for Led Zeppelin. It was this review in *Rolling Stone* that soured Zeppelin on the press and started one of the longest hate/hate relationships in rock 'n' roll. Even in interviews today the remaining members of the group talk about being hurt by the review. For being members of what was once the most successful performing group in the world, they sound remarkably sensitive. "We couldn't understand why or what we'd done to them," John Paul Jones recently told Q magazine. The band took it *personally*. On the other side, journalists seemed to take it personally when Page would describe their profession as one that practices "musical lobotomy." With those volleys fired, the press and the band squared off, and as Jones said, "We avoided them and so they started to avoid us." Even the seasoned vet Page took the reviews personally. He told Cameron Crowe in 1975, "I got really shattered by the press. . . . (So) I came down hard on the press for judging us. I once said that a lot of reviewers were frustrated musicians. And, through their own paranoia (the reviewers) came down on me personally, slamming me. And I was glad, because I knew I had hit their weak point." Page was right—most rock critics would die to be able to stand onstage and play the solo to "Heartbreaker"—but he didn't win the band any friends by saying so.

It wasn't that Zeppelin didn't get press—they got loads of it—it just wasn't the sort of press you'd want if you were a rock band. The critics really pissed the band off by calling both the band and their following "dumb." It was suggested more than once that Zeppelin's goal was to create a musical milieu to which their audience could get high. Most reviews were similar to this *L.A. Times* jab: "Their success may be attributable at least in part to the accelerating popularity among the teenage rock 'n' roll audience of barbiturates and amphetamines, drugs that render their users most responsive to crushing volume and ferocious histrionics of the sort Zeppelin has heretofore dealt in exclusively." *Variety* was no kinder even when the group was attracting the biggest box offices in history: "The combo has forsaken their musical sense for the sheer power that entices their predominantly juvenile following." This is just a sample of some of the things said about the band's music, not to mention the dirt written about their offstage antics.

Looking back at the press that the band received in their heyday, it is shocking to see how quick many critics were to dismiss the band. This is not to say that Led Zeppelin didn't occasionally deserve a critical roasting—any band with a half-hour drum solo in their live sets should be forced to listen to the solo every night, rather than be allowed to hang around backstage. And when critics pointed out the occasional overblown production and weak lyrics on the first two albums, they had a point. But rereading the reviews, and looking at them with 15 years of perspective, you wonder if anything Zeppelin ever could have done wouldn't have been trashed. No matter what direction they chose to go in they were met with caws, bellows, and whines. When they tried to establish an original heavy sound with their first two records, they were called "unoriginal" and even "slovenly." The third record, critics said, showed the group "going soft on us," and they were said to be trying to imitate Crosby, Stills, Nash, and Young. When they released their brilliant fourth album, critics called the effort "uneven." One of the deans of rock criticism, Lester Bangs, described "Stairway to Heaven" in *Creem* as "a thicket of misbegotten mush."

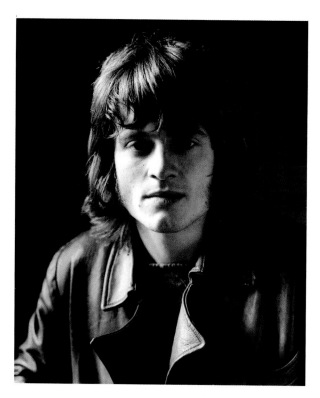

Houses of the Holy may have gotten the worst reviews of the band's long history, but it sold faster than any of their records had previously, and some writers had the nerve to knock the record simply because it was "just very good." *Physical Graffiti* was the first album to get a major review from *Rolling Stone*. (The review was lukewarm and the disc rated only three of five stars in *The Rolling Stone Record Guide*, but by the end of the 1980s the magazine was calling the record "the best double album in history.") *Presence* was routed all around, even by formerly sympathetic critics like Charles Shaar Murray from the *New Musical Express* who said, "I thought my razor was dull until I heard this album." Reviews of *In Through the Out Door* took an even more personal angle than the past: it was as if any record with Led Zeppelin on the cover was bound to get panned.

Paul Simonon of the Clash may have summed up the opinions of many journalists when he said, "Led Zeppelin? I don't need to hear the music. All I have to do is look at one of their album covers and I feel like vomiting." It was no surprise that Simonon's comment got wide circulation in the music papers.

Paradoxically, the 1990 boxed set contained the same Zeppelin music that had been on the band's albums over the years. But the boxed set, unlike the group's albums over the years, received almost universally excellent reviews. Could it be that if Jimmy Page had been able to do a little bit of remastering back in 1969 he might have gotten a positive response from the critics all along? It was the same damn music (and sometimes even the same damn critics) but like fine wine it seemed to go down a little better with age.

Something has happened over the decade since the demise of Led Zeppelin as a working entity. Once they stopped putting out new records, their critics stopped hating them so bad. The music industry has always been victim to a powerful nostalgia and some of that was at work in the reevaluation of Zeppelin by the media. No decade in the short history of rock 'n' roll was so quickly rejected and tossed aside as the seventies. Led Zeppelin was the quintessential seventies band so they were the first group thrown out the window in the early eighties. But as the eighties rolled down, the music

of the seventies began to seem idealistic and un-contaminated. And no group was reinvigorated as much as Led Zeppelin. What you might call the critical weight concerning Zeppelin took a dramatic shift.

In the music business it is not often that a group is critically reconsidered within such a short period of time, and the reemergence of Zeppelin's work is without precedent. Plenty of groups have released songs that bombed only to see them come back as hits a decade later. But Zeppelin's accomplishment was different since commercial success was theirs from day one. What this group was able to do since their break-up—and it is important to note that the remaining members of Zeppelin essentially did nothing to cause any of this shift, other than stay out of the spotlight and refuse to reunite—was watch music that had been routinely dismissed as populist sentiment suddenly become cutting-edge work. What had been considered the epitome of conformism was now fresh, admirable, and, in a word, cool. In the 1970s, Tanya Tucker, the Carpenters, Suzi Quatro, David Cassidy, Carly Simon, and Jackson Browne had all appeared on the cover of *Rolling Stone* magazine before the publication fi-

nally put Zeppelin on in 1975, despite the group's domination of the music industry during this period. And even though it wasn't until 1990 and the boxed set that Zeppelin again would appear on the cover of

the magazine (in a seventies retrospective issue), it must have felt tremendously satisfying to Jimmy Page to sit with a *Rolling Stone* reporter on that occasion and unself-consciously declare what at one point was an undeniable truth: "I thought I was in the greatest band in the world."

The Edgewater Hotel provides pretty spiffy accommodations. Page's former room is a stretched-out suite that and includes a sitting room and kitchen. This is a far cry from the Chateau Marmont in Los Angeles, the first place the band ever stayed in America on their initial tour of the States.

The room brings up an puzzling point: why did Page and the band even care what critics thought in the first place since by most measures they had achieved everything they ever dreamed of? Though it took a while for even the trade papers to report it, by the mid-seventies Zeppelin was the biggest thing ever to happen in rock 'n' roll, selling more tickets to shows than anyone had before, and selling albums on the day they were released at the rate of 300 copies an hour. And besides all that, they were fabulously wealthy. But Page did care, and that created one of the great ambiguities about this band: they forged ahead, ignoring the criticism of their naysayers but taking it personally nonetheless. Page once said that nothing about music came naturally to him—it was all a struggle—and perhaps he wanted to win something in this life without a fight.

I've cut off MTV since I'm sick of looking at pale imitations of Led Zeppelin. Perhaps the main reason the critical weight on Led Zeppelin finally shifted was because in the years since the band's departure from the scene, the shadow they cast has grown larger and taller. Zeppelin sold plenty of records and drew tremendous crowds to their concerts, but their most glorious feat was one they accomplished unintentionally: they were undeniably the most influential band of the last two decades.

For evidence, all you have to do is listen to rock radio, watch MTV, or take a peek at the *Billboard* charts. Heavy metal music was far and away the most popular genre of music over the past decade, and the successful bands of the eighties owe a tremendous debt to Zeppelin. To say that these bands were inspired by Zeppelin is not enough: Led Zeppelin virtually *invented* the entire form of metal rock 'n' roll in the eighties. So it comes as no surprise to learn that bands like Def Leppard attended the Knebworth shows or to see the guitar player from Guns N' Roses, Slash, wearing a Zeppelin T-shirt in publicity shots. (The largest merchandise firm in the United States reports that even in 1990 they sell more Zeppelin T-shirts than any other group.)

Everything from the way concerts are staged to the haircuts bands sport has been affected by Zeppelin, but what bands most wanted to emulate was the *sound* Zeppelin created. Jimmy Page's greatest achievements may have been as a producer. He not only made the recordings that still dominate rock radio, he produced a sonic sensibility that every

band in the eighties wanted. Hearing Zeppelin on the radio 15 years after Page produced the records, it is surprising how modern the music sounds. But part of the reason is that modern music sounds so Zeppelinlike.

Perhaps the ultimate irony of Led Zeppelin's career is that though the band refused to promote their singles, or to edit songs like "Stairway to Heaven" to meet AM radio standards, they still ended up dominating modern rock radio. In 1991 over 75 stations around the United States still feature weekly specialty sets of Led Zeppelin music. "Stairway to Heaven" is the single most-played song in the history of FM radio. One Florida radio station took Zeppelin's influence on radio a step further, deciding to switch to an all–Led Zeppelin format. Though the station eventually added other hard rock groups to their playlist, that any station would even consider limiting their music choice to the work of one group with only nine albums to their name is proof enough of the lasting impact and power of those albums. Modern sampling techniques have even made Zeppelin cloning a fine art, as drum and guitar riffs from the band continue to crop up in the work of other performers. Through sampling, John Bonham's drumming continues to live on to this day.

Zeppelin also changed the way the money flowed in the music industry by demanding a higher percentage of the profit than groups previously had sought. Eventually they even formed their own record label, proving that all bands really needed from the labels was distribution. Peter Grant, the group's manager, was a brilliant businessman and his savvy helped make the members of Zeppelin some of the first rock 'n' roll millionaires.

But if Zeppelin made big bucks, in concert they also delivered a big sound. The group was the first major rock act to use a quality sound system and to incorporate dynamic lighting and special effects into their performances. The Beatles were the only group that had previously toured giant stadiums, and they played through stadium P.A.s, which is why recordings of early Beatles concerts are unlistenable. Zeppelin cre-

ROBERT PLANT

CHICAGO, ILL.,

APRIL 8, 1977

ated a concert experience that was rivaled by no other band at the time and is memorable even today.

If you were to ask any of the remaining three members of Led Zeppelin what the key to understanding the band was, they would say it could be found in seeing the band live. As John Paul Jones told *Musician* in 1990: "To me the records were a starting point. The most important thing was always the stage shows. So many great nights. At our very worst, we were better than most people. And at out very best we could just wipe the floor with the lot of them."

The hotel manager has now phoned to complain for the third time and has warned me that the next time he has to call, I'm out on the street. Which is okay really since it's already four in the morning and I have to be getting to work soon. In homage to Jones I'm listening to "No Quarter" as recorded at the L.A. Forum on March 25, 1975. Jones's arrangement on mellotron was originally done in 1974, years before synthesizers made their mark on rock music. More than 15 years later it still sounds fresh and lively.

My friend Hugh first saw Led Zeppelin in concert when he was 13 years old, back in 1969. He now runs a record store in a university town and he says that nearly every college student he hires professes a love of Zeppelin, though some of them weren't even born back when Hugh was seeing the band perform. Hugh says that when his employees hear that he saw Zeppelin a dozen times they always stop and stare at him with awe, as if he had been witness to significant moments in the development of the world.

This reverence from the younger generation is why talk of a Zeppelin reunion tour is so constant. If the photos and letters sent in to Zeppelin fanzines like *Zoso* are an indication of the current following of the band, the majority of today's Zeppelin fans never had the opportunity to see the group perform live. The interest in a Zeppelin reunion tour is phenomenal, which is why promoters have talked offers of upwards of $150 million for the band to tour again. Robert Plant is the major stumbling block, but his attitudes about Zeppelin

tend to change over the years. When Plant first started his solo career, he swore he'd never do Zeppelin numbers in concert, yet by the late 1980s, he was even performing a few lines from "Stairway to Heaven" in concert.

This is how I justify my boom box blasting out Zeppelin concert tapes all night. "This stuff is history," I tell the hotel manager. In the late 1980s, some ticket agencies were already accepting deposits on seats for a rumored Zeppelin reunion. In 1990, with the appearance of the boxed set, a few ticket scalpers started advertising that Zeppelin tickets would be available soon. Time will tell if the action is premature, but what is evident is that the *desire* is there, and, strangely, seems to be building.

Until a reunion tour, the only way to capture the essence of the band is to listen to live tapes and bootlegged recordings. While supporting this sort of contraband seems illicit when it comes to many bands, with Zeppelin it seems almost appropriate. Even the band acknowledges that their live performances are the key to understanding the group and that understanding is not as easily conveyed by *The Song Remains the Same* soundtrack album as it is by the *Blueberry Hill* bootleg. A friend of mine reports meeting Jimmy Page a few years back and giving him a copy of a ten-album Zeppelin bootleg set. Page said, "Thanks," and continued walking on, as rock stars usually do when fans try to hand them momentos. But when he saw that the gift was a bootleg, Page stopped, went back to the fan, and said, "Thanks. This is great!" as if he'd just been handed the key to the city. That enthusiasm has not been shared by the band's management or record label (and at times not by Page himself), but it's the kind of response that shows Page to be as big a fan of Led Zeppelin as the next long-haired adolescent.

Listening to those tapes and bootlegs is proof that in concert, when they were good, Led Zeppelin were *very good*. When they were bad or mediocre, as Jonesy implies, they were still better than most. What this group attempted to create every night was nothing less than a monumental show: it was not your normal 45 minute rock 'n' roll set. They wanted to create a symphony of heavy

metal, a performance that with lights and sounds created "electric magic," as they described it at Earl's Court.

They asked more of themselves in concert than anyone else in rock and occasionally they weren't up to it. They played too long at times. During the 1975 tour they would occasionally stretch their concerts out for upwards of four hours but in that time they would only play 15 different songs. Page himself said he knew he could only play great one out of three nights. The band always seemed to come alive in Los Angeles, Boston, San Francisco, and New York, though, and recordings from those cities were almost always above par.

Whether you are a fan or not, one truth is undeniable about Led Zeppelin's live shows: they created a bludgeoning, powerful sound. Not only were they loud, for a four-piece band they sounded incredibly full. Though the group was, essentially, a power trio with a singer, the layers of melodies they laid down on stage rivaled that of a rock orchestra. And they could be very funky: as the group themselves described, they were "tight but loose" (a description that also provided the name for one of the first good Zeppelin fanzines from Britain). No major rock group has ever toured for so long without adding additional players to their stage show. This was testimony to the commanding musical prowess of Jones and Page, who created a wall of sound that Van Halen and Whitesnake together couldn't match. Page was phenomenal onstage, playing both rhythm and lead guitar on such guitar monoliths as "Kashmir" and "Achilles Last Stand." If the sound of their stage shows was occasionally a bit thin, it was limited only by what one man could create with one guitar (even if the guitar was a doubleneck).

Bonham was sensational behind a drum kit, taking the brute working-class English ethos he was born of and unleashing it every night on his skins. Jonesy once told *Musician*, "You can't help but swing if you've got John Bonham," and swing he did. It is the ultimate compliment that Jimi Hendrix offered to hire him away. At least part of the reason that Zeppelin disbanded after Bonham's death was because any other drummer would have been a step down from John Boham—there was no one better.

What Bonham did for Zeppelin in concert was to create a bottom, a monstrous and furious drum belly, from which the rest of the band could build their sound. This is exactly how a rock 'n' roll song is supposed to be built, but few bands ever follow the basic rules and do the hard work required to create a full and rich sound. Led Zeppelin never cut corners, building every track up from the basics. Even the signature tunes from the band designed to show off Page's phenomenal guitar riffs, songs like "Achilles Last Stand" and "Heartbreaker," all could stand on their own even without the guitar solos because they are so dense, so complete, so abundant. Even without guitar, the songs soared.

It was the punch of Led Zeppelin's bottom that popularized heavy metal music. Zeppelin didn't invent heavy metal but they refined it to an art form and perfected its execution. They hated the term when it was ascribed to their music, yet the bass and drum tracks on "Dazed and Confused" represent the epoch of heavy metal music. It is testament to Bonham and Jones that so few bands since have been able to create such thunder.

On top of it al there was Robert Plant, the quintessential front man for a British guitar band. Plant could sing anything from Elvis Presley to Robert Johnson. He could either recreate a song so perfectly that listening to tapes you'd wonder if it really was Elvis or Johnson singing, or he could take his voice and turn

whatever classic the band was covering into something all his own with his patented Zep-shrill.

Plant also had an incendiary sexual presence. He possessed a fondness for showing off his belly button, and he did this with such an innocence and lack of self-absorption, millions of teenaged girls fell in love with him. He also wore some of the tightest bell bottom trousers ever tailored, showing off bulges that figured in a decade's pubescent fantasies. Add to that package his aforementioned hair, which no matter when he was photographed, always looked perfect. Considering the band's exhaustive travel schedule you would have thought he'd wake up occasionally looking like Eraserhead, but instead he always had those hallmark ringlets.

Taken as a package, the four members of Led Zeppelin did what every great band does: together they created what they could never do individually. They described their first rehearsal of "Train Kept a Rollin' " as "magic" and the chemistry between the group was indeed extraordinary. Throughout it all they remained the best of friends, which was one of the reasons they couldn't go on when Bonzo passed away. Compare their harmony over the years with the Stones or the Who, and the band's unity seems even more remarkable.

Led Zeppelin also did something no other group in rock has ever accomplished: they quit with grace. At the time of Bonham's death the band was at their commercial zenith and had concert dates worth millions of dollars already booked in America. The newspapers went wild with speculation over who would replace Bonzo, and a dozen odd drummers were reported at one point to have gotten the nod. The band met in a hotel room in London and issued one eloquent sentence: "We wish it to be known that the loss of our dear friend and the deep respect we have for his family, together with the sense of undivided harmony felt by ourselves and our manager, have led us to decide that we could not continue as we were."

ROBERT PLANT AT THE SILVER- DOME, DETROIT, MICH., 1977

I am lying in bed now, a bed that once held the lanky frame of Jimmy Page. Page was fond of illuminating his hotel rooms with dozens of candles, rather than using the traditional lights, but I've decided not to go that far. The dawn is slowly breaking and more light is coming into the room.

Jimmy Page *was* odd. He was, and is today, a classic British eccentric, another product of the rigid English social system. Page quit art school to play rock 'n' roll, though I have to imagine that he would have been as weird an artist as he was a musician (and Zeppelin's album covers bear this out). It would be fair to call his interest in Aleister Crowley an obsession, but Page is an obsessive sort of fellow in everything he does, whether it is producing Zeppelin's albums or playing guitar. He is the ultimate control freak, and his approach to recording and producing records is shared by equally eccentric performers like Prince.

The idea for Led Zeppelin came to Page one day in the late summer of 1968. He had been a successful session player, he'd toured the world playing in a legendary group, he already owned a big house, and he had a great reputation as one of the hottest players on the scene. Page financed Zeppelin's first tour with his own money, risking his financial stability to take his new band on the road. In the first two years of Zeppelin's existence, the band did six tours of America, playing more nights in more cities than any other band had ever attempted previously. As Robert Plant would say years later in front of a crowd at the L.A. Forum, "We're playing our balls out," which is basically what the group did until they established themselves. They combined their talent with a work ethic that has never been matched, playing harder and longer than any group in history. They showed a willingness to play, and play, and they kept coming back to familiar markets, building word of mouth. Everyone who saw them came back next time with a friend. They enjoyed an exponential growth in fans after each visit.

Within two years, that hard work began to pay off as the band, and Page, met success that had never before even been suggested or considered possible for a rock 'n' roll group. From the moment their first album hit stores, without radio airplay, promotion, and much of a reputation, it had begun to sell and by the time their second album was released, advance orders were phenomenal. In contrast, the popularity of groups like the Beatles and the Stones was based on their hit singles, and not on the hard work of constant touring. When the Beatles did tour, they played for 30 minutes and followed several opening acts, and they played to kids who were already fans. Zeppelin used touring as a way to create an audience for themselves.

Over the ten years that would follow, Led Zeppelin found success on their own terms. Page refused to allow "Stairway to Heaven" to be released as a single. The group rewrote rock history by ignoring radio, ignoring the press and appealing directly to their audience.

Throughout it all, Jimmy Page remains an enigmatic figure, as unmovable as the rocks at Stonehenge, and as mysterious. When John Bonham died, the tabloids in England went nuts reporting stories with headlines like "Voodoo Mystery of Zeppelin Death" and "A Jinx That Haunts Led Zeppelin." One paper declared that "Bonham died as retribution for guitarist Jimmy Page's obsession with the occult." Another suggested that "Everyone around the band is convinced that dabbling in black magic is somehow responsible for Bonzo's death."

In *Hammer of the Gods* Stephen Davis quotes a French promoter named Benoit Gautier as saying that he "wouldn't be surprised" if Zeppelin did indeed make a pact with the Devil: "I wouldn't be surprised if you look at who died, and who suffered, and who survived. You have to believe that Satan is able to do that."

Rereading these comments, while lying in a room that Jimmy Page, the person—the human being—once occupied, I can't believe the heartlessness, the meanness, the utter inhumanity of those remarks. From mud sharks to pacts with Satan, the public seems to suspend normal human empathy when talking about Led Zeppelin, accepting preposterous malice of the sort that would never be

accepted if it were directed toward anyone outside of rock 'n' roll. Have you heard anyone describe a successful business executive as having sold his soul to Satan? Wouldn't we laugh this comment off instantly if applied to anyone else, anyone working in any other art form? Can one *really* believe that a pact with Satan is possible, and if so isn't *that* the big news story here?

There is no Devil in room 342 of the Edgewater Hotel, and I can't hear any voices saying, "Come to me sweet Satan," from underneath the bed. All I hear are the strains of my favorite Led Zeppelin song, "Tangerine," as it plays on my box. Page says this is one of the last songs he wrote without lyrical input from Plant and it is pure Jimmy Page. It is a gorgeous moment, a song that shows enormous humanity. "Tangerine, Tangerine," Robert Plant sings at first very quietly and then slowly increasing the power of his voice, "living reflection from a dream."

"Tangerine," like most great rock 'n' roll songs, is about one singular thing: the love between a man and a woman. There is no hidden meaning here, no secret messages, no grand themes, no arty statements. Robert Plant introduced the tune at Earl's Court as about "love at its most innocent." The song may mean more to me than it ever has to Jimmy Page, or to Robert Plant, or to John Paul Jones, or or than it did to John Bonham. But that's what music is supposed to do—create emotion in the listener.

To me, it is emotion that rests at the core of the music of Led Zeppelin. It speaks to my heart more than my head and my soul more than anything. It is this passion and ardor that remains the same, a full 20 years since Jimmy Page and Robert Plant sat around a campfire with acoustic guitars and first sang "Tangerine" together.

I crank it up another three notches on the boom box and wait for the knock on the door.

—Charles R. Cross

Part Two

OVER
THE
HILLS
AND
FAR
AWAY

YOUR TIME IS GONNA COME

The Blues and Other Inspirations

Its origins and its legend to the contrary, Led Zeppelin cannot with any accuracy be called a blues band. Their ventures into the strict twelve-bar blues form were few and for the most part tentative. Yet more than a decade after their demise, the notion that Led Zeppelin was a power-blues quartet remains commonly accepted.

Even when the group members did draw from the blues, they frequently showed a glaring want of taste (although it was precisely Led Zeppelin's lack of taste that often made them great). When the band's bassist and keyboardist, John Paul Jones, brought in an explicit blues idea to propel "Black Dog," he picked an idea off a cut from Muddy Waters' *Electric Mud*, one of that seminal bluesman's most pandering and least engaging records.

Jimmy Page was far more interested in, and adept at, filtering Indian and Celtic styles through his Marshall amplifiers than he was in updating Delta or Chicago blues styles. He had listened to the major bluesmen, all right, but he was no tradition-obsessed popularizer like John Mayall of the Bluesbreakers. At his greatest, Page was looking for-

ward into uncharted territory, not back toward the Mississippi Delta.

Unlike his predecessor in the Yardbirds, Eric Clapton, Jimmy Page was emphatically not a blues purist. Though fans of the Yardbirds wanted Page to follow in Clapton's footsteps, Page saw music through the widest of screens. He often spoke of the Everly Brothers and Ricky Nelson as early influences (especially Nelson's guitarist, James Burton, who also played with Elvis Presley), and he listed classical guitarist Andre Segovia as one of the shared passions that brought him together with his Yardbirds bandmate Jeff Beck. The first song that Page says ever moved him was "Baby, Let's Play House" by Elvis Presley, with Scotty Moore on guitar. "I heard that record and I wanted to be part of it," Page says.

Early on, folk was more important to Led Zeppelin than the blues, and not just the expected Celtic variety. American folk and folk-rock were integral in uniting Page and Plant. It's a matter of record that it was Joan Baez's version of "Babe I'm Gonna Leave You" that inspired their own, and the two of them often praised West Coast folk-rockers like Buffalo Springfield and Crosby, Stills, Nash, and Young. (Page once described CSNY as "real music," leaving some critics to

FACING PAGE: AN OUTTAKE FROM A 1967 YARDBIRDS CHRISTMAS CARD PHOTO SHOOT. PETER GRANT WAS DRESSED AS SANTA IN THE ACTUAL CARD. FOLLOWING PAGES: ROBERT PLANT, JOHN PAUL JONES, JIMMY PAGE, 1970

wonder just what he thought Zeppelin's music was.)

What set the young Led Zeppelin apart from other "heavy" outfits was, more than anything, their catholic tastes. Among the many cover versions they performed in concert in the early days were Joni Mitchell's "Woodstock," Curtis Mayfield's "Theme from Shaft," Roy Orbison's "Only the Lonely," the Ventures' "Walk, Don't Run," Neil Young's "Cowgirl in the Sand," Buddy Holly's "Peggy Sue," Paul Simon's "59th Street Bridge Song," Sly and the Family Stone's "Everyday People," Ben E. King's "Stand by Me," the Beatles's "I Saw Her Standing There," Little Richard's "Long Tall Sally," and Chuck Berry's "No Money Down." If Led Zeppelin was a blues band, why weren't they covering more blues tunes? Over the course of their performing history the group covered more songs performed by Elvis Presley than they did Robert Johnson tunes.

Early in their career, the group did make passes at some classic blues numbers, but the result was often either parody or self-parody, usually with some amount of arguable plagiarism as a confounding variable. It took a threat of legal action to compel writers Page and Plant to pay Willie Dixon for *Led Zeppelin II*'s "Whole Lotta Love," which even cursory examination reveals to be a knockoff of "You Need Love," a Dixon song popularized by Muddy Waters. They loved the blues, all right, but they did not know what to do about it except say so.

Needless to say, the group members were familiar with Dixon's work, having covered his "You Shook Me" on their debut LP, being familiar with the song both from the Muddy Waters original and the version they heard the Jeff Beck Group perform live. Another song from the debut, "How Many More Times," takes off from Howlin' Wolf's Memphis smash "How Many More Years," with a bit of Albert King thrown in. And "The Lemon Song," from *Led Zeppelin II*, grafts the "squeeze my lemon" line from Robert Johnson's "Travelling Riverside Blues," a song they were covering for a BBC recording session, onto Howlin' Wolf's "Killing Floor." In fact, the first British pressings of *Led Zeppelin II* credited the tune to "Burnett" (Howlin' Wolf's given name) until the issue was settled in an out of court agreement. The controversy over Jake Holmes's "Dazed and Confused," another similar Zeppelin track precursor, remains unresolved and when asked about the remarkable similarities between the two tracks Page avoids the subject.

You can call Led Zeppelin musical pilferers, or you can call them talented fans who could take others' ideas and expand on them. When John Bonham kicked off "Rock and Roll," from the fourth album, with the William O'Connor drumbeat from Little Richard's "Keep a Knockin'," he was taking something he loved and incorporating it into his own work. Rock 'n' roll is full of loving quotes, although Led Zeppelin quoted so frequently it was sometimes easy to wonder whether they were writers or copiers. The band members must have been aware of this, as reflected by the press photos shot around the time *Presence* came out, in which they prowl a recording studio floor full of albums they have pillaged. But even detractors of the band must acknowledge that they borrowed less as they developed, and their greatest work didn't come until they began to discover their own ideas.

Those ideas owed at least as much to soul as they did to the blues—it's no accident that the Albert King song interpolated into "How Many More Times" was written by members of Booker T. and the MGs, whose work at Stax defined most listeners' and players' idea of what soul music could be. Plant has reported that the first single he bought and loved was Smokey Robinson's double-sided monument, "Shop Around," backed with "Who's Loving You." Especially in its rhythms, soul music was a major influence on Led Zeppelin. Traces of the Al Jackson/Duck Dunn (Stax) and Benny Benjamin/James Jamerson (Motown) rhythm sections work their way into the beats that Bonham and Jones locked into. Both Jones and Bonham cited soul music as an inspiration, and Jones also had been greatly influenced by classical music. Page's rhythm guitar phrasings on the band's first two albums owe far more to Steve Cropper (Stax) than Jimmy Rogers (Chess). What Page picked up from Cropper was the notion that putting a song across was more important than any solo section. This soul aesthetic was one that served Page well during

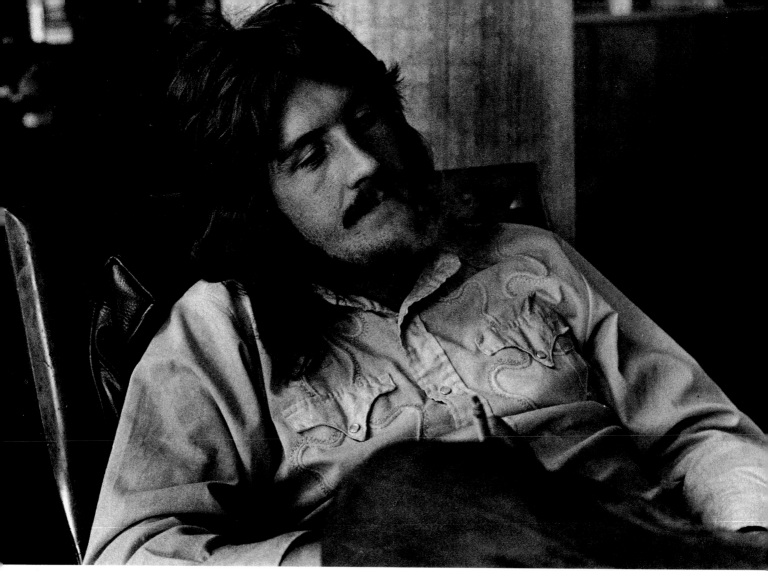

his days as a session player; in Led Zeppelin, it insured that his guitar mastery rarely detracted from the song at hand.

Yet the idea of Led Zeppelin as a blues unit remains remarkably persistent. It is encouraged by the former band members: as he ages, Robert Plant speaks more and more glowingly about people like Willie Johnson and Bukka White, folks he mentioned infrequently during the thousand-odd interviews he conducted during Led Zeppelin's heyday. The inclusion of a BBC-broadcast take of Robert Johnson's bottleneck "Travelling Riverside Blues" on the group's 1990 boxed set institutionalizes the judgment. Fifty million Led Zeppelin fans can't be wrong, so there must be something to the claim. What is it about Led Zeppelin that summons up the blues for many people? One can dismiss the charge by asserting that the vast majority of people who bought, say, *Houses of the Holy* never heard of Skip James, but even the group's more knowledge-

able fans (among them many musicians) claim their place in the blues.

JOHN BONHAM, SAN FRANCISCO, CALIF., 1970

The answer starts in an unlikely place, their 1976 album *Presence*. The group's seventh release, it was one of the few not immediately considered some sort of classic upon release, and although it was a substantial hit, it was their least successful album, as far as American chart action was considered, since their debut seven years earlier. Of all their collections, it was certainly the one pieced together under the most difficult circumstances. Plant was still recovering from a terrible auto accident (which prevented him from standing up during recording). The band spent much of their time putting finishing touches on the film and soundtrack to *The Song Remains the Same*, which came out a few months later, and even before it was released the group members acknowledged that the film, drawn from long-past Madison

Square Garden dates, did not come close to capturing what made Led Zeppelin at its peak at once both direct and mysterious from an arena stage. Yet they felt locked into the film, and plowed on.

While recording *Presence* they did far more than merely plow on out of a sense of duty. There is a far different attitude in *Presence* than its predecessor, the double *Physical Graffiti*. That set was all about excess (musical and lyrical) and how much the group members could stick into a song without it overflowing. Its premier cut, "Kashmir," epitomizes this idea. It is the most tense number Led Zeppelin ever recorded, guitars colliding and coalescing with synthesizers, John Bonham's massive drums holding sway over Plant's Middle Eastern visions. One extra element and that song would explode; one less and something important would seem to be missing—it would evaporate.

But when they went in to record *Presence*, Page, Plant, Jones, and Bonham acknowledged that they had taken the idea of more-is-more as far as it could go. (The first rumblings of punk in England around the same time probably also encouraged the process.) The next step, perhaps one partially directed by Plant's physical condition, was to step back, cut musical elements closer to the bone, and on cuts like "Candy Store Rock" and "Tea for One," listen to the Led Zeppelin that remained.

Blues is about stripping down to the essentials, both musically and lyrically, which accounts for much of the attraction it holds for many rockers. It is no romantic notion to suggest that the ideas that propel blues songs are more down-to-earth than those of nearly all other forms of American popular music; only hard country comes within shouting distance. After a thousand overlong guitar and drum solos, a thousand damaged hotel rooms, a thousand photo studios, a thousand airline terminals, Led Zeppelin was ready to shut itself off from the world and do nothing but lean into the music. They were stripping down, and the simple act of peeling away layers of self-consciousness brought them closer to the blues.

The opening salvo on *Presence*, "Achilles Last Stand," is typical Led Zeppelin in some ways (it's too long, Plant's lyrics don't survive close inspec-

tion), yet it is also something altogether different. It is not grounded in traditional twelve-bar blues form, yet it is as drenched in broad blues feeling as a straight-ahead rock song can get. Page bends into the song with a gnarled, distorted introductory figure that gets louder each time it is repeated, and then it resolves into the loudest boom of this band's anything-but-sedate career. This is a Big Noise, with Page's guitar comments slicing through Plant's narration, yet "Achilles Last Stand" is somehow different from what is on the half-dozen records that came before. The sympathy among the players is far less contingent on volume and tempo than it had ever been before; although the tune rocks as ferociously and straightaway as anything Led Zeppelin had recorded, this has a grace to it, a hint at least of a traditional blues base.

One could even refer to the interplay on *Presence* as friendly, the hard-rock equivalent of four mates on a back porch. Page's diverse lead lines and compact, compressed solos are a tour-de-force journey through dozens of styles (among the unlikely touchstones are Pete Townshend and Hubert Sumlin). At the same time, Plant's singing is his least affected: no upper-register showing-off, no callow asides, no gimmicks. For once, he's content to be only himself; for once, there's nothing between him and the microphone.

In rock 'n' roll that does not overtly ape the twelve-bar blues form, the blues shows up as an intensity more than a sound. Rock 'n' roll albums as diverse as Van Morrison's *Astral Weeks*, Neil Young's *Tonight's the Night*, and Bruce Springsteen's *Nebraska* look to the blues for inspiration, not specific ideas. Gifted white rockers all, Morrison, Young, and Springsteen hear the blues plaints of Charley Patton and Son House rattling in the back of their brains, and they respond to those sounds as signposts and goals. They know it is foolish for them to try to sound like a world-weary bluesman, but they are so attracted to the music that they cannot help but wish to claim some of its power. They can explore new frontiers this way, without pretending to be something they are not and will never be. They are in love with the blues, and their love is returned.

as famed blues stick men Willie Steele and Francey Clay. That's the only element Led Zeppelin needs to latch onto a tradition that suits them well only in altered form and turn in an outstanding performance.

Led Zeppelin expanded from there, got more original, and then collapsed in tragedy. The follow-up to *Presence, In Through the Out Door,* was their broadest record yet, and some of their later tracks collected on the posthumous *Coda* ("Ozone Baby," "Wearing and Tearing," "Poor Tom," "Bonzo's Montreux") indicated that they were still energetic and wily enough to exploit new sources.

But once in a great while, Led Zeppelin could attack blues form on its own terms. Rich in dark harmonica and Delta-inspired imagery, "When the Levee Breaks" (from the untitled fourth album) is perhaps the one time Led Zeppelin worked close to the constraints of twelve-bar form and flourished. (Granted, the tune originated with Memphis Minnie in 1929.) Blues for the members of Led Zeppelin was not a form so much as it was a dare from them to match the music they loved so much. So when fans (and former members of the band) refer to Led Zeppelin as a blues band, what they really mean is that the members of Led Zeppelin were blues fans who acted on their influences. And as a track like "Achilles Last Stand" screams out, for a band as ambitious as Led Zeppelin, that influence was sometimes all they needed to fly.

It's this high road that Led Zeppelin travels on a performance like "Achilles Last Stand." After more than a half decade of blues assays that verged on parody (even if some of them made Howlin' Wolf and Willie Dixon wealthy men), the group members learned that the only way for them to draw on the blues was to use that inspiration as a means to create something new, something their own. In fact the most overt blues element of "Achilles Last Stand" here is coming from, of all people, the drummer. At the end of each chorus, Bonham playfully but very

—Jimmy Guterman

THE CRUNGE

Jimmy Page Gives a History Lesson

You could describe Led Zeppelin's relationship with newspaper and magazine journalists in one succinct headline: "Led Zeppelin v. The Press." Though they were the biggest group in rock 'n' roll during their prime, you wouldn't have known it from the major music papers. Robert Plant once summed up the band as "Loved by their fans, and hated by their critics."

From their genesis in 1968, the band seemed to start on the wrong foot. "We had appalling press at the time," John Paul Jones said in 1990. "We got to America and read the *Rolling Stone* review of the very first album, which was going on about us as another hyped British band. We couldn't believe it. In our naivete, we thought we'd done a good album and were doing all right and then all this venom comes flying out. We couldn't understand why or what we'd done to them. After that we were very wary of the press, which became a chicken and egg situation. We avoided them, so they started to avoid us." That *Rolling Stone* review by John Mendelsohn, suggested that the band "find a producer (and editor) and some material worthy of their collective attention." Jones said the review "helped foster my general hatred of the press." The few journalists who didn't feel that hatred were ones like Lisa Robinson and Chris Welch who were so friendly with the band that one got the impression Lisa and

Chris were writing about friends, not musicians.

Led Zeppelin went through periods of not speaking to the press at all, then they would change their minds and do slews of interviews in one day. They occasionally took their dislike of journalists to extremes, as when John Bonham punched out a reporter for the English magazine *Sounds*. Most journalists knew better than to get in Bonham's way and few reporters seemed interested in hearing what John Paul Jones might have to say even though his insights into the band were frequently illuminating. "They want to interview the stars, not the rhythm section," Jones was fond of saying.

Robert Plant did more than his share of interviews and gained a reputation as the friendliest band member. Years later he would admit to frequently making up complete falsehoods to get interviewers off his back. And though Plant's involvement in the band was essential, he still lacked the perspective offered by Page, who had come up with the original concept for the band and had written most of the songs. "I'd lived every second of the albums," Page said in 1977, "whereas the others hadn't."

Jimmy Page's reputation for being a "tough interview" grew nearly as legendary as his reputation as a guitarist. He told more than one interviewer to take a hike and was known for responding to questions with "Don't ask me that question" or "Well, it's a fact, isn't it?" if the question didn't please him. As stories of the band's offstage antics began to creep into the press, Page became even more elusive. He got so sick of being asked

WITH COMPLIMENTS

JIMMY PAGE
PLUMPTON PLACE
PLUMPTON
SUSSEX

IN THE EVENING.
JIMMY PAGE
AT THE MYRIAD
IN OKLAHOMA
CITY, APRIL 3,
1977.

about Aleister Crowley and black magic in the late 1970s that he began turning down most interview requests from establishment newspapers.

Page showed a marked dislike for the larger music papers and daily newspapers but he would occasionally go out of his way to speak to journalists representing smaller publications, closer to the level of fanzines. Though the band refused for years to talk to *Rolling Stone* reporters, they frequently allowed fanzine editors to hang out backstage and on their jet. When Page sat down with the English fanzine *Zig Zag* in 1973, he explained the early years of the band with rare candor, and it was one of his best interviews of the period.

But the best interview Jimmy Page ever did was with a small fan-oriented rock magazine called *Trans-Oceanic Trouser Press* in 1977, at the height of the band's accomplishments. *Trouser Press* called itself "America's Only British Rock magazine" and that moniker, along with shoestring financing, limited the magazine's reach to about 20,000 hardcore record collectors in the United States. As the magazine noted in their original introduction to the Page interview, "We wondered whether he'd want to take the time to talk to a magazine whose circulation was not exactly in the same league with, say, *People*, or even *Rolling Stone*." But when *Trouser Press* asked for an exclusive and extensive interview with Page to span his entire career, the guitarist agreed. Swan Song publicist Janine Safer was a big fan of *Trouser Press* and, as it turned out, so was Jimmy Page.

Dave Schulps, senior editor of *Trouser Press*, spent more than six hours with Page, one of the longest interviews Page ever did. The interview was scheduled to happen on the East Coast after the band's 1977 Madison Square Garden gigs, but Page was too tired to talk. So Swan Song put Schulps on their chartered jet with the band and flew him to California. Schulps ended up snagging the guitarist on three separate occasions a few days later in Beverly Hills. The interviews took place at the Beverly Hilton Hotel, on June 16 and 17, 1977, while the band had a brief break from touring. The discus-

sion concluded on June 19, 1977 following a show earlier that night in San Diego. Schulps writes of the interview today, "Looking back on this interview nearly fifteen years later, two things strike me as remarkable about it. First, that in all the years since, there really hasn't been another one quite like it, and second, how rarely the Jimmy Page I saw has shown himself to journalists. The picture of Page that emerged during our three interview sessions was that of a physically frail, but extremely intelligent, man, very much in control of himself. He was patient, thorough and friendly, as well as extremely knowledgeable, up-to-date, and opinionated about virtually any musical topic. He was also open to any question that pertained to his *music*, though he was guarded about his private life and practices. Frankly, I wasn't there to talk about that and to this day could care less what he does in the privacy of his home."

Writing in 1977, at the time of the interview, Schulps described the guitarist as "remarkably thin and pale, his sideburns showing a slight touch of gray, his skin exhibiting a wraith-like pallor. I found it hard to believe this was the same person I had seen bouncing around the stage at Madison Square Garden earlier that week. Speaking slowly and softly, in a sort of half mumble, half whisper that matched his frail appearance, Page seemed to have an excellent memory for detail considering the time that had elapsed since the period we discussed."

During the interviews Page discussed everything from the early influence of Indian music to Bob Dylan's *Blood on the Tracks*, which he said he loved. "When you heard it," Page said of the Dylan album, "you realized it was the thing that was missing." Schulps says that during the interview Page made numerous references to demos and "instrumental versions" of Zeppelin songs and pulled out a box of tapes and played them for Schulps, including a demo for "Kashmir" featuring just Page and Bonham. The tapes included a strange number, yet to be released in any form, that Schulps describes as "a song featuring Page on guitar, Keith Richards on rhythm and vocal, Ronnie Wood on bass, and Charlie Watts, I think, on drums, recorded at

Wood's home." Page also played some of his favorite music of the moment during the interview, including the Damned, a group he couldn't say enough about.

Schulps now works in radio syndication on the popular shows *Rock Today, Metalshop,* and *Desert Is-*

PAGE AT THE ELECTRIC MAGIC SHOWS, LONDON, NOVEMBER 1971.

land Discs and is vice president of Talent Acquisition at MJI Broadcasting. He did get the chance to interview Page again ten years later during rehearsals for the Firm tour. "He didn't seem to remember me or *Trouser Press,*" Schulps notes, "but he was gracious enough to sign the cover of the magazine in which this interview first appeared."

DAVE SCHULPS: *What were your ambitions as a young guitarist? You kept out of the limelight for quite a while, not playing with any groups except Neil Christian until you joined the Yardbirds.*

JIMMY PAGE: Very early, once I started getting a few chords and licks together, I did start searching feverishly for other musicians to play with, but I couldn't find any. It wasn't as though there was an abundance. I used to play in many groups . . . anyone who could get a gig together, really.

This is before you joined Neil Christian?

Just before Neil Christian. It was Neil Christian who saw me playing in a local hall and suggested that I play in his band. It was a big thing because they worked in London, whereas I was from the suburbs. So there I was, the 15-year-old guitarist marching into London with his guitar case. I played with him for a couple of years.

Did he have a big local reputation at the time?

In an underground sort of way. We used to do Chuck Berry and Bo Diddley numbers, bluesy things, before the blues really broke. In fact, half the reason I stopped playing with Neil Christian was because I used to get very ill on the road, glandular fever, from living in the back of a van. We were doing lots of traveling, the sort of thing I'm used to doing now. I was very undernourished then. It wasn't working right either; people weren't appreciating what we were doing. At that time they wanted to hear Top 20 numbers. I guess you could put it pretty much akin to the pre-Beatles period in America, except that this was a couple of years before that. I was at art college for 18 months after I left Neil Christian, which was still before the Stones formed, so that dates it back a way. The numbers we were doing were really out of character for the audiences that were coming to hear us play, but there was always five or ten percent, mostly guys, who used to get off on what we were doing because they were into those things themselves as guitarists, record collectors. You'll find that nearly all the guitarists that came out of the '60s were record collectors or had friends that were collectors of either rock or blues. I used to collect rock and my friend collected blues.

Did you swap?

He wouldn't have any white records in his collection. He was a purist. I remember going up to a blues festival in the back of a van the first time a big blues package tour came to England. That was the first time I met Mick Jagger and Keith Richards . . . pre-Stones.

Were you into the blues as much as the Stones or was it more rock 'n' roll for you?

I was an all-arounder, thank God.

Do you think that's helped your career?

Immensely. I think if I was just labeled a blues guitarist I'd have never been able to lose the tag. When all the guitarists started to come through in America—like Clapton, Beck, and myself—Eric, being the blues guitarist, had the label. People just wanted to hear him play blues. I saw the guitar as a multifaceted instrument and this has stayed with me throughout. When you listen to the various classical guitarists like Segovia and Julian Bream, brilliant classical players, and Manitas de Plata doing flamenco, it's two totally different approaches to acoustic. Then there's Django Reinhardt and that's another approach entirely.

In those early days I was very interested in Indian music, as were a lot of other people too. Most of the "textbook" of what I was forced to learn was while I was doing sessions, though. At that point you never knew what you were going to be doing when you got to the session. In America, you were a specialist. For example, you would never think of Steve Cropper to do a jazz session or film session or TV jingles, but in Britain you had to do everything. I had to do a hell of a lot of work in a short time. I still don't really read music, to be honest with you. I read it like a six-year-old reads a book, which was adequate for sessions, and I can write it down, which is important.

What was your first guitar?

It was called a Grazioso. It was a Fender copy. Then I got a Fender, an orange Gretsch Chet Atkins hollow body, and a Gibson stereo which I chucked after two days for a Les Paul custom which I stuck with until I had it stolen . . . or lost by T.W.A.

What got you into guitar playing? You listened to a lot of music being a collector, so was it just hearing it on record?

Exactly. I've read about many records which are supposed to have turned me on to want to play, but it was "Baby, Let's Play House" by Elvis Presley. You've got to understand that in those days "rock 'n' roll" was a dirty word. It wasn't even being played by the media. Maybe you'd hear one record a day during the period of Elvis, Little Richard, and Jerry Lee Lewis. That's why you were forced to be a record collector if you wanted to be part of it. I heard that record and I wanted to be part of it; I knew something was going on. I heard the acoustic guitar, slap bass, and electric guitar—three instruments and a voice—and they generated so much energy I had to be part of it. That's when I started.

Mind you, it took a long time before I got anywhere, I mean any sort of dexterity. I used to listen to Ricky Nelson records and pinch the James Burton licks, learn them note for note perfect. I only did that for a while, though. I guess that after one writes one's first song you tend to depart from that. It's inevitable.

How old were you when you left Neil Christian and started going heavily into sessions?

I left Neil Christian when I was about 17 and went to art college. During that period, I was jamming at night in a blues club. By that time the blues had started to happen, so I used to go out and jam with Cyril Davies' Interval Band. Then somebody asked me if I'd like to play on a record, and before I knew where I was I was doing all these studio dates at night, while still going to art college in the daytime. There was a crossroads and you know which one I took.

Do you remember your first studio session?

I think it was called "Your Momma's Out of Town," by Carter-Lewis and the Southerners. Wait a minute; I'd played on one before that, "Diamonds" by Jet Harris and Tony Meehan, but that

didn't mean anything to me. They were both hits and that gave me the impetus to keep on doing it. If "Your Momma's Out of Town" hadn't been a hit, though, I might have abandoned it then and there.

In retrospect, you think you made the right move by doing sessions?

I think so. It kept me off the road until such time as it became stagnant and it was time for a change. I was doing pretty well with Neil Christian, as far as money went, and to come out of that and go to art college on a $10 a week would seem like insanity to a lot of people, but I'd do it anytime if it were necessary—make a drastic change if it had to be.

I'd be interested in your reminiscences of some of the groups you did or were supposed to have done sessions with. If you wouldn't mind commenting, I'll just run down a few of them. You worked with Them . . .

A most embarrassing session. Before we even start, I should say that I was mainly called in to sessions as insurance. It was usually myself and a drummer, though they never mention the drummer these days, just me. On the Them session, it was very embarrassing because you noticed that as each number passed, another member of the band would be substituted for by a session musician. It was really horrifying. Talk about daggers! God, it was awful. There'd be times you'd be sitting there—you didn't want to be there, you'd only been booked— and wishing that you weren't there.

I heard Shel Talmy used to keep you around Who sessions and Kinks sessions, just in case you were needed, without really planning to use you in advance.

Well, I was on "Can't Explain" and on the B side, "Bald Headed Woman," you can hear some fuzzy guitar coming through which is me.

Did you work concurrently with Big Jim Sullivan when you were doing these guitar sessions?

At one point, Big Jim was the only guitarist on the whole session scene. That's the reason they really picked up on me, because they just didn't know anyone else but Jim. Obviously, there were many people about, but I was just lucky. Anyone needing a guitarist either went to Big Jim or myself. It's a boring life. You're like a machine.

But you kept at it a pretty long while?

I kept at it as long as the guitar was in vogue, but once it became something that was a tambourine and they started using strings or an orchestra instead, I decided to give it up.

They stopped putting on guitar breaks?

Exactly. It just wasn't the thing anymore.

What about Fifth Avenue's "Just Like Anyone Would Do?"

That's a Shel Talmy thing, isn't it? Wait a minute, I produced that! What am I talking about? That's got a really good sound. I wrote that. It's not good because I wrote it, but it's got a fantastic sound on it. I used a double up-pick on the acoustic guitars. It had nice Beach Boys–type harmonies. The other side was "Bells of Rhymney."

Did you play guitar on it?

No, I just produced it.

Who was the band?

Just session musicians that were around. I think John Paul Jones was on bass.

Was that your first production?

No, but don't ask me what the other ones were. That was during the period I was producing for Immediate Records and Andrew Oldham.

How did you get involved with Oldham?

I just knew him . . . I know all the crooks. Better not print that, he might sue me. Actually, I love Andrew. He's one of the few producers I really respect. That's true, I really do respect him.

How did you come to work with Jackie DeShannon?

Just happened to be on a session. She was playing guitar and she said, "I've never found a guitarist who could adapt so quickly to the sort of things I'm doing." She had these odd licks and she said, "It's usually a big struggle to get these things across." I didn't know what she was talking about, because I'd been quite used to adapting.

We wrote a few songs together, and they ended up getting done by Marianne Faithfull, P. J. Proby, and Esther Phillips or one of those colored artists did a few. I started receiving royalty statements, which was very unusual for me at the time, seeing the names of different people who'd covered your songs.

What about "Beck's Bolero"?

Wrote it, played on it, produced it . . . and I don't give a damn what he says. That's the truth.

What about your solo single, "She Just Satisfies"?

I did it because I thought it would be fun. I played all the instruments except drums, which was Bobbie Graham. The other side was the same story.

Why didn't you do a follow-up to "She Just Satisfies"?

Because I wanted to do "Every Little Thing" with an orchestra, and they wouldn't let me do it.

So you refused to do anything else?

No, it was just left like that, and my contract ran out before I could do anything else. Simple as that.

What about Mickie Most? You worked on his single and then later he produced the Yardbirds?

"Money Honey" I did with him, but the B side, "Sea Cruise," wasn't me. It was Don Peek, who toured England with the Everly Brothers. He was bloody good. He was the first guitarist to come to England who was doing finger tremolo, and all the musicians were totally knocked out. Clapton picked up on it straight away, and others followed soon after. Eric was the first one to evolve the sound with the Gibson and Marshall amps; he should have total credit for that. I remember when we did "I'm Your Witchdoctor," he had all that sound down, and the engineer, who was cooperating up to that point (I was producing, don't forget), but was used to doing orchestras and big bands, suddenly turned off the machine and said, "This guitarist is unrecordable!" I told him to just record it and I'd take full responsibility; the guy just

couldn't believe that someone was getting that kind of sound from a guitar on purpose. Feedback, tremolo, he'd never heard anything like it.

Was Clapton the first guitarist to use feedback or were others using it before him?

No, there were a few guitarists doing it. I don't know who was the first, though, I really don't. Townshend, of course, made it a big feature of his scene, because he didn't play single notes. Beck used it. I used it as much as I could.

Do you like Townshend's style?

Oh, yeah. Lots of attack. Really good. He had his limitations, though. He was no Beck, but he was all right.

Were you getting off much on the other English guitarists at that time?

Sure. I really was, yeah. More so then than I do now.

Was it mostly Clapton, Townshend, and Beck?

Well, yeah. It was just like a little clan really.

Beck, myself, and Clapton were sort of "arch-bud-dies," and Townshend was sort of on the periphery. He came from another area of London. We were all in commuting distance from Richmond, which is where it was all going on. Townshend came from Ealing. Albert Lee was the only other guitarist real-ly worth noting. He was like a white elephant. He was so good . . . very much in the Nashville tradi-tion. One thing I've noticed, though, is that all the good musicians who've stuck to it from those days have come through.

You were originally offered the job as Clapton's replace-ment in the Yardbirds but you turned it down, suggesting Beck instead. How did that come about?

Giorgio Gomelsky approached me and said that Eric wasn't willing to expand and go along with the whole thing. I guess it was probably pretty appar-ent to them after they did "For Your Love." Clapton didn't like that at all. By that time they had already started using different instruments like harpsi-chords and at that point Clapton felt like he was just fed up. The rest of the band, especially Gomelsky, wanted to move further in that direction.

The very first time I was asked to join the Yardbirds, though, was not at that time, but sometime before then. Gomelsky said that Eric was going to have a "holiday," and I could step in and replace him. The way he put it to me, it just seemed really distasteful and I refused. Eric had been a friend of mine and I couldn't possibly be party to that. Plus Eric didn't want to leave the band at that stage.

When Beck joined the Yardbirds he was supposedly asked to play in Clapton's style, at least in the beginning.

A lot of things the Yardbirds were doing with Eric other people were doing at the same time, so it wasn't really hard for Beck to fit in. When you say "playing in his style," there were obviously certain passages and riffs that had to be precise and it was only a matter of time until the next recording, at which time Beck could assert his own identity.

You mentioned you were good friends with Beck before the Yardbirds. How did your friendship come about? Did you see the Yardbirds often when Beck was with them?

When I was doing studio work I used to go see them often, whenever I wasn't working. I met Beck through a friend of mine who told me he knew this guitarist I had to meet who'd made his own guitar. Beck showed up with his homemade guitar one day and he was really quite good. He started playing this James Burton and Scotty Moore stuff; I joined in and we really hit it off well.

We used to hang out a hell of a lot when he was in the Yardbirds and I was doing studio work. I remember we both got very turned on to Rodrigo's Guitar Concerto by Segovia and all these sorts of music. He had the same sort of taste in music as I did. That's why you'll find on the early LPs we both did a song like "You Shook Me." It was the type of thing we'd both played in bands. Someone told me he'd already recorded it after we'd already put it down on the first Zeppelin album. I thought, "Oh dear, it's going to be identical," but it was nothing like it, fortunately. I just had no idea he'd done it. It was on *Truth* but I first heard it when I was in Miami after we'd recorded our version. It's a classic example of coming from the same area musically, of having similar taste. It really pissed me off when people compared our first album to the Jeff Beck Group and said it was very close conceptually. It was nonsense, utter nonsense. The only similarity was that we'd both come out of the Yardbirds and we both had acquired certain riffs individually from the Yardbirds.

Under what circumstances did you finally join the Yardbirds when Paul Samwell-Smith quit in late summer of 1966?

It was at a gig at the Marquee Club in Oxford which I'd gone along to. They were playing in front of all these penguin-suited undergraduates and I think Samwell-Smith, whose family was a bit well to do, was embarrassed by the band's behavior. Apparently Keith Relf had gotten really drunk and he was falling into the drum kit, making farting noises into the mike, being generally anarchistic. I thought he'd done really well, actually, and the band had played really well that night. He just added all this extra feeling to it. When he came offstage, though, Paul Samwell-Smith said, "I'm leaving the band." Things used to be so final back then. There was no rethinking decisions like that. Then he said to Chris Dreja, "If I were you, I'd leave too." Which he didn't. They were sort of stuck.

Jeff had brought me to the gig in his car and on the way back I told him I'd sit in for a few months until they got things sorted out. Beck had often said to me, "It would be really great if you could join the band." But I just didn't think it was a possibility in any way. In addition, since I'd turned the offer down a couple of times already, I didn't know how the rest of them would feel about me joining. It was decided that we'd definitely have a go at it; I'd take on the bass, though I'd never played it before, but only until Dreja could learn it as he'd never played it before either. We figured it would be easier for me to pick it up quickly, then switch over to a dual guitar thing when Chris had time to become familiar enough with the bass.

How did Beck leave the group?

It was on the Dick Clark tour when there were a few incidents. One time in the dressing room I walked in and Beck had his guitar up over his head, about to bring it down on Keith Relf's head, but instead smashed it on the floor. Relf looked at him with total astonishment and Beck said, "Why did you make me do that?" Fucking hell. Everyone said, "My goodness gracious, what a funny chap." We went back to the hotel and Beck showed me his tonsils, said he wasn't feeling well and was going to see a doctor. He left for L.A. where we were headed in two days time anyway. When we got there, though, we realized that whatever doctor he was claiming to see must have had his office in the Whiskey. He was actually seeing his girlfriend and had just used the doctor bit as an excuse to cut out on us.

These sort of things went on and it must have revived all the previous antagonism between him and the rest of the band. I think that that, and a couple of other things, especially the horrible wages we were being paid, helped bring about his behavior, which had obviously stewed behind everybody's back. That quote you mentioned, that Keith Relf had said, "The magic of the band left when Eric left," I think really has to be taken into account. They were prepared to go on as a foursome, but it seemed that a lot of the enthusiasm had been lost. Then Simon Napier-Bell called up with the news that he was selling his stakes in the band to Mickie Most. I think they must have cooked it up, actually, the three of them: Napier-Bell, Mickie Most, and Beck. This way Beck could have a solo career, which he'd already begun in a way with the recording of "Beck's Bolero."

How did Peter Grant come to manage the Yardbirds?

Peter was working with Mickie Most and was offered the management when Most was offered the recording. . . . I'd known Peter from way back in the days of Immediate because our offices were next door to Mickie Most and Peter was working for him. The first thing we did with him was a tour of Australia and we found that suddenly there was some money being made after all this time.

I was only on a wage, anyway, with the Yardbirds. I'd like to say that because I was earning about three times as much when I was doing sessions and I've seen it written that "Page only joined the Yardbirds for the bread." I was on wages except when it came to the point when the wages were

more than what the rest of the band were making and it was cheaper for Simon Napier-Bell to give me what everybody else was getting.

How lucrative was it to be a session musician?

It was very lucrative and I'd saved up a lot of money, which is why it didn't bother me that I was working for a lot less money in the Yardbirds. I just wanted to get out of only playing rhythm guitar and have a chance to get into something more creative. As they were a really creative band, there were obviously possibilities, especially the idea of dual lead, that really excited me. Nobody except maybe the Stones had done anything that approached what we wanted to do, and even the Stones didn't really use dual leads, at least not the way we had in mind. I mean we immediately settled into things like stereo riffs on "Over, Under, Sideways, Down" and all kinds of guitar harmonies onstage. Everything fell into place very easily.

Why did the group finally split?

It just got to a point where Relf and McCarty couldn't take it anymore. They wanted to go and do something totally different. When it came to the final split, it was a question of begging them to keep it together, but they didn't. They just wanted to try something new. I told them we'd be able to change within the group format; coming from a sessions background I was prepared to adjust to anything. I hated to break it up without even doing a proper first album.

What about your own desire for stardom, did that have any role in your quitting sessions to join the Yardbirds in the first place?

No. I never desired stardom, I just wanted to be respected as a musician.

Do you feel the extent of your stardom now has become a burden for you in any way?

Only in relation to a lot of misunderstandings that have been laid on us. A lot of negative and derogatory things have been said about us. I must say I enjoyed the anonymity that was part of being one fourth of a group. I liked being a name but not necessarily a face to go with it. The film, *The Song Remains the Same,* I think,

JIMMY PAGE,
NASSAU COLISE-
UM, UNIONDALE,
N.Y., FEBRUARY
13, 1975

has done a lot to put faces to names for the group.

And after Relf and McCarty said they were quitting the Yardbirds, you planned to keep the group going with Chris Dreja and bring in a new drummer and singer, is that right?

Well, we still had these dates we were supposed to fulfill. Around the time of the split John Paul Jones called me up and said he was interested in getting something together. Also, Chris was getting very into photography; he decided he wanted to open his own studio and by that time was no longer enamored with the thought of going on the road. Obviously, a lot of Keith and Jim's attitude of wanting to jack it in had rubbed off on him, so Jonesy was in.

I'd originally thought of getting Terry Reid in as lead singer and second guitarist but he had just signed with Mickie Most as a solo artist in a quirk of fate. He suggested I get in touch with Robert Plant, who was then in a band called Hobbstweedle. When I auditioned him and heard him sing, I immediately thought there must be something wrong with him personality-wise or that he had to be impossible to work with, because I just could not understand why, after he told me he'd been singing for a few years already, he hadn't become a big name yet. So I had him down to my place for a little while, just to sort of check him out, and we got along great. No problems. At this time a number of drummers had approached me and wanted to work with us. Robert suggested I go hear John Bonham, whom I'd heard of because he had a reputation, but had never seen. I asked Robert if he knew him and he told me they'd worked together in this group called Band of Joy.

So the four of your rehearsed for a short time and went on that Scandinavian tour as the New Yardbirds.

As I said, we had these dates that the Yardbirds were supposed to fulfill, so we went as the Yardbirds. They were already being advertised as the New Yardbirds featuring Jimmy Page, so there wasn't much we could do about it right then. We had every intention of changing the name of the group from the very beginning, though. The tour went fantastically for us, we left them stomping the floors after every show.

Who actually named Led Zeppelin? I've heard that both

John Entwistle and Keith Moon claim to have thought up the name.

It was Moon, I'm sure, despite anything Entwistle may have said. In fact, I'm quite certain Richard Cole asked Moon for his permission when we decided to use the name. Entwistle must have just been upset that the original Led Zeppelin never took off.

What original Led Zeppelin?

We were going to form a group called Led Zeppelin at the time of "Beck's Bolero" sessions with the lineup from that session. It was going to be me and Beck on guitars, Moon on drums, maybe Nicky Hopkins on piano. The only one from the session who wasn't going to be in it was Jonesy, who had played bass. Instead, Moon suggested we bring in Entwistle as bassist and lead singer as well, but after some discussion we decided to use another singer. The first choice was Stevie Winwood, but it was decided that he was too heavily committed to Traffic at the time and probably wouldn't be too interested. Next, we thought of Stevie Marriott. He was approached and seemed to be full of glee about it. A message came from the business side of Marriott, though, which said, "How would you like to play guitar with broken fingers? You will be if you don't stay away from Stevie." After that, the idea sort of fell apart. We just said, "Let's forget about the whole thing, quick." Instead of being more positive about it and looking for another singer, we just let it slip by. Then the Who began a tour, the Yardbirds began a tour and that was it.

Remembering that session when we did "Bolero," the band seemed to be almost tied up; it was really close to happening.

What were the original ideas behind Zeppelin when the band first got together? Was it immediately decided to be a high energy thing?

Obviously, it was geared that way from the start. When Robert came down to my place the first time, when I was trying to get an idea of what he was all about, we talked about the possibilities of various types of things, "Dazed and Confused," for example. Then I played him a version of "Babe I'm Gonna Leave You." It was the version by Joan Baez, the song is traditional, and I said, "Fancy doing

this?" He sort of looked at me with wonder and I said, "Well, I've got an idea for an arrangement," and started playing it on acoustic guitar. That's indicative of the way I was thinking with regards to direction. It was very easy going.

How was the material chosen for the first Zeppelin album?

The stuff was all originally put forward by me as the material to include in the program we played in concert. It had all been well rehearsed as we'd tour Scandinavia as the New Yardbirds before recording the album. We also had a few other things we were doing at the time which never got recorded: "Flames," written by Elmer Gantry, was a really good number; "As Long as I Have You," was a Garnett Mimms number we had done with the Yardbirds which Janis Joplin had recorded. There were

a lot of improvisations on the first album, but generally we were keeping everything cut and dried. Consequently, by the time we'd finished the first tour the riffs which were coming out of these spaces, we were able to use for the immediate recording of the second album.

The first album is said to have been recorded in 30 hours.

That's right, about 30 hours of recording time. Before we started recording we had already played the numbers live and I already had a good idea of what was going to go on as far as the overdubs went.

There weren't many overdubs done on the album at any rate, were there?

Not many. On "Babe I'm Gonna Leave You," there's an acoustic guitar dubbed over and there's some pedal steel on "Your Time Is Gonna Come."

When did you learn to play pedal steel?

For that session. We also had worked out a version of "Chest Fever" in rehearsals, though we never played it onstage. That had organ and pedal steel on it.

What was the recording of the second album like? How long did it take you as opposed to the first album?

It was done wherever we could get into a studio, in bits and pieces, so I couldn't even tell you how long it actually took. I remember we did a vocal overdubs in an eight-track studio in Vancouver were they didn't even have proper headphones. Can you imagine that? It was just recorded while we were on the road.

Was it recorded entirely on the road?

No. "Thank You," "The Lemon Song," and "Moby Dick" were overdubbed on tour and the mixing of "Whole Lotta Love" and "Heartbreaker" was done on tour. In other words, some of the material came out of rehearsing for the next tour and getting new material together. The most important thing about *Zeppelin II* is that up to that point I'd contributed lyrics. Robert wrote "Thank You" on his own. That was the first one and it's important because it's when he began to come through as a lyricist. I'd always hoped that he would.

There was a bit of a fuss made at one point because on the first couple of albums you were using a lot of traditional and blues lyrics and tunes and calling them your own.

The thing is they were traditional lyrics and they went back far before a lot of the people that one related them to. The riffs we did were totally different, also, from the ones that had come before, apart from something like "You Shook Me" and "I Can't Quit You," which we attributed to Willie Dixon. The thing with "Bring It on Home," Christ, there's only a tiny bit of that taken from Sonny Boy Williamson's version and we threw that in as a tribute to him. People say, "Oh, 'Bring It on Home' is stolen." Well, there's only a little bit in the song that relates to anything that had gone before it, just the end.

Your next album, Led Zeppelin III, *presented a very different image of Led Zeppelin from the first two albums. Most importantly, it was predominantly acoustic. It was a very controversial album. How and why did the changes that brought about the third album take place?*

After the intense touring that had been taking place through the first two albums, working almost 24 hours a day, basically, we managed to stop and have a proper break, a couple of months as opposed to a couple of weeks. We decided to go off and rent a cottage to provide a contrast to motel rooms. Obviously, it had quite an effect on the material that was written.

Did you write the whole album there?

Just certain sections of it. "That's the Way," "Bron-Y-Aur Stomp," quite a few things. It was the tranquility of the place that set the tone of the album. Obviously, we weren't crashing away at 100 watt Marshall stacks. Having played acoustic and being interested in classical guitar, anyway, being in a cottage without electricity, it was acoustic guitar time. It didn't occur to us not to include it on the album because it was relative to the changes within the band. We didn't expect we'd get thrashed in the media for doing it.

Was there a rethink by the band about the stage act, since you were faced with having to perform material from a predominantly acoustic LP?

It just meant that we were going to have to employ some of those numbers onstage without being frightened about it. They were received amazingly well.

Had you wanted to bring in more of the English folk roots to Zeppelin or was it just the influence of living in the cottage that gives the album a pastoral feeling?

It has that because that's how it was. After all the heavy, intense vibe of touring which is reflected in the raw energy on the second album, it was just a totally different feeling. I've always tried to capture an emotional quality in my songs. Transmitting that is what music seems to be about, really, as far as the instrumental side of it goes, anyway. It was in us, everything that came out on *Zeppelin III* can still be related to the essence of the first album when you think about it. It's just that the band had kept maturing.

Were you surprised when the critical reaction came out?

I just thought they hadn't understood it, hadn't listened to it. For instance, *Melody*

JIMMY PAGE,

CHICAGO

STADIUM,

APRIL 7, 1977

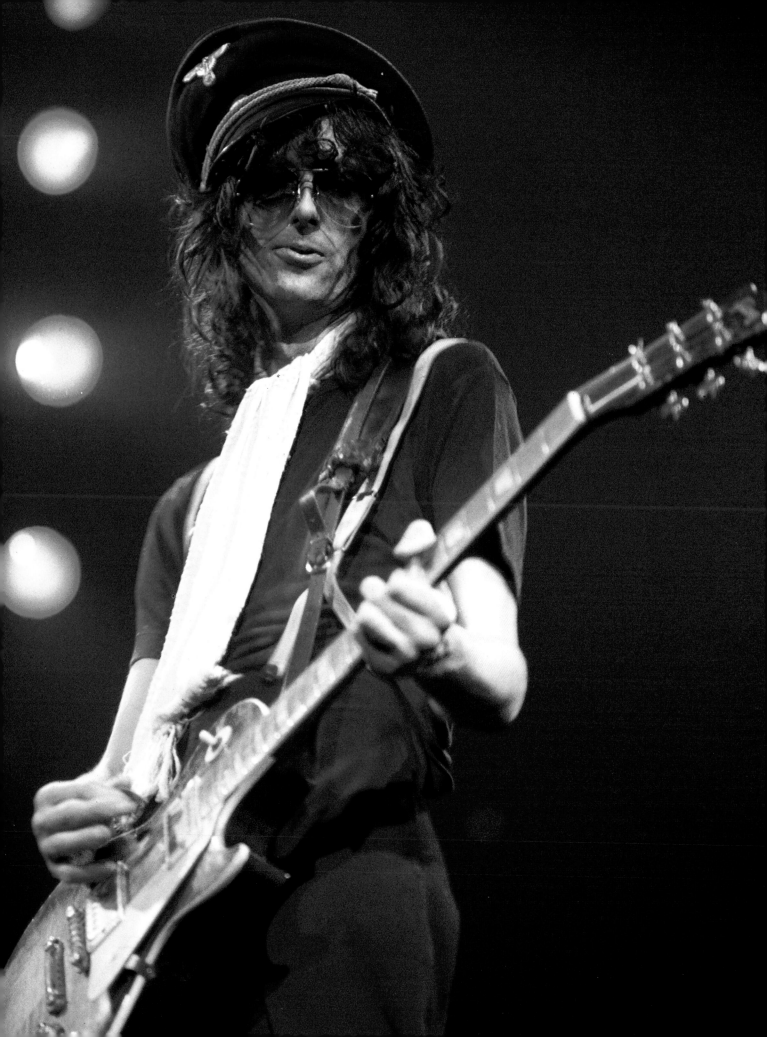

Maker said we'd decided to don our acoustic guitars because Crosby, Stills and Nash had just been over here. It wasn't until the fourth LP that people began to understand that we weren't just messing around.

You did take a lot of stock in the criticism of the third record. Personally, you seemed to be hit hard by it at the time.

To pave the way for 18 months without doing any interviews, I must have. Silly, wasn't I? That was a lot of the reason for putting out the next LP with no information on it at all. After a year's ab-sence from both records and touring, I remember one agent telling us it was professional suicide. We just happened to have a lot of faith in what we were doing.

Was the cover of the fourth album meant to bring out that whole city/country dichotomy that had surfaced on the third record?

Exactly. It represented the change in the balance which was going on. There was the old country-man and the blocks of flats being knocked down. It was just a way of saying that we should look after the earth, not rape and pillage it.

LED ZEPPELIN

62

Do you think the third record was good for the band, regardless of the critical reaction, because it showed people that the band was not just a heavy metal group, that you were more versatile than that?

It showed people that we weren't going to be a stagnant group. There were some people who knew that already and were interested to see what we'd come up with; there were others who thought we were just an outright hype and were still living back in the '60s. They just didn't take anything we did seriously. A lot of them have since come around. You should read that *Melody Maker* review, though, it's absolutely classic. I felt a lot better once we started performing it, because it was proving to be working for the people who came around to see us. There was always a big smile there in front of us. That was always more important than any proxy review. That's really how the following of the band has spread, by word of mouth. I mean, all this talk about a hype, spending thousands on publicity campaigns, we didn't do that at all. We didn't do television. Well, we did a pilot TV show and a pilot radio show, but that's all. We weren't hyping ourselves. It wasn't as though we were thrashing about all over the media. It didn't matter, though, the word got out on the street.

Once a band is established it seems to me that bad reviews can't really do anything to a band.

No, you're right. But you've got to understand that I lived every second of the albums. Whereas the others hadn't. John Paul and Bonzo would do the tracks and they wouldn't come in until needed. And Robert would do the vocals. But I'd be there all the time and I'd live and cringe to every mistake. There were things that were right and wrong on a subjective level.

You said that "Hats Off to (Roy) Harper" was written as a tribute to him. Did you hope to draw attention to him?

In a way. I mean hats off to anybody who sticks by what they think is right and has the courage not to sell out. We did a whole set of country blues and traditional blues numbers that Robert suggested. But that was the only one we put on the record.

It seems that of the big groups, only you and the Who have managed to stay together for such a long time without personnel changes, and the Who don't really seem to get on with each other very well.

Yeah, we've always had a strong bond. It became very apparent when Robert was injured before we made *Presence*.

The fourth album was to my mind the first fully realized Zeppelin album. It just sounded like everything had come together on that album.

Yeah, we were really playing properly as a group and the different writing departures that we'd taken, like the cottage and the spontaneity aspects, had been worked out and came across in the most disciplined form.

"Rock and Roll" was a spontaneous combustion. We were doing something else at the time, but Bonzo played the beginning of Little Richard's "Good Golly Miss Molly" with the tape still running and I just started doing that part of the riff. It actually ground to a halt after about 12 bars, but it was enough to know that there was enough of a number there to keep working on it. Robert even came in singing on it straight away.

I do have the original tape that was running at the time we ran down "Stairway to Heaven" completely with the band. I'd worked it all out already the night before with John Paul Jones, written down the changes and things. All this time we were all living in a house and keeping pretty regular hours together, so the next day we started run-

ning it down. There was only one place where there was a slight rerun. For some unknown reason Bonzo couldn't get the timing right on the twelve-string part before the solo. Other than that it flowed very quickly. While we were doing it Robert was penciling down lyrics; he must have written three quarters of the lyrics on the spot. He didn't have to go away and think about them. Amazing, really.

"Black Dog" was a riff that John Paul Jones had brought with him. "Battle of Evermore" was made up on the spot by Robert and myself. I just picked up John Paul Jones's mandolin, never having played a mandolin before, and just wrote up the chords and the whole thing in one sitting. The same thing happened with the banjo on "Gallows Pole." I'd never played one before either. It was also John Paul Jones's instrument. I just picked it up and started moving my fingers around until the chords sounded right, which is the same way I work on compositions when the guitar's in different tunings.

When did Sandy Denny come in to sing on "Gallows Pole"?

Well, it sounded like an old English instrumental first off. Then it became a vocal and Robert did his bit. Finally we figured we'd bring Sandy by and do a question-and-answer–type thing.

"Misty Mountain Hop" we came up with on the spot. "Going to California" was a thing I'd written before on acoustic guitar. "When the Levee Breaks" was a riff that I'd been working on, but Bonzo's drum sound really makes the difference on that point.

You've said that when you heard Robert's lyrics to "Stairway to Heaven" you knew that he'd be the band's lyricist from then on.

I always knew he would be, but I knew at that point that he'd proved it to himself and could get into something a bit more profound than just subjective things. Not that they can't be profound as well, but there's a lot of ambiguity implied in that number that wasn't present before. I was really relieved because it gave me the opportunity to just get on with the music.

Did you know you'd recorded a classic when you finished?

I knew it was good. I didn't know it was going to become like an anthem, but I did know it was the gem of the album, sure.

You recorded the fourth record at a few different studios, right?

It was recorded on location at Headley Grange in Hampshire. "Stairway" was done at Island, as were the overdubs. "Four Sticks" was done at Island because it had a lot of chiming guitars and things. "When the Levee Breaks" is probably the most subtle thing on there as far as production goes because each 12 bars has something new about it, though at first it might not be apparent. There's a lot of different effects on there that at the time had never been used before. Phased vocals, a backwards echoed harmonica solo. Andy Johns was doing the engineering, but as far as those sort of ideas go, they usually come from me. Once a thing is past the stage of being a track, I've usually got a good idea of how I'd like it to shape up. I don't want to sound too dictatorial, though, because it's not that sort of thing at all. When we went into Headley Grange it was more like, "Okay, what's anybody got?"

And it turned out that you had more than anyone else?

It usually does.

Was the idea of the symbols on the cover of the fourth album yours?

Yeah. After all this crap that we'd had with the critics, I put it to everybody else that it'd be a good idea to put out something totally anonymous. At first I wanted just one symbol on it, but then it was decided that since it was our fourth album and there were four of us, we could each choose our own symbol. I designed mine and everyone else had their own reasons for using the symbols that they used.

Do you envision a relationship between Zeppelin cover art and the music on the albums?

There is a relationship in a way, though not necessarily in a "concept album" fashion.

Does Robert usually come into sessions with the lyrics already written?

He has a lyric book and we try to fuse song to lyric where it can be done. Where it can't, he just writes new ones.

Is there a lot of lyric changing during a session?

Sometimes. Sometimes it's more cut and dried, like on "The Rain Song."

There are a few tracks on the fifth album that seemed to exhibit more of a sense of humor than Zeppelin had been known for. "The Crunge" was funny and "D'yer Mak'er" had a joke title which took some people a while to get.

I didn't expect people not to get it. I thought it was pretty obvious. The song itself was a cross between reggae and a '50s number, "Poor Little Fool," Ben E. King things, stuff like that. I'll tell you one thing, "The Song Remains the Same" was going to be an instrumental at first. We used to call it "The Overture."

You never performed it that way.

We couldn't. There were too many guitar parts to perform it.

But once you record anything with overdubs, you end up having to adapt it for the stage.

Sure. Then it becomes a challenge, a tough challenge in some cases. "Achilles" is the classic one. When Ronnie Wood and Keith Richard came to hear us play, Keith said, "You ought to get another guitarist; you're rapidly becoming known as the most overworked guitarist in the business." Quite amusing. There are times when I'd just love to get another guitarist on, but it just wouldn't look right to the audience.

The Houses of the Holy album was the last one that came out on Atlantic before you formed Swan Song. How did the label get started?

We'd been thinking about it for a while and we knew if we formed a label there wouldn't be the kind of fuss and bother we'd been going through over album covers and things like that. Having gone through, ourselves, what appeared to be an interference, or at least an aggravation, on the artistic side by record companies, we wanted to form a label where the artists would be able to fulfill themselves without all of that hassle. Consequently the people we were looking for for the label would be people who knew where they were going themselves. We didn't really want to get bogged down in having to develop artists, we

wanted people who were together enough to handle that type of thing themselves, like the Pretty Things. Even though they didn't happen, the records they made were very, very good.

The Physical Graffiti album was not all new material. Why was this?

Well, as usual, we had more material than the required 40-odd minutes for one album. We had enough material for one and a half LPs, so we figured let's put out a double and use some of the material we had done previously but never released. It seemed like a good time to do that sort of thing, release tracks like "Boogie With Stu" which we normally wouldn't be able to do.

Who's Stu?

Ian Stewart from the Stones. He played on "Rock and Roll" with us.

Which other tracks on Physical Graffiti had been recorded previously?

"Black Country Woman" and "The Rover" were both done at the same time we did "D'yer Mak'er." "Bron-Yr-Aur" was done for the third record. "Down by the Seaside," "Night Flight," and "Boogie With Stu" were all from the sessions for the fourth album. We had an album and a half of new material, and this time we figured it was better to stretch out than to leave off. I really fancied putting out a song called "Houses of the Holy" on the album.

Do you consider "Kashmir" one of your better compositions?

Yeah. There have been several milestones along the way. That's definitely one of them.

If you were to put together a "Best of Zeppelin" album, what tracks would you choose for it?

That's very difficult to say. I haven't thought about it.

What other milestones would you mention?

"Communication Breakdown." . . . It's difficult, only because I don't know the running times and if you mean a single LP or a double. It would probably be about three songs from each LP. I'd be very conscious of a balance of the sides. There are some tracks which are obvious.

Are there any plans to put out an album like that?

Not at this moment.

KEZAR
STADIUM, SAN
FRANCISCO,
JUNE 2, 1973

Do you think that you'll do one eventually?

I'm going to work on a quad thing. I have one idea of a chronological live LP which would be two or three albums going back through "Communication Breakdown," "Thank You," and all those sorts of numbers. We've got recordings starting with the Albert Hall in 1969 and 1970 with two a year from then on. It would go all the way through.

The Presence album was recorded after Robert's accident and you've said it was the album you were most intensely involved with since the first album.

As far as living it uninterrupted from beginning to end, yeah, definitely. I did 18-hour sessions, 24-hour sessions to complete it.

Is there any reason that Presence is a totally electric guitar-oriented album?

I think it was just a reflection of the total anxiety and emotion at the period of time during which it was recorded. It's true that there are no acoustic songs, no mellowness or contrasts or changes to other instruments. Yet the blues we did, like "Tea for One," was the only time I think we've ever gotten close to repeating the mood of another of our numbers, "Since I've Been Loving You." The chordal structure is similar, a minor blues. We just wanted to get a really laid-back blues feeling without blowing out on it at all. We did two takes in the end, one with a guitar solo and one without. I ended up sitting there thinking, "I've got this guitar solo to do," because there have been blues guitar solos since Eric on *Five Live Yardbirds* and everyone's done a good one. I was really a bit frightened of it. I thought, "What's to be done?" I didn't want to blast out on the solo like a locomotive or something, because it wasn't conducive to the vibe of the rest of the track. I was extremely aware that you had to do something different than just some

B. B. King licks.

You've always seemed to be conscious of not repeating blues clichés.

I probably do it more onstage than on record. It's evident on the live album when we do "Whole Lotta Love."

I'll tell you about doing all the guitar overdubs to "Achilles Last Stand." There were basically two sections to the song when we rehearsed it. I know John Paul Jones didn't think I could succeed in what I was attempting to do. He said I couldn't do a scale over a certain section, that it just wouldn't work. But it did. What I planned to try and get that epic quality into it so it wouldn't just sound like two sections repeated, was to give the piece a totally new identity by orchestrating the guitars, which is something I'd been into for quite some time. I knew it had to be jolly good, because the number was so long it just couldn't afford to be half-baked. It was all down to me how to do this. I had a lot of it mapped out in my mind, anyway, but to make a long story short, I did all the overdubs in one night.

Do you know how many tracks you did?

No, I lost count eventually. Not many people picked up on that number but I thought as far as I can value tying up that kind of emotion as a package and trying to convey it through two speakers, it was fairly successful. Maybe it's because it was a narrative, I don't know.

Were you upset that the first live LP was a film soundtrack?

Dead right. It was a shame. For a time, the movie was shelved and we were going to come over here with what we'd learned, and do some more footage, but after Robert's accident we were forced to tie it all up. We'd done work with it already and it had to come out. It was recorded across three nights, but in fact the music for the footage mainly came from the first night. It was the best vocal performance. It wasn't like they had drop-ins and that sort of thing, but they just didn't have complete footage. So we had to come up with the fantasy sequences to fill it up. Had we been a band that's the same every night, it would have been very easy for them to link one night's performance with another. As far as live albums go, most groups will record over half a dozen nights and take the best of that, but as it was a visual, we couldn't do that.

Do you like the movie?

Oh, it was an incredible uphill struggle. We'd done a bit of work on it and stopped, did more, then stopped again. Three times in all. At that point, we'd decided to redo the thing, making sure the filmmakers did have everything covered properly. As far as it goes, I'm really pleased that it is there. Purely because it's an honest statement, a documentary. It's certainly not one of the magic nights. It was not one of the amazing nights you get now and again, but you'd have to have the entire film crew traveling with you all the time to catch one. That would be just too costly to do. We'd gotten to the point where we were so far into it we couldn't pull out. We'd put so much money into it. By that point, we knew it was going to be all right, but the director was very stubborn and it would have been a lot easier had he just done what he'd been asked to do.

Getting back to your original question, though, it was frustrating because I did have this concept of this chronological live LP which really would have been a knockout.

It still sounds like a viable thing for you to do in the future.

I'll get to it. I'll do it eventually.

—Dave Schulps

Part Three

WEARING
AND
TEARING

I CAN'T QUIT YOU BABE

Collecting Led Zeppelin

Legend has it that in September 1959 James Patrick Page bought a record by Elvis Presley called *A Date With Elvis*, listened to a song called "Baby, Let's Play House," and received divine inspiration that playing the guitar was his calling. Scotty Moore's riff was certainly inspirational to Page, as it was to every teenager at the time, but Page has also noted that hearing some of his buddies playing in school had an equal effect. Whatever the source of his calling, less than three years later Page was already the hottest guitar session player in London and within ten years he had formed Led Zeppelin, a band that would eventually rank in the same category with Presley in terms of influence and massive popularity.

Though Page was an early collector of live concert tapes of blues performers and was an avid record collector himself, if he had been a real Elvis nut he would have picked up the import copy of the RCA Victor single that came out in the United States almost four years earlier. Page missed that piece of vinyl, but in the years that followed, few records by any major artists escaped his hands. His collection of records and tape recordings is legendary. And so it is only appropriate that when Page found himself creating his own band and his own piece of history with Led Zeppelin, he approached their recordings thinking like a record collector.

Robert Plant was also a fanatical record collector, buying as many U.S. singles as he could afford on his meager budget. John Paul Jones had made music his living for a number of years and also had a wide collection of recordings. And though John Bonham had struggled financially in his early years to such an extent that he'd had to quit smoking to save a few quid, his knowledge of music ran far beyond that of most drummers. Considering the attitude and background of the four members of the band, and the marketing genius of manager Peter Grant, it should come as no surprise that every single item ever released by Zeppelin was planned so as to be essential to any fan of the band. Few bands had so much control over how their recordings were released and perhaps for that reason the material in the Zeppelin catalog seems tailor-made to appeal to the collector mentality. Being fanatics of a sort themselves, this band made sure that every release of their recordings would rank as a collectible in its own right, even if millions of copies were issued.

More than a decade after their demise, Led Zeppelin remains one of the most collected groups in the history of rock 'n' roll. Demand for their rarest recordings and promotional items only grows

THEY'LL SPACE YOUR BRAINS OUT!!!

LED ZEP

HOW THEY BECAME THE METAL MONSTERS OF THE '70s

THE MAGAZINE EVERY ZEP FREAK SHOULD OWN!!

100 FRAMABLE PHOTOS!!

with time. The group ranks just below the Beatles, the Rolling Stones, Bruce Springsteen, and Elvis Presley in terms of the numbers of collectors who still follow them. All the superstars of rock 'n' roll have inspired legions of followers but it is an indication of Zeppelin's fanatical following that more than ten years after their breakup, at least four monthly fanzines continue to cover the group's legacy around the world (by contrast, the Beatles have only one monthly fanzine). Prices for Zeppelin collectibles continue to go up in value whenever they go on the collector's market and their material is now in the league where their rare collectibles are sold along with Ming vases in stuffy fine art houses like Sotheby's. In early 1991 the string arrangements done by John Paul Jones for "Kashmir," one of the most primeval of all of Zeppelin's rock 'n' roll songs, sold for several thousands of dollars in an auction along with classic old movie posters, some shoes of Marilyn Monroe's, and more of the prestigious sort of art you expect to find in such offerings. It may have taken years for Zeppelin to find the critical respect they deserved all along, but record dealers have known for years that this is a group that commands top dollar and ranks in the highest pantheon of collecting.

Perhaps one reason that Led Zeppelin has been so popular with record collectors is the finite number of records in their catalogue. Though the group existed for 12 years, with a couple of posthumous releases that followed, their entire catalog consists of only ten full-length albums, ten singles in the United States and one boxed set. All of the group's albums remain in print (at least in the compact disc format) and for less than $300 a collector can walk into a record store and come out with CD copies of every single thing Led Zeppelin ever officially issued. By contrast, the sheer amount of official material available from the Rolling Stones or the Beatles is overwhelming: both groups have officially released more than three times as much material as Zeppelin.

Despite the limited amount of material in the catalog, Zeppelin collectors have found that collecting this band means more than just buying the officially released albums. The band did issue nu-

merous 45s in foreign markets, as they were popular all around the world, and the number of promotional items and posters featuring the group is staggering. And while the sheer number of albums may be small, the group's control over their product—and their commitment to making every record a collectible in and of itself—makes the available material highly sought after.

Led Zeppelin's involvement in designing and creating each album was unique in the industry. They can even be considered the forerunners of today's practice of involving musicians in the packaging of their music. In early rock 'n' roll, record companies paid virtually no attention to what artists thought about how they should be marketed and generally issued whatever records they thought would sell the most in the variations that would be most financially rewarding for the company. RCA issued virtually every song Elvis ever recorded on several different albums with the sole purpose of getting the maximum number of dollars from fans. EMI/Capitol's treatment of the early Beatles albums is another classic example: to get all of the group's recordings, fans found themselves having to buy both the U.K. and U.S. releases since these issues didn't match up in title, design, or song selection.

Jimmy Page and Peter Grant helped change all that. The concept behind Zeppelin was so strong and so well thought out that when the band began negotiations with their label, they had power that few artists had ever had. They insisted on control over design of album jackets and over how the band was marketed. To their credit, Atlantic trusted Page and Grant to put together their own records. Zeppelin wasn't allowed to do whatever they wanted without input from the record company; the battles between the group and their label were as legendary as Zeppelin's offstage antics. Eventually strain between the group and their label, and debates over royalties, led the group to start a record label of their own called Swan Song, which was distributed by Atlantic.

The biggest debate between the band and the label con-

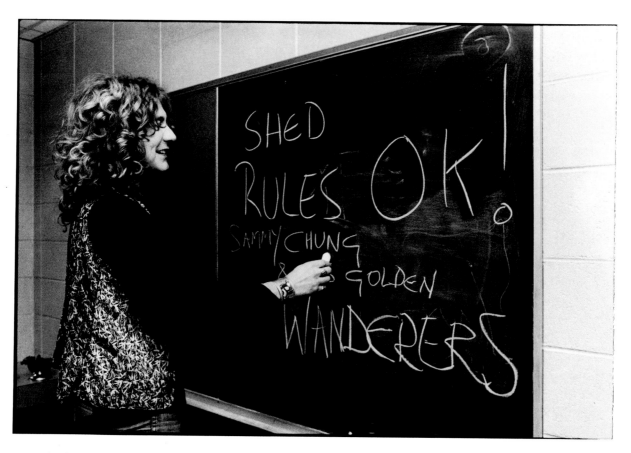

cerned releasing singles. In the early 1970s, the 45-rpm single still played a major role, getting groups airplay and boosting record company profits. Though all four members of Led Zeppelin had had singles released in the United Kingdom during the late 1960s, no one saw the concept of Led Zeppelin lending itself to the single format. Singles were inevitably short, poppy tunes produced to sound good on car radios and jukeboxes and as such they were everything that Led Zeppelin wasn't.

The band did manage to retain artistic control over the cosmetics of their album releases, but they eventually lost the singles feud with the label. The compromise Atlantic worked out was that Zeppelin singles would be released in the United States but not in their native England, but even this was not to the band's liking. Ten 45s were eventually released in the United States, but their biggest song, "Stairway to Heaven," was never commercially available in America as a 45.

And unlike most other bands, the group also re-

fused to release a "greatest hits" package, though the label constantly lobbied for such a release. The 1990 boxed set was a phenomenal success and serves as a retrospective of hits, but the band says that their main motivation was remastering the material for compact disc release. That may sound somewhat disingenuous, but considering the commercial success a greatest hits package would have had if released in the late 1970s, the group can't be faulted for grossly marketing their material. It took almost eight years of playing and recording before the group would issue a live record and that release served more as a soundtrack to the film *The Song Remains the Same* than it did as a legitimate live recording (something many fans still suggest is forthcoming).

The group did almost no television appearances,

though they were offered millions for such work, and apart from their film, they made only one promotional rock video (there was no place to show it back then). After *Rolling Stone* ripped their first album to shreds, they almost never gave interviews and when they did talk to the press Jimmy Page gave reporters such a hard time they wished they'd never heard of the band. Though they were considered by critics during the 1970s to be a band fueled by hype and hyperbole, the crass hucksterism associated with hype in the music industry was never found coming from the band themselves or their management. In an effort to dispel such accusations, when their fourth record was completed the group insisted that the cover not mention the band, or the record label—in fact, it had no type at all. There was not even a catalog number printed on the spine of the first pressing of the fourth record. Atlantic executives freaked out and told the band it was committing commercial "suicide," hence the nickname for the record, the "Suicide Album." (Others in the industry suggest that maybe the group knew their noncommercial stance would make them even more commercially successful. It did.)

The best place to start a Led Zeppelin collection is with the official albums themselves. Zeppelin designed their albums with an appreciation for graphic design and marketing that was years ahead of their time, and no collection would be complete without one copy of each of the vinyl album releases. Though the band's music has been digitally captured on compact disc, the CD releases of Zeppelin albums miniaturize the original artwork and greatly lessen the visual impact. The majority of the album covers in the Zeppelin catalog also contain either die cuts or special printing that have not been replicated on the CD releases. The cost of making these die-cut album covers is considerably more than the expense of making a plain album cover but all re-pressings of Zeppelin albums up through early 1991 (when a vinyl pressing of any title became hard to find) featured the original album packages. Even if these albums are not available new, consider picking up used copies since they were designed to be seen and experienced in the 12-inch album jacket format in all their glory.

The band worked hard to assure that their standards of quality were maintained in every release around the world, but the logistics of foreign record companies created a number of unique collectibles. The most evident differences in the album cover to the group's first album, *Led Zeppelin*, was the variety of different colors used for the type and the group picture on the back. The Canadian pressing of the album reproduced the back album photo by Chris Dreja without the brown tint found on the U.S. copy. A Korean pressing of the record, which is probably a pirate release pressed without authorization, deletes the song "How Many More Times" from the record and consequently "I Can't Quit You" fades out at the end instead of leading into the missing song. The original Nippon Grammaphon pressing from Japan came with a gatefold cover, the only such issue of this worldwide. Like other Japanese releases from the group, this album was also sporadically packaged with a lyric sheet and poster. An early German record club pressing combined the first two albums into a gatefold double record. This release was issued without the band's consent and was withdrawn quickly, though not before it became a valued collectors' item.

The most notable exception to the second album, *Led Zeppelin II*, was an Austrian pressing with a unique cover. The pressing was put together for a record-of-the-month club and appears to have been created with no input from the band. The other collectible element involving the second record came out of one of Zeppelin's frequent controversies over songwriting credits. The original U.K. pressing of the album credited "The Lemon Song" to "Page, Plant, Jones, and Bonham," but later U.K. copies credited the song as being composed by Howlin' Wolf, while the record label, but not the jacket, retitled the song as "Killing Floor" and credited it to "Burnett."

FOLLOWING PAGES: JIMMY PAGE, MINNEAPOLIS TOUR REHEARSAL, JANUARY 17, 1975. ROBERT PLANT, AT CHICAGO, APRIL 7, 1977

The third Zeppelin album was designed by Page to feature an elaborate spinning inner cover, called a "farmer's wheel," that showed different images as it was spun inside the die cut outer cover. Although it is extremely expensive to create, Atlantic continues to issue the LP with the original die cut. Other overseas record companies were not so generous and many pressings simply featured a flat cover without the die cuts. The second German release of the LP discontinued the inner spinning wheel idea and pictures of the band appear in what would have been the holes in the jacket if it had contained a die cut.

One of the strangest elements in the Zeppelin discography concerns messages scratched into the dead wax near the label of the record on *Led Zeppelin III*. For the first few years of its release, U.S. copies had an Aleister Crowley quote, "Do What Thou Wilt," scratched into the wax on one or both sides. The 45 pressing of "Immigrant Song" featured a similar quote. Most Zeppelin fans take this as a testament to Page's fascination with the legendary occultist.

The untitled fourth album was pressed on colored vinyl in the United Kingdom and was also reissued there with a booklet in a box put out by the record chain HMV in 1989. The second German pressing went one step farther and even took the name of the group off the label of the record. This meant that on this particular pressing the group's name did not appear anywhere on either the jacket or the label. Pirate pressings from the Far East were not so illusory: the Taiwanese pressing stuck a giant logo declaring "Led Zeppelin IV" on the front cover.

Houses of the Holy was Zeppelin's follow-up to their biggest record to date and the band stuck with their pattern of subtle identification. Early pressings in the United States and Japan came with a paper wraparound that displayed the title, as no type was on the actual cover itself. This album represented the first and last time a lyric sheet was included in a Zeppelin album, reproduced on the inner sleeve. Pirates from the Far East again put the band's name

ROBERT PLANT,

CHICAGO,

APRIL 8, 1977

on the cover and printed the lyrics on the back cover of the album, rather than on the album sleeve. Another interesting overseas variation is the Brazil pressing that has the title of the record emblazoned on the front cover in Spanish.

As if Jimmy Page hadn't already given record manufacturing plants enough trouble, he decided that *Physical Graffiti* would feature a die-cut cover with windows through which different images would appear as the sleeve was pulled out of the cover. In Spain the record company didn't quite figure this double album out and it was issued there with sides one and three back to back. The Taiwanese pirates chose to confound Page once again and issued the album as a gatefold minus the expensive die cuts.

As the band's reputation and popularity grew, so did its ability to control overseas variations. By the time of 1976's *Presence* and *The Song Remains the Same*, the group was successful in overseeing all the various worldwide pressings, with the exception of the pirate copies from the Far East. The title on the original U.K. and U.S. pressings of *Presence* was embossed with a sticker on the shrink wrap. A record club issue in the United States printed the title in gray on a white background. For *The Song Remains the Same* the group went back to putting their name on their albums again, this time perhaps because they were so proud of the package. Though the collection is thought to be one of the group's weakest sets of music, the album cover itself is a monumental achievement. Early issues featured an embossed cover and custom-printed black inner record sleeves. The inner gatefold featured an eight-page booklet with color pictures and was finely printed. The Japanese pressings of the album were even more elaborate, with the booklet printed as a separate item and the photos on the cover spot varnished.

If record retailers imagined that Zeppelin had become more conventional, they would not have been ready for the group's next release, *In Through the Out Door*. The album was initially packaged in six different covers, each one contained in an outer brown paper bag. Each of the six covers features a different variation of the same scene in a bar with

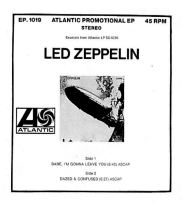

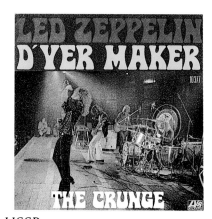

the letters A through F on the spine being the only indication on the outside of the package of the differences. The group was already huge with the record collectors of the world and many fans actually bought all six variations, making this one of the more successful marketing gimmicks of all time. And as if the different covers were not enough, the group also had the inner sleeves printed up on "magic" paper that changed colors when exposed to water. One error was notable on early U.S. pressings of the actual album: writing credits for "I'm Gonna Crawl" were given to "Grant" rather than "Plant." Though no one knew it at the time, *In Through the Out Door* represented the last album from Zeppelin while the group was together and the packaging alone made this an appropriate swan song release.

Since the band's demise there have been two releases, neither of which produced any interesting variations worldwide. *Coda* was an album of studio outtakes and the design and packaging was subdued by Zeppelin's standards, perhaps to emphasize for fans that this was an outtake Zeppelin album. The boxed set also titled *Led Zeppelin*, which saw release in 1990, featured an elaborate package and an excellent booklet complete with liner notes and photos. For the CDs and albums in the boxed set, the band had new covers designed featuring pictures of nature rather than the complicated images they had previously been associated with. Hidden in the nature scenes were the band member's symbols from the fourth album.

Other vinyl releases from around the world collected various tracks on compilations and promotional records. Perhaps the most curious was a release from the USSR, post-Glasnost, where a compilation of tracks from the third and fourth albums was issued on the state-controlled label Melodiya. The record was distributed openly in state-run record stores throughout Eastern Europe and was also sold by reputable companies like Czechoslovakia's Supraphon Records. In a recent interview, Robert Plant claimed no knowledge of the release having been officially approved, so it may be a pirate. Counterfeits are common in Eastern Europe.

Led Zeppelin released only one non-LP B side during the course of their career, "Hey Hey What Can I Do," which came out as the B side of the single "Immigrant Song," in the United States and Japan. There are also two previously unreleased live tracks on the boxed set, "Travelling Riverside Blues," and "White Summer/Black Mountain Side." The group released a total of ten singles in the U.S. market and most of those releases were issued in foreign markets. In the United States, none of the band's 45s ever came with picture sleeves, another compromise Atlantic made to help appease the noncommercial attitude the band wanted to put forth.

In foreign markets almost every Zeppelin single released did feature a picture sleeve and these sleeves were usually exclusive to each country. Collecting these picture sleeves is one of the main goals for most serious Zeppelin collectors.

LEFT: U.S PROMOTIONAL EP ISSUED TO RADIO STATIONS PRIOR TO THE RELEASE OF THE FIRST ALBUM. CENTER: U.S. PROMO 45 FOR "STAIRWAY." RIGHT: GERMAN SLEEVE FOR "D'YER MAK'ER."

LEFT: GERMAN
SLEEVE FOR
"THE OCEAN."
CENTER: SPAN-
ISH SLEEVE FOR
"WHOLE LOTTA
LOVE." RIGHT:
GERMAN SLEEVE
FOR "ROCK AND
ROLL."

The single rarest Zeppelin single, and additionally the single rarest Zeppelin item, is the original Japanese 45 pressing of "Immigrant Song" manufactured in Japan by Nippon Grammaphon on the Atlantic/Polydor label with the album cut "Out on the Tiles," on the B side. It is unclear why Japan issued the 45 with this B side since they almost immediately recalled it and put out the standard issue B side of "Hey Hey What Can I Do." The 45 also features a unique picture sleeve that is considered one of Zeppelin's finest. Only one copy of the original "Out on the Tiles" 45 is known to exist outside of Japan and the value of this item would exceed a thousand dollars because of its rarity.

Other foreign releases that are specific to a country include "Heartbreaker" backed with "Bring It on Home," as released in Italy; "Bron-Y-Aur Stomp" backed with "Out on the Tiles," from Holland; "Babe I'm Gonna Leave You," with "How Many More Times," on the B side from Greece; "The Ocean" paired with "Dancing Days" from Germany; and "Whole Lotta Love" backed with "Thank You" from Japan. Zeppelin singles have so far been issued in more than two dozen countries around the world, creating a job for collectors in just figuring out what's been released where.

Both Mexico and Australia released special EPs of the band, which was surprising since extended-play releases had fallen out of favor with record companies by the early 1970s. The Australian EP

includes "That's the Way," "Going to California," and "Stairway to Heaven," which is notable since it marks the only official commercial issue of "Stairway to Heaven" on a seven-inch format. (There are several promotional versions but the single was never sold to the public.)

Led Zeppelin never thought they needed much promotion to get their music heard, but they were the subject of numerous promotional issues designed to appeal to radio stations. The most sought-after promo items are the four U.K. seven-inch singles, which indicate that Atlantic wanted at least to get airplay for the band even if they couldn't get them to press a commercial single. The singles are "Communication Breakdown" backed with "Good Times Bad Times"; "Whole Lotta Love" backed with "Living Loving Maid"; "D'yer Mak'er" backed with "Over the Hills and Far Away"; and "Trampled Under Foot" backed with "Black Country Woman." The "Trampled Under Foot" single is the most common since 5,000 were given away to retail stores prior to the Earl's Court concerts. The promotional 45s from the U.K. represent the only way Zeppelin's music was ever available in their native country in the seven-inch format.

There are numerous U.S. promo pressings that are valuable, including white label promotional pressings of all the LPs. The U.S. pressing of the promo 45 "Babe I'm Gonna Leave You," backed with "Dazed and Confused," complete with picture sleeve, is considered one of the earliest

FOLLOWING
PAGES: 1973
PROMOTIONAL
POSTER FOR
HOUSES OF THE
HOLY; POSTER
FOR 1980 EURO-
PEAN TOUR

LED·ZEPPELIN·HOUSES of THE·HOLY

THE EFFECT IS SHATTERING...

LED·ZEPPELIN
TOUR OVER EUROPE 1980

ROTTERDAM
AHOY
JUNE 21ST

BREMEN
STADTHALLE
JUNE 23RD

BERLIN
EISSPORTHALLE
JULY 7TH & 8TH

HANNOVER
MESSEHALLE
JUNE 24TH

BRUSSELS
FOREST NATIONAL
JUNE 20TH

DORTMUND
WESTFALENHALLE
JUNE 17TH

KÖLN
SPORTSHALLE
JUNE 18TH

FRANKFURT
FESTHALLE
JUNE 30TH

MANNHEIM
EISSTADIUM
JULY 2ND & 3RD

NÜRNBERG
MESSEZENTRUM HALLE
JUNE 27TH

ZURICH
HALLENSTADION
JUNE 29TH

MÜNCHEN
OLYMPICHALLE
JULY 5TH

VIENNA
STADTHALLE
JUNE 26TH

and rarest U.S. Zeppelin collectibles. Two jukebox EPs were issued in the United States consisting of "Dancing Days," "D'yer Mak'er," "The Song Remains the Same," and "The Crunge," and "Rock and Roll," "Black Dog," and "Stairway to Heaven." Both had picture sleeves, though they were only issued as promotional items to get jukebox play. To promote "Stairway to Heaven" to radio stations it was issued as a promotional 45 (with a mono version of the song on one side and a stereo mix on the other). This promo, which came with a picture sleeve, is considered one of the single most valuable Zeppelin rarities and is worth over $100.

Radio promos are particularly sought after by Zeppelin collectors since many contain live or rare cuts that were not issued on commercial releases. The band was infamous for their BBC radio appearances in England and several of these have made their way onto promotional or syndicated radio show albums and CDs. The rarest radio items would have to be the original BBC transcription discs of the several shows Zeppelin agreed to broadcast over the radio. The most common of these discs is from the legendary show at the Paris Theatre on March 25, 1971, which aired again on April 4, 1971, and through the magic of bootlegging is one of the most reproduced Zeppelin live shows. Also notable is the BBC broadcast from the Playhouse Theatre on June 27, 1969, which again has been bootlegged extensively. Both of these shows have been subsequently licensed to the Westwood One radio network in the United States and have aired in various forms on American radio. The Westwood One albums are far more common than the BBC pressings (there are a lot more radio stations in the United States than in England), but they still command a price of around $100 a disc. The complete uncut shows from the BBC have never been aired in the United States.

Other BBC sessions have never been officially pressed on vinyl, though they have aired on radio and exist on tape. These include the studio performances for Dave Symonds "Symonds on Sunday" show recorded on June 9, 1969, and broadcast on June 15, 1969, and John Peel's Top Gear from June 24, 1969. These two sessions were rebroadcast in their entirety by the BBC in early 1979 and have also been extensively bootlegged. "Travelling Riverside Blues" from the Peel show was also finally officially released on the boxed set in 1990, though much of the rest of these shows remains unreleased and constitutes some of the most sought-after Zeppelin material.

Led Zeppelin split up before the advent of the compact disc, but a few CD rarities have surfaced over the years. The first Zeppelin album to be released on CD was the fourth album, which came out on CD in 1982. It has subsequently been packaged in several different cardboard sleeves and these have attracted the attention of collectors. Atlantic took advantage of the popularity of the CD format and has since pressed all of Zeppelin's album catalog on CD, though this move has not been without controversy. The early CD packages have been criticized for their poor sound quality and for the shabby production used on the CD booklets—which is one reason that the original pressings of the Zeppelin LPs remain collectible. The boxed set did clean up the sound on the cuts included and Atlantic is working to issue remastered CDs of all the albums in the near future. There were even plans in 1990 in Japan to release several CD singles du-

plicating the original Japanese seven-inch releases but the CDs have yet to appear.

The original pressing of *Physical Graffiti* contained an error that cut off the end of "In My Time of Dying." This mistake was reportedly on the master tape used for the CD pressing and was eventually corrected but not before this CD became a collectible itself.

In 1990, when the boxed set was released around the world a double CD set was released in Europe titled *Remasters*. The cover art was similar to the boxed set but the contents were different. The material from the boxed set, which took up four CDs, was edited down to a two CD collection also featuring "Good Times Bad Times" presented in a remastered version for the first time. This song was not on the boxed set itself and has yet to appear in

the United States in its remastered form. The double CD set also does not include any of the non-LP tracks featured on the four CD version. To promote the boxed set, a four-track CD EP was issued in the U.K. that came in a gold blimp-shaped box and included "Good Times Bad Times" plus three other songs.

Another promo CD for the boxed set was an interview disc titled *Profiled*, which was issued in the United States. It contained interviews with the three remaining band members and a profile of their work.

One of the rarest and most valuable Zeppelin-related CDs is a radio promo disc called *Rarities Precious Gems* from Radio Today that includes the first CD issue of "Hey Hey What Can I Do." The track is included on the disc, though the cover only lists it as a "mystery track." Another radio station promo CD of note is a recent six CD set from Westwood

One titled "It's Been a Long Time" hosted by Jason Bonham and featuring a couple of notable tunes from the BBC sessions. This CD set sells for over $300, indicating the tremendous power the group still has with collectors.

Though it is unreleased or live music that interests most collectors of Zeppelin, there's no doubt that what looks the neatest is the sometimes bizarre promotional materials Atlantic issued to push the group. These include the three inflatable blimps that were issued for the first three records, which are extremely rare and valuable items. Japan also issued a promo inflatable blimp to promote *Physical Graffiti* and this item is among the most valuable Zeppelin collectibles.

The music of Led Zeppelin always had a three-dimensional feel to it so it comes as no surprise that their label issued a number of mobiles and cardboard standups in addition to the blimps. These include a very rare silver cardboard mobile for the first record, a similar mobile for *Houses of the Holy*, a three dimensional window display featuring the famous tenement cover to *Physical Graffiti*, and a counter standup promoting *In Through the Out Door* with a picture of the group taken at Knebworth in England.

Perhaps the most significant piece of Zeppelin paraphernalia is called "The Object." This promotional item reproduces the object shown on the cover of *Presence*. The small black counter ornament was meant to represent the mystical nature of the band's music. The original promo piece was limited to 1,000 pieces and they were packaged and numbered by Atlantic. This item alone commands prices of several hundred dollars. Not surprisingly, considering the interest in Zeppelin bootlegs, even "The Object" was not free from the wrath of the bootleggers and counterfeit copies exist. The counterfeits are also numbered and supposedly less than 1,000 were made, though their value would be considerably less than the original. The counterfeit is very difficult to tell from the original and only differs in that the finish of the ornament is significantly

rougher than the finish on the original ornament.

Zeppelin posters represent another subcategory to collecting the band that alone could occupy the a collector's entire attention. Promotional posters for the group are difficult to come by, partially because Atlantic didn't issue them in great quantities and because the group first formed so long ago.

Even rarer than promotional posters and more sought after are the numerous posters done to advertise concert appearances. Some of these posters from the late 1960s and early 1970s represent valued items just for their design, apart from their Zeppelin connection. The famous Fillmore posters commissioned by promoter Bill Graham are perhaps the most commonplace of the early Zeppelin concert posters. There are four posters for Zeppelin gigs in the Graham archives and the most important three are from January, April, and November 1969, designed by Randy Tuten. The fourth poster is from Zeppelin's September 2, 1970 show at the Oakland Coliseum and this lists a host of other Bill Graham-promoted attractions. As with all collectibles, price is determined by a combination of supply and demand, and though the first three posters are far more attractive, the 1970 poster is the hardest to find and hence the most valuable. Zeppelin played numerous shows all over the world on more than a dozen organized tours so hundreds of posters announcing the band's performances are in existence.

Other Zeppelin collectibles of note include magazines and paper goods. Some early and rare magazines with Zeppelin covers exchange hands for over $100 and even old newspapers fetch tidy sums if they feature Zeppelin reviews or features. The early songbooks are considered prime Zeppelin items since they feature some otherwise unpublished photos of the group and they are quite valuable. Sheet music is also sought after printed matter for Zep fans, both because it looks great framed and because many Zeppelin fans are musicians themselves. The color songbook for *In Through the Out Door* is already commanding over $50 on the collector's market.

Surprisingly, there were no biographies written about Led Zeppelin until 1975. The first, titled

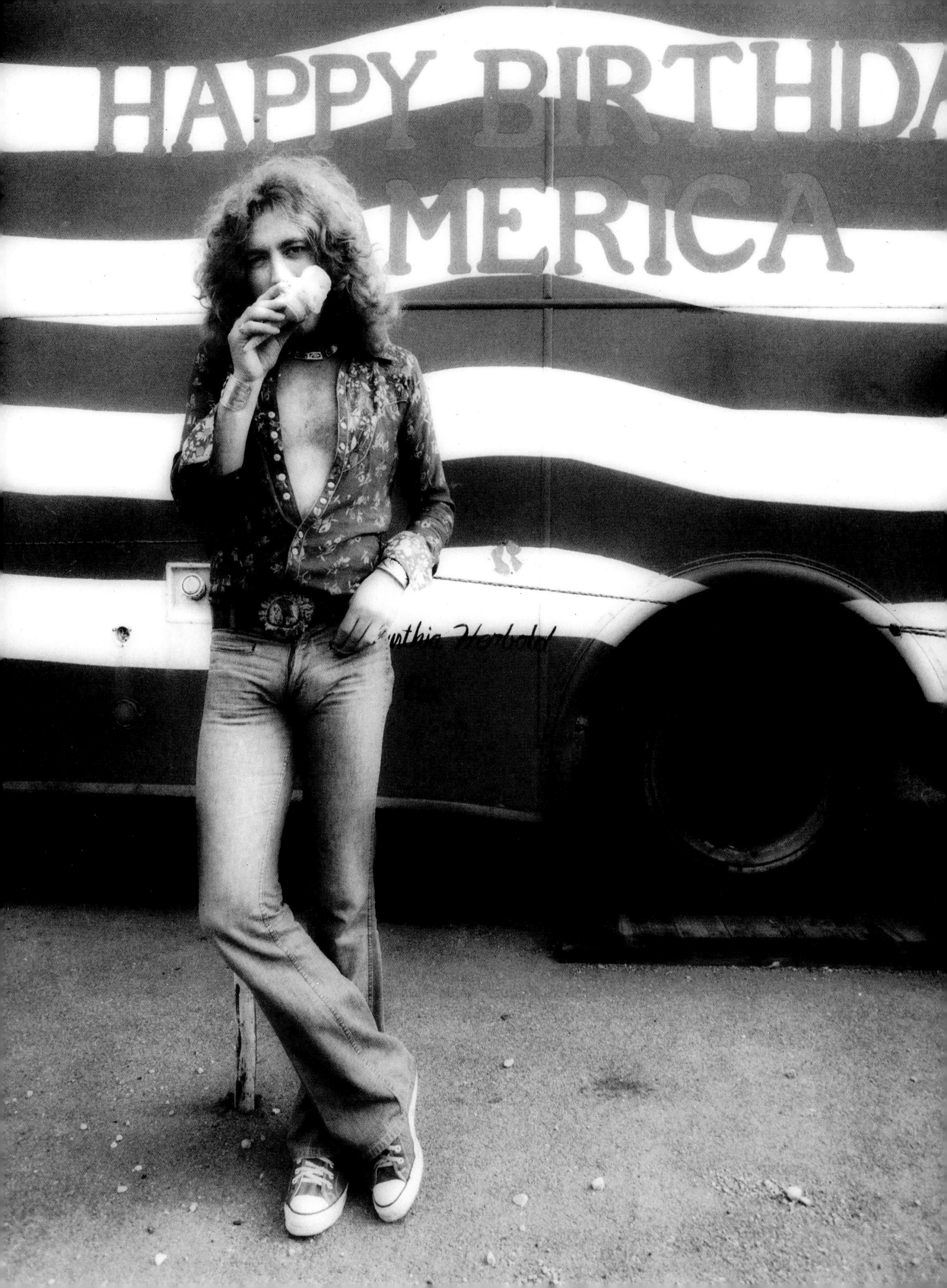
HAPPY BIRTHDA
MERICA

Robert Plant, was published by *Circus* magazine and is unquestionably one of the worst publications ever devoted to the band, but because of its scarcity it still interests collectors. This book strangely is no more about Robert Plant than it is about Jimmy Page, but the theory must have been that Plant's name would sell more copies. Richie York began to do some justice to the subject with his 1976 book *The Led Zeppelin Biography*, which is also rare these days and is worth as much as $30 to a collector.

Other books on the band include *A Visual Documentary* by Paul Kendall, which is a useful and mostly accurate reference work. Stephen Davis's *Hammer of the Gods* is by far the most successful book on the band (and incidentally one of the best selling rock 'n' roll books of all time), yet many serious collectors refuse to value this sordid look at the band's offstage activity. Neal Preston's photo book, *Portraits*, is an extremely attractive piece that features some of the real "hammer of the Gods" imagery that Jimmy Page was always in search of. There are two versions of Preston's book: the first is signed and numbered and worth at least $60 on the collectors' market.

Led Zeppelin has also inspired numerous fanzines, as previously mentioned, most of which spend some of every issue pondering the unponderable: when will this band reunite? The most notable fanzine was *Pure Blues*, which debuted in January 1979 in the United States and lasted a couple of years. The first issue is most valuable and prized by fans. *Proximity*, one of the most professional efforts, was around for a number of years in the 1980s. Dave Lewis edited the short-lived *Tight But Loose* magazine in the late 1970s, ending around the time the group split up. Other titles from around the globe include *The Rover* for the United States, *The Australian Led Zeppelin Connection*, *The Ocean*, *Oh Jimmy* from Italy, and *Electric Magic*, an excellent glossy monthly publication from Canada that is still an ongoing concern. *Zoso* is the best-circulated current fanzine. Starting in 1987 with a relatively limited base, it has

blossomed into a well prepared monthly journal with a worldwide readership.

Those with big bucks and the inclination may want to chase after industry awards, the gold and platinum records issued by record companies to record sales. A number of these attributed to Zeppelin are on the market and with this group, and many other artists, numerous fakes exist. The best rule of thumb for a collector of these types of items is to be sure of your source: if you're buying a gold record for the "Stairway to Heaven" single, you're getting taken.

The same can be said of autograph collecting, which is harder when it comes to Led Zeppelin than most other groups. During the apex of their career the band was not easily accessible so autographed articles signed by all four members are extremely valuable. In recent years it has become easier to get Plant's or Page's autograph but Jones's continues to be relatively hard to come by.

Finally there is also the selling and buying of stage paraphernalia such as drumsticks, stage clothes, or even the band's stage amps and other equipment. These are obviously one-of-a-kind items, though they do occasionally come up in auctions at Sotheby's or Christie's. On odd occasions members of the band have given articles, such as guitars, to charity auctions. Page complains that over the years many rare Zeppelin items have been stolen from him, which shows you the insanity that collecting will lead some fanatics to.

There are literally thousands of collectors who specialize in Led Zeppelin material and all are competing for an ever-dwindling supply of true collectibles. The best word of advice would be to deal with reputable dealers and concentrate on easily obtainable material before going out to purchase an "Immigrant Song" original 45 from Japan. The one thing that all Zeppelin collectors eventually learn is that you can never have everything because of the group's huge worldwide impact. But still, wouldn't it be nice to have the copy of *A Date With Elvis* that made Jimmy Page pick up the guitar?

—Charles R. Cross and Robert Godwin

WE'RE GONNA GROOVE

Led Zeppelin on Bootleg

In late 1968 a couple of California teenagers stumbled upon several reels of tape that had been recorded in Bob Dylan's house. How they came to acquire these tapes has never exactly been explained and is the stuff of legend. Before the 1960s, record companies usually held onto all tapes from artists' recording sessions. But artists like Dylan and the Beatles took more control of the process of making records, recording where they felt like it—in a house in Woodstock, for example—and the record labels lost control of the process.

The tapes these two teenagers stumbled upon contained some previously unreleased Dylan songs and alternate versions of some songs that had already been released. Open-reel tape decks were expensive at the time, and beyond the budget of these kids, so they approached a record manufacturing plant to master and press the tapes in the lowest quantity allowed, which was 100 pieces. In the 1960s, cassette tapes were not commonly available, and everyone had a turntable, so it was not unusual for people to make records to pass on information as they do with tapes today. High school bands made records of their annual concerts and church groups made records of their favorite hymn performances. Pressing 100 records was considerably cheaper than buying a tape deck and at the time there was nothing illegal about it.

The kids made these 100 Dylan records, thinking of them more as novelties rather than as albums per se. They gave them away to friends and soon friends of friends began to inquire about them. People began to offer money for the discs, which were packaged in JIMMY PAGE AT KNEBWORTH, AUGUST 4, 1979 a plain white sleeve. A record store approached the kids to ask if they could have 100 copies at $4 apiece. So the kids made 500 more, started to sell them for a few bucks each, and the modern American bootlegging industry was born. The record became known as *The Great White Wonder* and over the next decade it sold so many copies some claimed it should have made it onto the *Billboard* charts. The teenagers went on to form the Trade Mark of Quality (TMQ) record label and to become the biggest bootleggers in music history.

Today we recognize *The Great White Wonder* as the first significant bootleg album. Bootlegging itself began back with the invention of the cylinder phonograph; the earliest bootlegs were of opera legend Enrico Caruso. But bootlegging didn't begin as an industry until the late 1960s and it continues to this day as a quasi-underground record industry. And with the exception of the Beatles and the Rolling Stones, no other group in history has interested bootleggers as much as Led Zeppelin.

When bootlegging began in the late 1960s, it was not illegal. Those first copies of *The Great White Wonder* were sold in legitimate record stores over the counter and were stuck in the Dylan section in the record racks. In the early 1970s, every hip record store in town had stacks of bootlegs for sale, and many times they were cheaper and occasionally better than the regular record company releases. The

law changed in February 1972, when the U.S. Congress passed a bill that outlawed the exhumation of pet cemeteries for the purpose of road construction. In an effort to quickly pass a law to deal with the increasing number of bootleg albums, the recording lobby persuaded Congress to attach an amendment to the pet cemetery bill making it a felony to manufacture bootleg, pirate, or counterfeit sound recordings for the purpose of resale. The law has been open to interpretation over the years and though court cases are still occasionally fought over the specifics of copyright infringement involved, bootlegging remains illegal.

It is important to distinguish between the different forms of music piracy. A "bootleg" is defined as an illegally manufactured disc or tape that includes previously unreleased live or studio recordings. A "pirate" is considered a copy of a commercially available recording that has been repackaged in its own unique packaging. A "counterfeit," finally, is a copy of a commercially available recording that duplicates all aspects of the original official copy, including the packaging. These distinctions are important because the perpetrators of each different level approach the project with a different intention. Pirates and counterfeits are usually made by professionals with the sole intent of high profits.

Most bootlegs are manufactured by fans. Even the Recording Industry Association of America (RIAA, the body that actually takes bootleggers to court) admits that bootlegging is small potatoes compared to the millions of dollars in losses record companies face from pirates and counterfeits. Usually the RIAA does not distinguish between the various forms of bootlegging when they report on raids or actions they have taken, so when you read about 100,000 records being seized they usually aren't talking about copies of *The Great White Wonder*. Though the moral question of bootlegging is one best answered individually, the debate generally comes down to whether the buying of bootleg albums hurts the sales of legitimate albums (as the record companies argue) or whether anyone who would spend money on a bootleg is bound to have all the legitimate releases already (as many bootleg collectors suggest).

Shortly after the release of *The Great White Wonder*, the Rolling Stones played a concert at the Oakland Coliseum that was the talk of the West Coast. The show was taped and released in bootleg form with the title *Liver Than You'll Ever Be*. It was an outstanding recording of a great performance and it was immediately recognized by fans, and by critics, as far superior to the official Stones live album. The record was reviewed in many publications and treated with all the seriousness that a legitimate release would warrant. The record sold even faster than *The Great White Wonder* and the legitimate record companies began to take notice. Two or three more titles followed in the next few months, a Donovan disc and a couple more Dylan titles, and rumor began to spread through the grapevine about a forthcoming disc from an exciting new live band by the name of Led Zeppelin.

The grapevine was something that Zeppelin manager Peter Grant stayed in touch with—he had virtually created all the excitement for his new band by word of mouth to start with. Grant heard about this Zeppelin bootleg and immediately thought it would take money out of his pocket. The group's label, Atlantic, also was concerned since Zeppelin already accounted for a high percentage of company profits. Grant set off to stop the bootleggers before they got started.

Grant reportedly traveled extensively through England and America, went to every studio that the band had recorded in and to every radio station that had done a broadcast, and reclaimed any tapes he could find. Shortly thereafter Atlantic drafted up a stack of cease-and-desist orders and made it known that they were ready to deliver them to any stores that sold bootlegs. In the October 3, 1970, issue of *Melody Maker* the headline read "Led Zeppelin Hammer Bootlegs." The story reported that "two new Led Zeppelin albums will shortly be in the shops—both unofficial, illegal bootlegs. But Zeppelin's management immediately blasted back with a denial that any tapes were in private hands, and added the threat that anyone who tries to bootleg the group will be promptly sued. One Zeppelin album is alleged to be studio recorded tracks, never released, and the other is a live album

from Germany. Phil Carson, European general manager of Atlantic records told me, 'We will be taking positive legal action against anyone who is found pressing, marketing or retailing these albums,' and Zeppelin manager Peter Grant declared this week, 'As far as I know there can be no tapes of Zeppelin available. After hearing some time ago that there was going to be an attempt to bootleg some tapes of the band, I flew to America. We've managed to retrieve all the tapes and we know of nothing in existence that can be issued.' " Perhaps no greater misstatement has been uttered in music business history.

It was an understandable mistake to make, though. Up to that time no one believed that you could make a good tape of a band from a seat in the audience. It was *Led Zeppelin Live on Blueberry Hill* that changed that misconception forever. The Dylan bootlegs had been recorded from either the famous "basement tapes," which were studio-quality recordings, or from television outtakes. The Stones' *Liver* album was so good that everyone assumed it was recorded by someone associated with the band, perhaps straight from the mixing board. But there were no illusions about *Blueberry Hill*. This was definitely an audience recording, complete with whistles and cheering, but despite that it sounded great. Legend has it that the recording was made using a two-track Nagra portable open-reel tape deck with a Sennheiser shotgun microphone. Some argued that this recording from the audience actually sounded closer to the experience of the show than the sterile sound on most legitimate live recordings.

Blueberry Hill opened the floodgates. The bootleggers realized that they could get as much material as they wanted, and more important, they realized that there was a tremendous audience for these recordings. *Blueberry Hill* is still recognized by many Zeppelin collectors as being one of the very best Zeppelin bootlegs. It has several unique fea-

IN THE STUDIO,

LOS ANGELES,

CALIF., 1970

tures: it was the best recording from the era (recorded September 1970 at the L.A. Forum, one of the band's favorite venues); it is still the only bootleg with a decent live recording of "Bring It on Home;" it is the only bootleg with live versions of "Out on the Tiles," "Blueberry Hill," and "I Saw Her Standing There;" and the original tape included a live version of Page's instrumental "Bron-Yr-Aur," which wasn't released on the original vinyl bootleg, though it was recently included on a CD release of the bootleg as a bonus track.

There have been literally hundreds of Led Zeppelin bootlegs since that first one in late 1970. Even ten years after the group's demise, Zeppelin bootlegs appear on the collector's market at the rate of about 30 different titles a year. Though bootleg CDs are still relatively new, there are already over 150 different Zeppelin titles out on CD. The number of vinyl Zeppelin bootleg titles is over 325 and that is for titles alone—consider that many of these titles have been re-pressed in ten or more

different editions. Most Zeppelin titles are double records and there are at least four ten album bootleg sets. One infamous Zeppelin bootleg set contains a full 70 different discs. Adding it all up and stacking them side by side would mean more than 12 feet of Zeppelin bootlegs with a total number of discs in the neighborhood of 1,000. All this from a group that released ten official albums!

The original TMQ bootlegs from the early 1970s are still some of the most desirable and the most valuable. There were three original TMQ single albums, *Mudslide*, *BBC Broadcast*, and *Stairway to Heaven*. The label originally issued five double albums: *Blueberry Hill*, *Going to California*, *Bonzo's Birthday Party*, *Three Days After*, and *V 1/2*. *Mudslide* was actually a reissue of another bootleg titled *Pb* (reissuing bootlegs is a very common occurrence and something that you'll see confuses the number of Zeppelin titles greatly) that had been recorded off the radio in Vancouver, Canada, and is an exceptional mono recording of a tremendous performance. *BBC Broadcast* was the first of a multitude of bootlegs taken from the performance at the BBC's Paris Theatre in March 1971. *Stairway to Heaven* was a combination of material from BBC concerts in March of 1971 and June 1969. *Going to California* was issued right after *Blueberry Hill* and was touted as being recorded in Los Angeles, though it actually was from a show at the Berkeley Community Theatre on September 14, 1971. Bootleggers frequently mislabel the date and place of the shows contained on their discs, sometimes out of incompetence, sometimes to purposely throw off authorities as to who recorded the show, and occasionally simply to try to sell more copies since shows from the bigger markets usually have more interest for collectors since the market is larger.

The next title of note went on to become legendary, perhaps because the title itself was such a classic. It was called *Bonzo's Birthday Party* and it featured the performance from the L.A. Forum on May 31, 1973. The boot contains outstanding live performances of "Heartbreaker," "Whole Lotta Love," and "The Ocean." It was followed up with the title *Three Days After*, recorded at the same venue on June 3, 1973. This release also included some of the leftover material from the *Blueberry Hill* tape. The next TMQ title was *V1/2* which was recorded in Seattle on June 17, 1973. The recording is not outstanding but the performance makes up for it.

These TMQ titles are considered to be the mainstays of any Zeppelin bootleg collection, though not every release came out first on TMQ. *Blueberry Hill* was originally issued before the inauguration of the TMQ label, so the first very pressings were on Blimp Records and were packaged in two single plain white sleeves with two insert covers printed in two colors. It was later reissued on TMQ innumerable times and on several different colored pressings of vinyl. Colored wax in the early days was a good indication of a title being an early pressing of a bootleg (and therefore having better sound than a bootleg of a bootleg), though in modern times it is not always the case; some first

editions of bootlegs are on black wax while later pressings are on colored wax and are mistaken for original pressings.

The next major bootleg label on the scene was the Amazing Kornyphone Record Label (TAKRL), a business that issued a ton of records though only a few of their titles were Zeppelin discs (supposedly the people behind the label weren't big Zeppelin fans). The label released three single Zep albums: *Ballcrusher*, a reissue of an album by the same name from Flat Records and taken from the 1971 BBC concert; *Live in England 1976*, a reissue of the excellent European bootleg recorded at Earl's Court on May 24, 1975; and *Cellarful of Noise*, a poor recording from the performance at Osaka Festival Hall in Japan on September 29, 1971. The label released two double albums of Zeppelin material: *Live in Seattle*, a reissue of the TMQ *V1/2* title and *The 1975 World Tour*, from Montreal, Canada, on February 6, 1975. Kornyphone's releases were some of the most widely distributed Zeppelin bootlegs and pop up in most collections, but they are not known for being high quality recordings.

Another early bootleg label was Wizardo Records. The only Zeppelin titles put out by Wizardo were *Plant Waves* (the title was a takeoff on the Bob Dylan album *Planet Waves*), and *Caution Explosive*. *Plant Waves* was a compilation of tracks from Detroit and New York shows on the 1975 tour and the sound quality was variable. *Caution Explosive* fared a little better since the source material included, once again, the infamous *Blueberry Hill* material along with some of Winterland in San Francisco from 1969.

By the mid 1970s a whole host of smaller bootleg labels had sprung up including Contraband Music, Idle Mind Productions, K&S Records, Berkeley Records, Smilin' Ears, and Ze Anonym Plattenspieler. Most of these labels offered up Zeppelin titles that were little more than reissues of the early TMQ stuff, though there were a few notable new releases. Idle Mind rereleased a Japanese bootleg of the show from Osaka 1972 and called the album *My Brain Hurts*, which should win an award for best title of a Zeppelin boot. The release included a rare and interesting version of the band

covering Ben E. King's "Stand by Me." K&S was the first label to release the legendary Knebworth shows on bootleg, and their version of these shows also included material from the BBC studio sessions and Montreux 1970. Smilin' Ears distinguished itself by being the first bootleg label to release a four-record Zeppelin box set, titled *Destroyer*. The set was originally listed as a Seattle recording, though it actually featured a concert from Cleveland in 1977. The set has become one of the best known and loved of all Zeppelin titles and has been reissued many times.

In 1979 two new labels debuted with Zeppelin releases that stood above the others available at the time. Phoenix and Toasted Records put more effort into packaging their material than other labels had, with full-color deluxe covers that rivaled the official album jackets. The labels issued a whole slew of double albums, with four-color covers and featuring artwork by the noted artist Giger, including *Absence* (BBC and Earl's Court 1975), *Spare Parts* (BBC and Copenhagen 1969), *Knebworth II* (Knebworth August 11, 1979), *Seattle '73;* and *Knebworth '79* (Knebworth August 4, 1979). Most of the material on these labels had been previously released, but the packaging on these records made them desired collectors' items.

In 1980 the RIAA and the Canadian Recording Industry Association, in conjunction with the FBI, mounted a massive campaign to put an end to the bootlegging problem in North America. The publicity surrounding raids staged all across the continent sent bootleggers even further underground. Around this period most major bootlegging operations moved to Europe or Japan, where bootlegs continued to come out and get imported into the United States at ever greater cost to the collector.

OUTTAKE SHOTS FROM THE *IN THROUGH THE OUT DOOR* PUBLICITY PHOTO SESSION, SUMMER OF 1979

In 1985 a new bootleg label called Rock Solid/International Records came into operation and in a very short time issued more Zeppelin work than most other labels put together, most of it previously unreleased.

The single albums included a reissue of a Japanese album called *White Summer* from a show in Hamburg 1970; a Honeydrippers show from 1981; and *John Henry Bonham Session Man*, a boot that included all of Bonham's known recordings for other artists. The multi-album sets included *Listen to this Eddie*, from Los Angeles June 21, 1977; *Duckwalks and Lasers*, Fort Worth 1977 and New York 1973; *In Person*, New York 1977; *In Concert*, Osaka 1971; *Live on the Levee*, Chicago 1975, including "When the Levee Breaks;" *Custard Pie*, a triple from Offenbach 1973 and Earl's Court 1975; *Alpha and Omega*, a four-record set from Oakland 1977 and Spokane 1968 that featured the first ever foldout on a Zeppelin bootleg; *214*, Seattle 1975; *207.19*, Boston 1970; and *Winterland*, from the infamous San Francisco venue, recorded in April 1969. The label even issued two ten-record sets: *Strange Tales from the Road*, which featured tracks from seven different sources, all previously unreleased; and *Led Zeppelin—The Can*, which was a 14-inch film can numbered and stickered with live versions of almost every original song the band ever played live. One of the strange things you'll notice about Zeppelin bootlegs is that the bootleggers weren't afraid to mix material from dramatically different time periods on the same record (including a 1969 performance on a disc of mostly 1977 stuff), which confuses many fans as to the original source material.

As if the material from Rock Solid/International wasn't impressive enough, many of the original bootleggers got back into action in the late 1980s again and Zeppelin was one of their favorite groups. TMQ returned and, using the original master plates, re-pressed *Blueberry Hill*, this time with a deluxe color cover. Toasted also returned to the scene, this time with a number of titles made from unreleased soundboard recordings of the band, and the quality was phenomenal. Available around this time were rehearsals for *Physical Graffiti*, *In Through the Out Door*, and the legendary campfire sessions from Bron-Yr-Aur. Also released in this period were boots of the legendary performance of "Friends" with the Bombay Symphony Orchestra, Plant and Bonham's recordings with the Band of Joy, outtakes from the third record, and dozens of live concert

recordings. On the back of an album called *Last Stand*, featuring the band's Berlin 1980 show, Toasted publicly announced they would stop making vinyl bootlegs, though other manufacturers have continued to press their wares on vinyl.

In the late 1980s, Zeppelin bootlegs, and perhaps bootlegs in general, hit their zenith with the release of the ultimate bootleg of them all, a package titled *The Final Option*. This set featured 70 different albums of Zeppelin material and included pressings of almost every Zeppelin bootleg previously made, all seemingly stamped from the original master plates. This set included material from Rock Solid, Screamin' Oiseau, TAKRL, Toasted, Waggle, and other labels and represented a major organizational effort on the part of the bootleggers. The set came in a black acrylic box with black and gold stickers over it. Only 150 copies were pressed and they sold out immediately. *The Final Option* is now considered one of the rarest collectibles in Zeppelin record lore and commands extraordinary prices on the collector's market.

The Final Option could hardly be topped and that together with Toasted's announcement essentially spelled the end to Zeppelin vinyl bootlegs since the compact disc soon became the format of choice, both for legitimate record releases and for bootleggers. The first Zeppelin CD bootleg was a European issue of the BBC Paris Theatre show and though it was incomplete, the sound quality was outstanding. By early 1991, over a 125 Zeppelin CD titles were on the market, though most of them were reissues of material previously out on vinyl.

The Neutral Zone bootleg label has won accolades from several Zeppelin fanzines for their three discs titled *Classics Off the Air*. This series features the complete BBC performances, all four shows. As a set they represent the best way to get the complete BBC catalog. Other new bootleg CD labels that have produced Zeppelin material include Living Legend, Great Dane, Pyramid, World Productions, and Golden Stars. Many of these labels operate out of Europe where laws allow the bootlegging of concert tapes from performances a decade old as long as royalties are paid to the performers. These loopholes in the European laws have made Europe a hotbed for bootlegging activity and this material inevitably finds its way around the world.

Though the formats now include vinyl, tape, and compact disc, there are still only a limited number of recordings of Zeppelin that rank as top rate and deserve a second look from the collector. What follows is a list of the outstanding recordings available, most of which have now made their way out on CD. It can serve as the basis for a collection of underground Led Zeppelin recordings. All these titles have their merits; some are included because they are perfect recordings, others because they capture historical performances .

Classics Off the Air. These three CDs capture the complete BBC performances recorded on June 9, 16, and 27, 1969, along with March 25, 1970. Also included are parts of the Vancouver 1970 radio broadcast.

Dallas '75. A superb mono soundboard recording, these two CDs document the Dallas show from March 4, 1975. While the entire concert is not included, this set does capture the band at its best, with excellent sound quality.

Destroyer. This is almost the complete soundboard recording from the Cleveland show on April 27, 1977. The recording quality is superb and is the best available from the 1977 tour, though the band's performance is only average.

Final Touch and Last Stand. The band's final performance is documented in soundboard quality.

Rock and Roll. This collection features 65 minutes of soundboard-quality material from the band's legendary Earl's Court show on May 24, 1975.

Stockholm. Featuring only 22 minutes of soundboard recording done in mono, this set nonetheless captures one of the band's best early shows from March 14, 1969.

Studio Daze. One of the few Zeppelin discs to feature studio outtake material, this includes working mixes from the third and fifth albums with some unreleased material. Also included is some live soundboard recording from an L.A. show on June 3, 1973.

Tour over Europe 1980. The material here is from Zurich, June 29, 1980, and features over 88 minutes of soundboard quality. This show is recog-

nized by fans as being one of the band's best performances on what would be their last tour.

Bonzo's Birthday Party. From the L.A. Forum on May 31, 1973, this collection documented a concert on John Bonham's birthday and was a particularly memorable performance.

Central Park. This set is two picture discs from the show on July 21, 1969.

V1/2. Titled to poke fun at the names of the group's albums, this was the first bootleg from the enormously successful 1973 American tour. The recording is from Seattle June 17, 1973, and documents one of the group's best shows on the tour.

For Badge Holders Only. These two double sets document the band's L.A. forum show on June 23, 1977, shows that were a triumph on many levels.

Jenning's Farm Blues. This outstanding CD features outtakes from the third record combined with a soundboard recording from Toronto on September 4, 1971. The title track is an extended electric instrumental version of "Bron-Y-Aur Stomp."

Knebworth. The complete and uncut show, this set from August 4, 1979 is considered the best document so far of this band at their peak.

Bonzo's Last Stand. This single LP of studio rehearsal material was done in Windsor prior to the canceled 1980 tour of America. An excellent recording, it may be the last time the band played together prior to Bonham's death.

Listen to This, Eddie. This is an outstanding performance from the L.A. Forum on June 21, 1977 and though the sound quality is average, the enthusiasm of the band is unmatched.

Live on Blueberry Hill. A double CD or double album set from the L.A. Forum September 4, 1970, this is one of the best performances captured by early tapers and is of historic importance to boot.

Mudslide. A single disc from Vancouver in March 1970, this tape features the excellent mono recording from FM radio.

Tangible Vandalism. This set featured studio rehearsals for the legendary *Physical Graffiti* album and also included outtakes from the third record and some live material from Liverpool 1973.

JIMMY PAGE,

PONTIAC

SILVERDOME,

APRIL 30, 1977

Ballroom Blitz. The legendary performance from London's Lyceum on October 12, 1969. Only an average recording but notable for the venue.

In Through the Outtakes. This set features very good stereo recordings of the working mixes for Zeppelin's last original studio album.

San Francisco. An excellent stereo recording of the date at the Fillmore West on April 27, 1969, the nearest thing to a complete show from the era.

Wild Side and World Tour. This set from the Osaka show on September 29, 1971, is another excellent soundboard tape from the early days.

This list of recordings is just the tip of the iceberg from this band since any group that can see the release of a 70-album bootleg has plenty of material out there. Ironically, during the last five years of the 1980s, more Zeppelin bootlegs were released than were issued in the band's 12 year existence. This may have contributed to the massive upswing in the popularity of this group over those same years as the group's reputation has grown.

As for the band's opinion on bootlegs, Peter Grant no doubt would still like to grab any bootleggers he could find and practice some of his old wrestling moves on them. Grant's opinion on bootlegs will be well remembered if only because in the movie *The Song Remains the Same* he can be seen arguing extensively with a security guard who failed to catch someone selling bootleg photos inside the hall. And though Grant would probably never admit it, being heavily bootlegged also probably helped the connection between Led Zeppelin and their numerous teenaged fans: it made them seem cool and cult and kept them on the cutting edge of danger even if they were the most popular band in the world during their day.

Atlantic Records probably feels the most pain from the numerous Zeppelin bootlegs on the market. Zeppelin accounted for a large share of Atlantic's profits, and seeing the sheer number of

LONDON,

ENGLAND,

JANUARY 1970

Zeppelin bootlegs was evidence to Atlantic executives of what they suspected all along, that a live Zeppelin album would be a best-seller. The release of *Coda* after the band's breakup was an attempt by Atlantic to cut off any bootlegs of studio outtakes that might surface, and, some fans argue, an effort to produce another studio Zeppelin album from material left over in the can. Jimmy Page says today in interviews that "*Coda* was released, basically, because there was so much bootleg stuff out. We thought, 'Well, if there's that much interest, then we may as well put the rest of our studio stuff out.' "

Over the years the remaining band members themselves have mellowed considerably when it comes to bootlegs. Robert Plant has been known to autograph a bootleg now and again without making a big stink, and Jimmy Page himself even comes off these days as a fan. In 1985 when the British metal magazine *Kerrang* asked him if there was the possibility of another release coming out along the lines of *Coda*, he said, "Ah, no. There's some great live stuff. But there's also some great live bootlegs, ha ha. Thank god they're there and thanks to the people who send me these things. I listen to them and go, 'My god, that was good. I wish it had been recorded on the line.' Because our performances changed so much through all those years, it shocks you sometimes to hear what happened." Speaking with *Musician's* Charles M. Young in 1988, Page said about the possibility of a Zeppelin live album, "There are so many bootlegs around that people who are that interested have probably made up their own compilation. They've got their own favorites and it's a very personal thing." Later in that year Page was a little less understanding when he reported that some bootlegs had been made from soundboard tapes stolen from his home.

Although bootlegs continue to be a sensitive subject for the band, there can be little doubt about fans' delight in acquiring bootleg Led Zeppelin. A whole generation of new fans never got to see the band in their prime and they are inclined to snatch up anything that brings a bit of the old hammer of the gods into their living rooms.

—Robert Godwin

Part Four

THE
SONG
REMAINS
THE
SAME

THE SONG REMAINS
THE SAME

Tales from Led Zeppelin's Recording Sessions

Glyn Johns, who engineered the record, says Led Zeppelin's first album was recorded in nine days. John Paul Jones is a little more specific, saying that the entire process took 30 hours, which Jimmy Page confirms: "It took about 30 hours of recording time. Before we started recording we had already played the numbers live and I already had a good idea of what was going to go on as far as the overdubs went." The band received a $200,000 advance for the record, which at that time was one of the largest advances ever awarded a group for its debut record. The advance seemed particularly large in light of the fact that the recording costs for the entire album were less than $3,000.

According to Page and others, the group's name had been given to them by the Who's drummer, Keith Moon, who had suggested that the group would go over like a lead balloon. The Who's bass player, John Entwistle, steadfastly maintains it was he who came up with the name. A number of other names were considered prior to coming up with Led Zeppelin and at one point the band thought of calling themselves Mad Dogs. The "a" was taken out of Lead to make sure Americans pronounced it correctly.

The press had a hard time from the start spelling the name of the group correctly. To make sure the English press got it straight from the start Jimmy Page himself walked a press release into the Melody Maker office in 1968. "No it's Led," Jimmy told the reporters there

LED ZEPPELIN,

SAN FRANCISCO,

CALIF., 1970

who had written the name down as "Lead." "You know the old gag about swinging like a lead balloon?" Page said in way of explanation for the name.

Led Zeppelin I

The album cover made use of a United Press International photo of the Hindenberg Zeppelin catching on fire in 1937 in Lakehurst, N.J. The original British pressings listed an address for a Led Zeppelin fan club, which was never mentioned again on any other record.

The album was recorded in October 1968 at Olympic Studios in London. Before going into the studio the band had rehearsed all the tunes live on their tour of Scandinavia billed as "The New Yardbirds." Page called the studio conditions crude, telling *Musician's* Matt Resnikoff, "I was playing through a little tiny Supro amp with a 12-inch speaker on the whole of that first album, with a Telecaster and just a couple of pedals."

Led Zeppelin was released in the United States on January 12, 1969, and in the United Kingdom on April 1, 1969.

Good Times Bad Times: This track made use of an elaborate kick drum that instantly helped establish John Bonham's signature. The unusual syncopation on a single bass drum was one of the many trademarks that made Bonzo's drumming stand out. Bonham used a single Ludwig drum on this cut and created a sound that many drummers couldn't recreate using two bass drums. Jimi Hendrix was impressed enough with Bonham's drumming here that Page reported Hendrix said Bonham had "a right foot like a pair of castanets."

Babe I'm Gonna Leave You: Though it sounds strange when you consider that Jimmy Page and Robert Plant went on to create what is thought of as the ultimate heavy metal band, both were fans of Joan Baez, who had previously recorded "Babe I'm Gonna Leave You" (as had Quicksilver Messenger Service). Page says he learned this song "in the days of sitting in the darkness, playing my six-string behind Marianne Faithfull." Page described the Zeppelin version of the tune as "a good example of drama, of light and shade and everything."

This was one of only two songs on the debut record, according to Page, that made use of overdubs, this time on the acoustic guitar. (Page may not consider his studio work on the other tracks to be overdubs since there appears to be a number of background tracks added to several of the songs) Robert Plant spoke later in his career about how this track represented one of the first times he and Page were able to successfully work together: "I don't think Jimmy was dominating anything as some have suspected. I was able to suggest things and the two of us rearranged 'Babe I'm Gonna Leave You.' When we heard it back in the studio we were shaking hands with our brains because it turned out to be so nice. It was really good to be able to get it off like that." Page described the simplicity of the recording process on the record: "We recorded the songs almost exactly as we'd been doing them live. Only 'Babe I'm Gonna Leave You' was altered as far as I can remember." Page had rehearsed a somber version of this earlier in 1968 with Steve Winwood on organ that has never been officially released.

You Shook Me: This song had also been recorded by Jeff Beck, though Page claimed the inspiration for Zeppelin's version was a Yardbirds jam. He defended the sound of the song like this: "It really pissed me off when people compared our first album to the Jeff Beck Group and said it was very close conceptually. It was nonsense. Utter nonsense. The only similarity was that we'd both come out of the Yardbirds and we had both acquired certain riffs individually from the Yardbirds." Plant echoed that theory, saying, "Beck's always moaned about Pagey by saying things like, 'He knew what we were doing, Rod Stewart and I. He got this guy from the Midlands (Plant). They were doing "You Shook Me."' We were all doing 'You Shook Me'! It was more famous than 'God Save the Queen' in England at the time."

The song represents the first call-and-response blues tune from Zeppelin, a style they would adopt frequently in the future. The Zeppelin version of the song was inspired by the Willie Dixon tune written when he was the bass player with Muddy Waters and recorded by Waters, as well as by the Yardbirds version. Plant recalled the vocal styling he used on the track: "I never consciously had the idea of mirroring the guitar work with my voice, but I remembered Robert Johnson had done it, and when I started singing with Jimmy, it just seemed natural. There were no spoken instructions about it for that first album, but we broke into it on 'You Shook Me' and we all broke into smiles."

Dazed and Confused: This song began as the tune "Dazed and Confused," originally done by Page back with the Yardbirds and recorded on the album *Live Yardbirds*, though both the Yardbirds track and the Zeppelin version are essentially identical to a song called "I'm Confused" done acoustically by Jake Holmes in 1965. Though the lyrics are different, the music to the song is surprisingly similar to Holmes's version. Page has been asked about this bit of "borrowing" before and he's said he was unaware of the Holmes track, though many critics have noted that the resemblance is beyond coincidence. When asked about the song later Holmes recalled, "I said, what the hell, let him have it."

"Dazed and Confused" represents some of the only bow-

of the few on the first record worked out by all four members of the group. Because of contractual obligations Robert Plant does not receive any songwriting credits on this record, as he was still under contract to CBS.

Jimmy Page plays a ten-string Fender 800 pedal steel guitar on this track, which he says is the first time he ever played pedal. "We had also worked out a version of 'Chest Fever' in rehearsals, though we never played it onstage. That had organ and pedal steel on it." This tune was never played live by Led Zeppelin.

Black Mountain Side: A Yardbirds tune called "White Summer" influenced this cut. The song features an unusual open tuning, a technique Page says Al Stewart taught him during his period as a session musician. Bert Jansch's vocal tune "Black Water Side" is also thought to be an influence on this track, and the melody to Jansch's tune sounds very similar to the Zeppelin number. The tabla drums on this track are played by Viram Jasani, who is credited on the album sleeve, one of the few times an outside musician ever recorded with the band.

Communication Breakdown: Page says this is one of the first things he and Robert ever wrote together. It also represents one of the few Zeppelin tracks on record where Page can be heard singing background vocals. In interviews Page talked about how hard this song was to play since it required so much rapid down stroking with the guitar pick. The riff of the tune was inspired by the Eddie Cochran song "Nervous Breakdown."

"Communication Breakdown" was released as a single in the United States in March 1969, backed with "Good Times Bad Times," and the single did not chart in the Top 40.

I Can't Quit You: The band revealed in early interviews that this track was influenced by a version of the tune recorded by Otis Rush. It was Plant's suggestion they attempt to record it.

How Many More Times: Critics had suggested this shares some of the same feel as "Beck's Bolero," a tune that Page had previously produced. It also gained some inspiration from Albert King's "The Hunter" and Howlin' Wolf's "How Many More Years." The song was played live by the Yardbirds,

ing with guitar done by Jimmy Page on a Led Zeppelin record, though he did use this trademark technique at every Zeppelin concert (it was probably used on "How Many More Times" on record). Page later said guitar bowing was something he'd learned while doing a studio session when a musician named McCallum suggested trying the technique. (McCallum's son was the actor David McCallum, who appeared on the popular television program "The Man from U.N.C.L.E.")

The song was issued as a promotional single in the United States complete with a picture sleeve, and backed with "Babe I'm Gonna Leave You," in January 1969, two weeks prior to the release of the album. The tune instantly became a concert staple for the group, and is one of the songs they played most often. As Page developed lengthy solos to insert into the song it began to grow longer and longer in concert, and frequently lasted from 30 to 40 minutes. At a Seattle concert on March 21, 1975, the song ran nearly 45 minutes.

Your Time Is Gonna Come: This song was one

who unsuccessfully attempted to record it. Strangely this song was credited on the record as being 3:30 long when the song is actually over 8:30. Plant said that his previous group had done this song in concert, saying it "was something that Bonzo and I did together in the Band of Joy anyway. A lot of excerpts from it anyway. It came from a lot of ad libs and improvisations, things that Page had been doing with the Yardies and that Bonzo and I had been doing together. That sort of freeform, branching out into different tangents."

Led Zeppelin II

Much of the second album was recorded live in the studio and though it was recorded rather quickly, Jimmy Page still complained afterward that "the album took such a long time to make. It was quite insane really." The band was touring extensively at this point, so they ended up recording the record in numerous studios around the world and patching the material together into one whole. Page commented on the process: "We've been so busy that we just weren't able to go into one studio and polish the album off. It's become ridiculous. We put a rhythm track down in London, add the voice in New York, overdub harmonica in Vancouver, and then come back to New York."

Studios at which *Led Zeppelin II* were recorded include A&R Studios in New York, Olympic Studio in London, Morgan Studios in London, Juggy Sound Studio in New York, Mystic Studios in Los Angeles, Mirror Sound in Los Angeles, Mayfair Studios in New York, and other studios in various locations including Vancouver, B.C., where Robert Plant described the studio as "a hut." Recording took place from July to September 1969. The album was mixed at A&R Studios in New York by Eddie Kramer in one weekend.

The album cover used a photo of the members of the Jasta division of German pilots featuring the infamous Red Baron, who can be seen seated on the wing of the plane. The original photo was from 1917, though the graphic designer retouched all the faces in the picture for the album cover and replaced the pilot's faces. Included in the photo are the band members along with several members of the group's road crew including road manager Richard Cole. The woman in the photo is the English actress Glynis Johns, who played the mother in the film version of *Mary Poppins*. One would have to guess her appearance in the photo is an in joke referring to Glyn Johns, the producer and engineer who had worked with the band on the first album.

Led Zeppelin II was released in the United States on October 22, 1969, and the United Kingdom on October 19, 1969.

Whole Lotta Love: This was the band's first real signature piece and, until "Stairway to Heaven" replaced it, it was the band's concert showpiece. Jimmy Page sings background on this song again. Robert Plant's lead vocal was done in only one take. "For 'Whole Lotta Love,' " Page said, "I had the section worked out already before entering the studio. I had rehearsed it. All that other stuff, sonic wave and all that, I built up in the studio and put effects on and things, treatments. The descending riff was done with a metal slide and backwards echo. I think I came up with that first before anybody. I know it's been used a lot now, but not at the time. In fact, some of the things that might sound odd have in fact backwards echo involved in them as well." Eddie Kramer, who engineered the album, attributed the sound on "Whole Lotta Love" to "a combination of Jimmy and myself just flying around on a small console twiddling every knob known to man." Robert Plant said years later that this song was one of the first Led Zeppelin tunes he contributed lyrics to.

Willie Dixon thought the song sounded familiar when he heard the tune, and in 1986 his lawyers sued Zeppelin, claiming the song borrowed from his "You Need Love." Dixon's lawyer Scott Cameron said Dixon first heard "Whole Lotta Love" in 1983 though the song had been issued originally in 1969. The Dixon song had first been recorded by Muddy Waters in 1962 and was a blues classic. The lawsuit was settled out of court even though the members of Led Zeppelin were not personally liable for the damages since they had already sold their publishing rights.

"Whole Lotta Love," backed with "Living Loving Maid," was released as a single in the United States in November 1969. It rose to number four on the *Billboard* charts, representing the highest position ever for a Zeppelin single in the United States.

What Is and What Should Never Be: Like many of Zeppelin's tunes, this song made extensive use of stereo separation.

The Lemon Song: First issues of the U.K. copy of the album credited this song to the band but in later pressings it was retitled "Killing Floor" and was credited to Howlin' Wolf (under Wolf's real name, Burnett). Presumably an out-of-court settlement over songwriting credit was reached, though never announced, since later pressings again credited the song to the band. Whoever wrote the actual song, Zeppelin's version is inspired lyrically, if not stolen, from Howlin' Wolf's "Killing Floor." The end of "The Lemon Song" is actually real time echo, meaning that no devices were used. When Plant sings "killing . . . floor . . . floor . . . floor . . . " the echo was one he made with his voice alone.

When Robert Plant was interviewed in 1990 around the time of the release of the charity album *The Last Temptation of Elvis*, which included a Plant cover of an Elvis tune, he said "The Lemon Song" was the Zeppelin number he would have most wanted to have heard Elvis sing.

Thank You: This song features one of the few times Page played a solo on acoustic guitar on record. It also was the first time Robert Plant had written lyrics on his own, and he wrote this song for his wife Maureen. Page described the process of urging Plant to write like this: "It took a lot of ribbing and teasing actually to get him into writing. It was funny, on the second album, he wrote the words of 'Thank You' because he said, 'I'd like to have a crack at this and write it for my wife.' " Page has frequently cited this song

ROBERT PLANT, OUTDOORS AT OAKLAND STADIUM, JULY 23, 1977

as the point at which he turned over most of the chores of Zeppelin's lyric writing to Plant.

Heartbreaker: Perhaps Page's first guitar signature piece and a tune that became a concert favorite over the years. In concert Page would frequently insert bits and pieces of other tunes into this, including "Greensleeves" and once even the "59th Street Bridge Song" by Simon and Garfunkel.

Living Loving Maid (She's Just a Woman): Jimmy Page again sings back-up on this tune.

Ramble On: The lyrics to "Ramble On" were the first of several Plant writings to show some inspiration from the works of J. R. R. Tolkien. Page used backward echo on this cut as he had on "Whole Lotta Love."

Moby Dick: Recorded in two parts, this song was remastered to segue into "Bonzo's Montreux" by Jimmy Page on the boxed set. Though Page spoke in interviews for the boxed set as if that remixing was a great accomplishment, the original studio tapes indicate that the drum solo was recorded separately from the beginning. The full band sections that precede and follow the drum

solo on record were recorded in one pass, with the band stopping after the first section and then counting in immediately to the end section. The next take featured just the drum solo and the engineer can be heard saying, "Drum insert, take one." The drum solo that was recorded during the original studio session was also longer than the version used on the second record.

Prior to "Moby Dick," Bonham frequently performed a drum solo called "Pat's Delight," which bore some similarities to "Moby Dick," though there the band did not start or end the tune and it featured Bonham's drumming alone. Pat was the name of Bonham's wife. In June of 1969, the band did a BBC radio session and included a vocal track called "The Girl I Love," and this song used a similar band track to the one that starts and ends "Moby Dick."

Bring It on Home: Heavily influenced by an-

other Willie Dixon song also called "Bring It on Home" and recorded by Sonny Boy Williamson.

Led Zeppelin III

The design of this record sleeve came from an idea of Jimmy Page's to recreate a "Farmer's Wheel," an old almanac device that would tell farmers when to plant based on the position of the moon. The complicated design of the record caused numerous problems for Atlantic and its release was held up for some time while the covers were fabricated. Page later described the sleeve as "intended to be something like one of those garden calendars or the zoo wheel things that tell you when to plant cauliflowers or how long whales are pregnant. But there was some misunderstanding with the artist, who in fact is very good but had not been correctly briefed, and we ended up on top of a deadline with a teeny-boppish cover which I think was a compromise." Advertisements for the album told buyers, "After you play the album, play the jacket."

The images featured on the spinning wheel include the band members and Aleister Crowley, the English author and magician who Jimmy Page was fascinated with. Page's fascination had reached its peak earlier in the year when he had purchased Crowley's former house, Boleskine, near the shores of Loch Ness. Page defended the purchase, saying, "There were two or three owners before Crowley moved into it. It was also a church that was burned to the ground with the congregation in it. And that's the site of the house. Strange things happened in that house that had nothing to do with Crowley. The bad vibes were already there."

In addition to the Crowley image on the sleeve, scratched into the dead wax on the vinyl of some of the album's first pressings was an inscription of Crowley's written by Page: "Do what thou wilt shall be the whole of the law." Other pressings had another Crowley saying, "So mote be it," scratched into the wax. These scratchings also showed up on some of the early pressings of the "Immigrant Song" single. Page explained the message in an early interview by saying the inscription "is meant as a philosophical statement. I hoped nobody would see it and none of the group knew about it."

He told another interviewer at the time, "That sprang from me. I suppose you could say that it was instructed, but under a strict cloak of secrecy. I hoped that nobody would see it and nobody did except you. One other person, to my knowledge, saw it because Robert came up to me one day and said that someone had written to Atlantic about a strange inscription on the record." Few critics noticed the scratching but many hard-core fans saw it and word of the message fed fuel to the rumors that the group was involved in the occult.

Years later when Plant was asked about Page's interest in Crowley, he said: "I don't think that Jimmy was particularly interested in the occult, but only in Aleister Crowley, as a great British eccentric. All eccentrics are interesting, but Crowley was a very clever man. Jimmy had an innocent interest in him, just as many people have fixations on individuals at one level or another."

The record itself came together after Page and Plant had spent time at Bron-Yr-Aur cottage, in the south of Wales, near Aberstwyth. The cottage was named for the way the sun shone on the valley every morning. Page described the experience like this: "Robert suggested going to this cottage in South Wales that he'd been to once with his parents when he was much younger. He was going on about what a beautiful place it was and I became pretty keen to go there. I'd never spent any time at all in Wales but I wanted to. So off we went, taking along our guitars of course. It wasn't a question of 'let's go and knock out a few songs in the country.' It was just a case of wanting to get away for a bit and have a good time. We took along a couple of our roadies and spent the evenings around log fires, with pokers being plunged into cider and that sort of thing. As the nights wore on, the guitars came out and numbers were being written. It wasn't planned as a working holiday, but some songs did come out of it."

In 1975, Page and Plant were asked to look back on the recording of the record and on the cottage itself. They reported that the cottage was now surrounded by a fence. Page: "It was so tranquil but there's a fence now." Plant: "We went back to live once, after the musical period, and obviously the place had been sold to somebody. The farmer had roped it off with a fence so the sheep wouldn't come up to the door, and suddenly it had lost its beauty."

Most of the album itself was recorded in Headley Grange, an old country house in Hampshire with a mobile recording studio rented from the Rolling Stones. (The band later bought Headley Grange.) Recording was also done at Island Studios in London and at Ardent Studios in Memphis. The record was recorded between June and August of 1970. Mixing was done at Ardent Studios in Memphis, and at Island and Olympic Studios in London by Andy Johns.

Led Zeppelin III was released in the United States on October 5, 1970, and in the United Kingdom on October 21, 1970.

Immigrant Song: Inspired by Plant's interest in Celtic lore. "The hiss at the beginning is a tape build-up," Page said. "But it's not really tape hiss, it's echo feedback." In rehearsals for the record this song was played as part of "Out on the Tiles."

"Immigrant Song," backed with the non-LP cut "Hey Hey What Can I Do," was released as a single in the United States in November 1970. It was one of Zeppelin's most successful 45s, and spent a total of 10 weeks on the *Billboard* Hot 100, going as high as number 16.

Friends: This is one of the few Zeppelin studio tracks to use strings. The influence is clearly East Indian, though the tune was also influenced by Gustav Holst's "Planets." Holst was an influential classical composer at the turn of the century. When Jimmy Page was selecting the music to introduce the band during his first tour with the Firm he chose "Mars" from Holst's "Planets."

"Friends" was one of two tracks recorded by Plant and Page with the Bombay Symphony Orchestra. Plant described the recording session: "We'd got a sort of disheveled gang of musicians together in Bombay and we recorded two Led Zeppelin tracks. The session went very well until I got

a bottle of brandy out, and there's nothing like a good Indian, and there were no good Indians in that room at the end of the bottle."

The track on the album did not make use of the Bombay Orchestra, though. "The idea was to get an Indian style with the strings," Page said later. "The string players were not Indian, however, and we had to make some on-the-spot changes. John Paul Jones wrote an incredible string arrangement for this and Robert shows his great range, incredibly high. He's got a lot of different sides to his voice which come across here. It has a menacing atmosphere. A friend came into the studio during the recording and it was bloody loud and he had to leave. He said, 'You've really done something evil.' "

Celebration Day: "The reason the voice is alone," Page said, "is the tape got crinkled in the studio and wouldn't go through the heads, so the end got ruined. But it worked out all right by using the idea of bringing the synthesizer down in pitch to the voice. It was either that or leave the track out altogether."

Since I've Been Loving You: The inspiration for this tune was "Never" by Moby Grape off of their album *Grape Jam*. Robert Plant ended up sticking a small segment of the vocal from this song into the end of "White, Clean and Neat," on his solo album *Now and Zen*. Plant frequently spoke in interviews of his great respect for Moby Grape saying that he was "hung up" on them. Page said, "This was a 'live' track. John Paul plays organ and foot bass pedals at the same time. My guitar solo? It could have been better." Plant once told an interviewer that the live in the studio sound on this track is what bootleggers should try to emulate. "The sound is great," he said of the track, "and if pirate albums got it together, instead of waving evil mics on the ends of broomsticks, that is the kind of sound they could get at a live concert." This song was originally considered for the second album but was bumped to make room for "Whole Lotta Love." "Since I've Been Loving You" was infrequently played live.

Out on the Tiles: The title is slang in Britain for "a night on the town." "This is Bonzo's riff," says Page. "Originally we had a set of lyrics to go with this relating to a night going out on the tiles."

Gallows Pole: This is the only Zeppelin track to feature banjo. "I'd never played one before," Page said. "It was John Paul Jones's instrument. I just picked it up and started moving my fingers around until the chords sounded right which is the same way I work on compositions when the guitar is in different tunings." The original inspiration was a traditional song called "Hangman." Page says "I first heard 'Gallows Pole' on an old Folkways record by Fred Gerlach, a twelve-string player who was, I believe, the first white to play the instrument. I used his version as a basis and completely changed the arrangement." Plant talks about this song being one of the first times the band took a tune and started it off acoustically before ending it electrically, a production technique reprised on "Stairway to Heaven," "Over the Hills and Far Away," and "Ten Years Gone." The song was played live only once, in Copenhagen. In an interview prior to the record's release, Page said this was his favorite track on the record.

Tangerine: Page played pedal steel guitar on this track which had been originally recorded by the Yardbirds, at the time of the *Little Games* session. Page described it as being "written after an emotional upheaval." In 1971 Page said this song was the last one he'd written all the lyrics on.

As for the infamous false start, Page said, "It was a tempo guide, and it seemed like a good idea to leave it in, at the time. I was trying to keep the tempo down a bit. I'm not so sure now it was a good idea. Everybody asks what the hell is going on." The band offered no further explanation.

That's the Way: Plant's lyrics on this song reflected his growing skills as a songwriter. According to Page this was one of the songs written in Wales, "after a long walk and we were setting back to the cottage. We had a guitar with us. It was a tiring walk coming down a ravine, and we stopped and sat down. I played the tune and Robert sang a verse straight off. We had a tape recorder with us. That sounds a bit strange but it was part of the kit. And we got the tune down." Prior to the record's release this song was introduced in concert with the title "The Boy Next Door." Demo tapes from the studio sessions indicate the band also tried and rehearsed several electric versions of this song.

Bron-Y-Aur Stomp: After the release of the record but prior to going on the road, Plant said of this song, "It was my influence really. I love folksy things, especially with a beat like that. I don't know if we'll do these numbers onstage. I'm sure the audience wouldn't mind. It depends on if they let me play guitar. I didn't play on the album and I'm not very good, but I've been playing the odd rhythm things. I mean, I could never compete with Page." An electric instrumental version of this song was also cut during the sessions for the album.

The song is about Plant's collie dog Strider. When asked about the meaning of the tune by a critic in 1970, Plant said "It's just about my dog." At the January 7, 1973, show in Oxford, England, Plant explained the tune to the crowd: "It's about a dog that refuses to be bathed, washed, brushed, and spends a lot of his time doing nothing." Strider made his film debut romping around the English countryside at the start of the film *The Song Remains the Same*.

Note the difference in spelling on this title from the song "Bron-Yr-Aur," which was also recorded for the third record but wasn't released until *Physical Graffiti*. The correct spelling of the name of the cottage is Bron-Yr-Aur.

On the recording of the track, Page says that Jones plays "an acoustic bass. It's like an acoustic guitar with a reasonable body. John Paul took the frets out and he plays it acoustically." Page said when the track was mixed, they threw everything they could find on it. "This has got the rattling of the kitchen sink. We overdubbed Bonham on castanets and spoons!"

Hats Off to (Roy) Harper: The song's rough mix is a result of Plant and Page playing together on distorted amps. The background percussion is from various Zeppelin roadies who were in the rehearsal hall at the time. The song is credited as being a traditional tune from "Charles Obscure," another inside joke from the band.

Roy Harper was a late 1960s English folk rocker and a genuine eccentric whom both

JOHN BONHAM ON TAMBOURINE, OAKLAND STADIUM, JULY 23, 1977

Plant and Page respected. He opened up some Zeppelin concerts and Plant and Page played on a number of Harper's recordings, though even the presence of the Zeppelin members failed to produce a hit for Harper.

Plant said, "When we played it for Harper, he didn't know what to say. But his time will come. I personally think Roy Harper is one of the best spokesmen this generation has. Despite the subsequent confusion of critics who somehow misconstrued the meaning and thought it was some kind of put-down, 'Hats Off to (Roy) Harper' is just an acknowledgment of a friendship." Around the time of the boxed set release, Plant described Harper as "a crucial chum, a sage and muse; that's not to say he didn't enjoy some of the Led Zeppelin by-products, like the occasional blow job."

Page also expressed his appreciation of Harper's music if not his offstage antics: "Harper's album *Stormcock* was a fabulous album which didn't sell anything. Also they wouldn't release his albums in America for quite a long time. For that I just thought, 'Well, hats off to you.' As far as I'm concerned, though, hats off to anybody who does what they think is right and refuses to sell out." The song was never played live by Led Zeppelin.

Hey Hey What Can I Do: Led Zeppelin's first, and only, non-LP B side, released as the flip side to "Immigrant Song." The song was also released in England on a sampler album called *The New Age of Atlantic* in 1972, the only 12-inch release of the tune, until it came out on the boxed set in 1990. The band said this was the only song in their repertoire they wrote intentionally as a single. Peter Grant told a British newspaper, "They'd written a special number intended as their first British single which they are recording this week." The song was never released as a single in Britain and was only issued as a B side. This song was never played live by Led Zeppelin.

Led Zeppelin IV

The fourth, or untitled, Zeppelin album was an elaborately thought-out album package. One of the original designs called for a foldout jacket that would feature the face of one band member on each of the sides, though the idea never got far enough along for a decision about which member's picture would be on the front cover. Out of this idea came the decision not to put the band's name on the cover since it seemed inappropriate to have the name "Led Zeppelin" over one band member's picture. Even though the four-picture idea was abandoned, the concept of the record having no name persisted. Page says not having a name on the cover of album was the band's response to the charges that they had been overhyped, though once again Zeppelin's anticommercialism ended up making them all the more commercial in the long run.

The image of an old man on the foldout is a rendition of the Hermit character from the Tarot, the ninth card in the Tarot and the one bearing the message "wisdom offered." The original artwork used here was drawn by a friend of Page's, Barrington Colby. The inclusion of the lyrics to "Stairway to Heaven" on the inner sleeve (this is the only Zeppelin LP to reproduce lyrics to only one song) indicates that the band knew in advance that this song was going to be a monster.

The old man on the front cover plays on the image of the Hermit from the Tarot, but it also may represent one of the most mysterious of Jimmy Page's inside jokes. The old man on the cover was chosen, or was made up, depending on how devious you think Page was, to bear a remarkable resemblance to one George Pickingale. Also, in the background of the photo there is a blue haze that some argue is significant.

Who was George Pickingale? He was one of the most famous occult masters in England in the early 1890s. Pickingale came from Canewdon County in the Essex area of England and he ruled the district like a feudal lord. He was nicknamed "Old George," and the oldest villager at the time of "Old" Pickingale's death said Pickingale had always looked the same. He carried a carved walking stick with him and villagers believed that he could curse someone with just a

touch of the stick. He was revered by students of the occult who came from all over Europe to learn witchcraft from him. One of those students was Allan Bennett, who later taught his occult knowledge to Aleister Crowley. Some students of the occult even suggest that Crowley met Pickingale back in the 1880s. Pickingale died in 1909 when, according to local legend, his home was struck by lightning. The electrical strike didn't kill him however but the next day when walking down the street, his hat flew off his head and landed on the steps of Canewdon Church. When Pickingale entered the churchyard to retrieve it, the shadow of the cross from the church fell on him and he fell dead to the ground.

The blue haze? It has been suggested by some fans who have studied ancient English folklore, though the subject has never even been addressed by Jimmy Page, that the haze is an indication that Druid activities are taking place in the woods. Back in the early days of England, folk tales said that blue haze in the sky represented the Druids at work (probably caused by the burning of powders and oils). Druid legend is now treated as folklore in England though a thousand years ago Druid priests worshipped Gods similar to those of the Greeks and Romans. The strange rock formations at Stonehenge are thought to be remains of a structure used by Druids for worship.

The photograph on the cover was shot at a photo session in early 1972, so it clearly was not an actual photo of Pickingale. (In a 1971 interview, though, Page claimed the photograph was one that he and Plant had found intact. "I remember he bought it in a junk shop in Reading," Page said. "I was with him at the time.") The old man used for the session is either someone made up to look like Pickingale, or the resemblance is remarkable. Only a couple of photographs of Pickingale are known to exist and whether Jimmy Page planned the cover, or it was just coincidence, is a matter of debate but the man on the cover and Pickingale look identical. If Page did plan out the cover to picture Pickingale, surely the concept went over the heads of the other band members, and the choice of the image was never explained to them or to anyone

else except in some elusive comments made by Page around the time of the record's release. "The old man on the cover," he said, "carrying the wood, is in harmony with nature. He takes from nature and gives back to the land. It's a natural circle. It's right. His old cottage gets pulled down and they put him in slums, old slums, terrible places. The old man is also the Hermit of the Tarot cards, a symbol of self-reliance and mystical wisdom. Unfortunately the negatives were a bit duff so you can't quite read an Oxfam poster on the side of the building on the back of the jacket. It's the poster where someone is lying dead on a stretcher and it says that every day someone receives relief from hunger. You can just make it out on the jacket if you've seen the poster before. But other than that, there's no writing on the jacket at all.

"We decided that on the fourth album we would deliberately play down the group's name," he continued, "and there wouldn't be any information whatsoever on the outer jacket. Names, titles, and things like that do not mean a thing. What does Led Zeppelin mean? It doesn't mean a thing. What matters is our music. If we weren't playing good music, nobody would care what we called ourselves. If the music was good, we could call ourselves the Cabbage and still get across to our audience. The words Led Zeppelin do not occur anywhere on this cover. And all the other usual credits are missing too. I had to talk like hell to get that done. The record company told us we were committing professional suicide." Based on the record company's response, the album has gained the nickname the "suicide record."

Everyone involved with the band seemed to have a different response when asked what the name of the record was. Peter Grant's answer is notable since he was responsible the marketing of the group. "There is no name to it. All we had on it were those symbols. That's all. We had a lot of fun with that. For $15 a block, we had the symbols actually printed in the *Billboard* and *Cashbox* charts. The rack jobbers used to call us up and ask how do you pronounce this or what language is this? Is this old Arabic or something? Things like that. It was incredible. It was a very successful thing. We never

THE SONG

REMAINS THE

SAME PREMIERE,

FOX THEATER,

LOS ANGELES,

OCTOBER 21,

1976

let anyone know what symbol represented which member of the group until they came on tour and the symbols were on the stage with each one." Grant says the idea of having no title was his: "I'm the one who said forget the title. Let's not have any title at all."

Since the record officially has no title, what it should be called has always been a matter of debate. Atlantic has always referred to it as "Led Zeppelin IV" within their catalogs or simply as "Led Zeppelin" (also the official title of the first record and the recent boxed set, leading to some confusion). Robert Plant calls it "Led Zeppelin IV" or "Four Symbols." Some fans call it "The Runes," in reference to the four symbols. Runes are linguistic symbols developed by early Gaelic civilizations and through the centuries they have developed

mystical associations and are used on charms. (Page says only the center two symbols are actually runes.) *Creem* magazine called the record "Atlantic SD 7208" after the record's catalog number. Many hard-core fans call it the "suicide album," and some call it "Zoso" or "Untitled." In the Zeppelin discography at the back of the boxed set, no title is reproduced, and the space is left blank.

If Jimmy Page is to be considered the final word on the group, the record should be called "Led Zeppelin IV." Prior to the release of the record Page told an interviewer that "it might be called 'Zeppelin IV.' Everybody expects that, but we might change it. We've got all sorts of mad ideas. I was thinking at one time of having four EPs." Page was a little more to the point when he explained his theory in 1990 with the release of the boxed set. When

FOLLOWING

PAGES:

SPORTS ARENA,

SAN DIEGO,

CALIF.,

MAY 28, 1973

asked what the untitled record should be called, he replied, "Well, 'Led Zeppelin IV.' That's it really. I'll tell you why the album had no title—because we got fed up with the reactions to the third album, that people couldn't understand why that record wasn't a direct continuation of the second album. And then people said we were a hype and all, which was the furthest thing from what we were. So we just said, 'Let's put out an album with no title at all!' That way, either people like it or they don't."

Peter Grant says that Page came up with the idea for the symbols. "It was Jimmy Page's idea to use symbols, but he also thought it would be confusing to be without a title." The four symbols themselves were designed to represent each band member (possibly as an extension of the original idea of having one member's face on each side of the record). As Plant explained around the release of the record, "We decided the album couldn't be called 'Led Zeppelin IV' and we were wondering what it should be. Then each of us decided to go away and choose a metaphysical type symbol which somehow represented each of us individually—be it a state of mind, an opinion, or something we felt strongly about, or whatever. Then we were to come back together and present our symbols."

Plant explains his symbol, the feather in the circle at far right, "was drawn from sacred symbols of the ancient Mu civilization which existed about 15,000 years ago as part of a lost continent somewhere in the Pacific Ocean between China and Mexico. All sorts of things can be tied in with Mu civilization, even the Easter Island effigies. These Mu people left stone tablets with their symbols inscribed into them all over the place in Mexico, Egypt, Ethiopia, India, China, and other places. And they all date from the same time period. The Chinese say these people came from the east and the Mexicans say they came from the west. Obviously it was somewhere in between. My personal symbol does have a further meaning, and all I can suggest is that people look it up in a suitable reference work."

Bonham's symbol of three circles was open to a couple of different interpretations according to Plant: "I suppose it's the trilogy—man, woman, and child. I suspect it has something to do with the mainstay of all people's beliefs. At one point, though, in Pittsburgh I think, we observed that it was also the emblem of Ballantine beer." Page was a little more concrete about Bonham's symbol and Jones's (the second from the left), saying, "Jones's symbol was found in a book about runes and was said to represent a person who is both confident and competent, because it was difficult to draw accurately. Bonzo's came from the same book. He just picked it out because he liked it."

Page's symbol, as with everything involving this band, remains the greatest mystery. He says it is not a word and that he designed it. "My symbol was one which I designed myself but a lot of people mistook for a word 'Zoso,' and some people in the states still refer to the record as 'Zoso,' which is a pity because it wasn't supposed to be a word at all but something entirely different." Exactly what that might be remains known only to Page himself, though Plant says that the guitarist once actually told him the secret meaning behind the symbol. "Pagey once took me aside," Plant says, "and said, 'Look, I'm going to tell you the meaning of this once, and then I shan't ever mention it again, or at least not for a long, long time anyway.' And would you believe that I have since forgotten what it was and now Pagey won't tell me. If I know Pagey, it'll turn up in some long lost book. That's the only light I can throw on it." Not much light.

Recording for the record began in December 1970 at Island Studios in London and the amount of work on the actual recording process makes the production of the album jacket seem minor in comparison. The group also recorded in Headley Grange, using the Rolling Stones's mobile unit, and additional recording and mixing was done in several studios, including Sunset Sound in Los Angeles and Olympic Studios in London. The record had been originally scheduled for release in April 1971. Problems with mixing delayed the project and it wasn't released until November 1971.

FOLLOWING PAGES: PLANT AND PAGE BEFORE SHOWTIME AT KEZAR STADIUM, SAN FRANCISCO, JUNE 2, 1973

The group's untitled fourth album was released in the United States on November 8, 1971, and in the United Kingdom on November 19, 1971.

Black Dog: John Paul Jones says he came up with the riff to this song while messing around in the studio. The vocal track was cut in only two takes. Page says he influenced the track by suggesting Jones check out a Fleetwood Mac record. "I suggested 'Oh Well' by Fleetwood Mac," he said. "How do you get the breaks with the vocals? That was the idea. The noise at the start is the guitars warming up—jing, jing, jing, an engine, the guitar army waking up. Rise and shine!" The band also said the drum riff used here was inspired by Little Richard's "Keep a Knockin'." The name of the tune came from a black dog who kept walking in and out of the studio during recording.

An acoustic version of this song exists on a bootleg 45 but there is some doubt as to whether it represents a legitimate studio outtake, or some bootlegger has created it by mixing the Plant vocal with a freshly cut acoustic guitar track.

"Black Dog," backed with "Misty Mountain Hop," was released as a single in the United States in December 1971. The 45 peaked at number 15 on the *Billboard* charts.

Rock and Roll: Jimmy Page says this song came out of a rock 'n' roll jam the group did on Little Richard's "Good Golly Miss Molly." Ian Stewart, who toured with the Stones, played piano on this track, one of the few times the Stones and Zeppelin mixed on record.

"Rock and Roll," backed with "Four Sticks," was released as a single in the United States in March 1972 and it reached number 47 on the *Billboard* charts.

The Battle of Evermore: Sandy Denny is featured as a guest vocalist on this track and she said she practically went hoarse trying to keep up with Plant. Plant had grown up in the same area of England as Sandy Denny and knew her from her work with Fairport Convention. Denny had also attended Kingston Art College, the same art school where Jimmy Page studied prior to becoming a session player full-time. Plant says the lyrics were affected by a book on the Scottish wars he read just prior to the recording sessions. "After I wrote the lyrics, I realized that I needed another completely different voice as well as my own to give the song its full impact. So I asked Sandy Denny to come along and sing on the track. I must say I found it very satisfying to sing with someone who has a completely different style to my own. So while I sang about the events in the song, Sandy answered back as if she was the pulse of the people on the battlements. Sandy was playing the role of the town crier, urging people to throw down their weapons."

Page played mandolin on the tune after picking up John Paul Jones's mandolin in the studio and thinking he'd give it a try. "It was my first experiment with mandolin," he said, "and those chords just came out. I suppose all mandolin players would have a great laugh, because it must be the standard thing to play those chords. It was just one of those things where I was governed by the limitations of the instrument. It sounded like a dance around the maypole number, I must admit, but it wasn't purposely like that."

Stairway to Heaven: "This song broke the rules," Jimmy Page says. "It purposely accelerates. It's supposed to do that. It's atmospheric but that's the whole point." When playing this song live, Page used his cherry red Gibson SG Doubleneck, serial number 911117. He demoed the song on an eight track home recording system called a New Vista, using the exact same deck that the Who had used to record *Live at Leeds*. Page says that Plant came in with most of the vocals on the spot when the band began actual recording, though Plant has said in interviews that "the song is the result of an evening when Jimmy and I sat down in front of the fire. We came up with the song which was later developed by the rest of the band in the studio."

Page says the guitar solo used is one of three he cut in the studio at the time and that he "winged" the solo, rehearsing the overall structure of the guitar parts in advance but improvising on the spot the actual notes of the solo. "When it came time to record the solo, I warmed up and did three of them," he told *Guitar World* in late 1990. "They were all quite different from each other. But the one we

used was the best solo, I can tell you that."

The song remains the most popular of all of Zeppelin tunes, and some argue that it is the single most played tune in the history of rock radio. Like everything about this band, though, it remains a controversial topic with Plant and Page both taking dramatically different positions on how it stands the test of time. Plant has said in numerous interviews that he never liked the tune. "When we used to rehearse with Zeppelin, we'd do 'Stairway to Heaven' as a reggae tune because Page could never get me to sing it," Plant said in 1990. "I loathed it so much!" It has been suggested that one of the reasons the band has not reunited since Bonham's death is Plant's reluctance to sing the group's signature tune. Peter Grant recently confirmed rumors that Plant had been unwilling to play the tune at the Atlantic Records Anniversary Concert. "I know for a fact that right up until five minutes before the band was due to go onstage, Robert was refusing to sing 'Stairway to Heaven,' " Grant told an interviewer.

John Paul Jones is much kinder. "I actually like 'Stairway,' " he says today. "I know that's really corny. But it encompasses a lot of the elements of the band, from the acoustic start to the slightly jazzier section, even, and then to the heavier stuff towards the end. It was a very successful song. I'm not talking about successful in commercial terms, but successful in that everything worked well and fell into place. Everything built nicely." Jones, incidentally, is playing the recorder at the start of the song, an instrument rarely used by Zeppelin.

Page, for his part, loves the track and frequently has said, "If ever we get together with Robert again in the future I hope we do that number." Even around the time of the release of the record, Page understood the popularity this track already had with Zeppelin fans and he seemed to share that. "I thought 'Stairway' crystallized the essence of the band," he said. "It had everything there and showed the band at its best—as a band, as a unit. I'm not

BONHAM, KEZAR STADIUM, SAN FRANCISCO, JUNE 2, 1973

talking about solos or anything. It had everything there. We were careful never to release it as a single. It was a milestone for us. Every musician wants to do something of lasting quality, something that will hold up for a long time and I guess we did it with 'Stairway.' "

Plant and Page continue today to debate the merits of "Stairway" and the reception it has received. In interviews for the boxed set Plant downplayed the song, saying, "When we played it at the beginning, before the album came out, you could often see people settling down to have 40 winks." Page was quick to respond when interviewers told him of Plant's comments: "Apparently, Robert's made some statements to the effect that the song wasn't well received originally. It's not true! Because I remember we played it at the L.A. Forum before the record had even come out, and there was this standing ovation. I think Robert would remember that."

BONHAM, RIVERFRONT COLISEUM, CINCINNATI, OHIO, APRIL 19, 1977

Misty Mountain Hop: Inspired by a big love-in near London that was busted by the police. Plant introduced the song onstage a couple of times, saying it was "about a bunch of hippies getting busted." At a show in Newcastle, Plant compared the tune to Chuck Berry's "My Ding-a-ling," adding that "the vice squad should have checked this one out before it was released." The title relates to Tolkien again, and to Druid legend.

Four Sticks: There are two theories on the title of this track, neither of which has been confirmed by a band member. Some argue that Bonzo plays with four drumsticks in his hands on this track while others suggest the title is a stab back at a critic who had described the band as "sticks in the mud." The band said the original master tape of this cut was lost so the song had to be recut a second time in the studio to include it on the record.

The tune was only played live once during the band's history, along with "Gallows Pole," in Copenhagen in 1970. Along with "Friends," this was re-recorded with the Bombay Symphony in

1972, though these versions have never been released.

Going to California: This song is one of Robert's sensitive love songs, inspired by singer/songwriter Joni Mitchell, who had recorded a tune of her own titled "California" on her album *Blue*. Both Page and Plant were big fans of Mitchell's and Page talks about meeting her in 1975 as one of the high points of his career. Page has said wrote this song on acoustic guitar prior to the forming of Zeppelin.

When the Levee Breaks: The guitar effect on this song is created by a phased twelve-string on the riff combined with a backward echo on the fade. Only one drum mike was used during recording, giving it a live sound. Page says the drums were recorded in a hallway in Headley Grange. This tune was only played in concert a handful of times. The song was originally performed by Memphis Minnie, and Plant described it as "something I have on an old album by Kansas Joe McCoy and Memphis Minnie in 1928. There are so many classics from way, way back which we can give a little of ourselves to take them through the years."

Plant used this song in a 1990 interview as an example of the unique sound that only Zeppelin could accomplish. "It was a giant step," he said. "We got the most amazing drum sound and we played to it. It was an old tune but once the drums were miked up and we heard that sound, we had to submit. We could have played anything and it would have sounded good. Nobody other than John Bonham could have created that sex groove, and many have tried."

Houses of the Holy

Houses of the Holy was the first Zeppelin album with a descriptive title, taken from a song that did not even appear on the album. The title refers to the nickname the group had for the coliseums and hockey arenas they were playing at the time.

The album cover again did not feature the name of the band or the name of the album on the original pressings, though the band did allow Atlantic to issue a wraparound banner with the title. The cover was the first Zeppelin cover to be designed by the revolutionary English graphics studio Hipgnosis (best known for their Pink Floyd covers), who went on to do all the rest of the band's records. For years the rumor was passed among fans that the nude children on the cover were Robert Plant's children but in fact they were professional models.

As was frequently the case with Zeppelin records, problems with color separations and proofs of the cover delayed the album several months. Page's complaints summed up the band's frustration: "The colors were so different from what we had anticipated. We had to compromise because the sky started to look like an ad for Max Factor lipstick, and the children looked as if they'd been turned purple from the cold."

Recording began in April 1972 at Stargroves, one of Mick Jagger's homes, done with the Rolling Stones's mobile recording unit again. Sessions continued later that spring and summer at Olympic Studios in London and at Electric Lady in New York City.

Houses of the Holy was released simultaneously in the United States and the United Kingdom on March 28, 1973.

The Song Remains the Same: This tune went on to become one of Zeppelin's most popular numbers and ended up as the title to their movie. "Every time I sing 'The Song Remains the Same,' " Robert Plant said, "I picture the fact that I've been round and round the world, and at the root of it all there's a common denominator for everybody. The common denominator is just what makes it good or bad, whether it's Led Zeppelin or Alice Cooper. I'm proud of the lyrics, somebody pushed my pen for me, I think. There are lots of catalysts which really bring out these sorts of things; working with the group on the road; living where I live; having the friends I've got; my children; my animals." Page has said that he originally planned this song to be an instrumental and that the original title was "The Overture." The track was also referred to as "The Slush" in some interviews prior to release. In concert and on the 1972 Japanese tour, before the track was officially released, it was introduced as "The Campaign."

The Rain Song: As featured in the film *The Song Remains the Same*, this song serves as the best single video clip the band has done. The primary setting for the song in the movie was filmed at Raglan Castle, a historic monument in South Wales.

Page says that some of the inspiration for this song's melody came after Bonzo had met George Harrison and the Beatle had said, "The problem with your band is that you don't do any ballads." In response, Page and Plant came up with "The Rain Song," and Page also thought of Harrison in crafting the start of the song. Page said, "I purposely stuck the first two notes of 'Something' on 'The Rain Song.'"

Plant said the lyrics came to him quickly. "It was sort of a little infatuation I had," he told a writer. "The next morning I scribbled it out. If I had done it the day after, it would have been no good."

Over the Hills and Far Away: Plant described how this and some of the other songs on the record came together, saying, "We would have backing track tapes worked out and somebody would say, 'We've got no bloody lyrics.' Some of the tapes would be quite intricate and I couldn't sing along instantly. So I had to take them away and listen to them on my own. Then a week later I'd come back with 'Over the Hills' or 'The Crunge.'" In an interview with Matt Resnikoff, Page said, "I guess my Celtic roots come out in that 'Over the Hills and Far Away' type of thing."

"Over the Hills and Far Away," backed with "Dancing Days," was released as a single in the United States in May 1973, peaking at number 53 on the *Billboard* charts.

The Crunge: Page first worked on the riff to this song in 1964 and 1965 and even recorded it in the studio then without releasing it. In early Zeppelin concerts he would frequently the riff into "Whole Lotta Love," and in a few rare instances Plant would sing it. Page explained the song "just happened spontaneously. Bonzo started playing, Jonesy came in next and then I joined in. It happened as quickly as that. At the time it seemed to be undanceable, because it keeps crossing over from the on to the off beat, as opposed to James Brown things, which are totally danceable. That's why we called it 'The Crunge.' We thought of putting steps on the cover to help you do the dance."

Dancing Days: Plant described this song as being "all about summer" though, because of delays, the album it appears on did not appear until winter. "I wrote the lyrics in mid-summer," he said. "It was like a weird summer-like sort of sound." At a June 19, 1972 show, the band played this song twice.

D'yer Mak'er: Plant says this was one of the first songs recorded for the album when the band was working at Stargroves. Page said that some fans took this song and "The Crunge" too seriously: "I would never say that it was reggae as a lot of people who've lifted their eyebrows at it have said. I think real reggae is rude, dirty music. That's what makes it great, but it only works when the Jamaicans do it, not the Whiteys. It doesn't have the same spirit at all." Before the record's release Plant told one journalist that the band had cut a "reggae number which will be on the next record but I would like to have it out as a single."

Engineer Eddie Kramer said the drum sound was created by using three mikes placed fairly distantly from the drums. Kramer said after the cut was finished he could "remember Bonham, Page, Plant, and Jones out on the lawn (at Stargroves) listening to playbacks, all walking like Groucho Marx, in sync, with back steps and forward steps in time to the music, like kids."

The lyric sheet that came with the album reproduced the lyrics to this song with one strange addition: one line in parentheses reads, "Whatever happened to Rosie and the Originals?" Rosie and the Originals were a 1950s vocal group who scored one hit with "Angel Baby," released in December of 1960 and going as high as number five on the *Billboard* charts. Lester Bangs, writing in *Creem*, answered the question for the band: "They had one hit and died the mung fade because they weren't so hot in the first place."

"D'yer Mak'er," backed with "The Crunge," was released as a single in the United States in October 1973, and hit number 20 on the *Billboard* charts.

No Quarter: Plant would frequently introduce this song in concert as "a song about a journey." At one of the legendary Earl's Court shows in 1975 he described it as something that would "lead you to different levels of consciousness."

The Ocean: The title of this song refers to the nickname the band had for the audiences they played to. This is the first song in the Zeppelin catalog that puts John Bonham's name at the front of the writing credit. Bonham does the vocal intro to the song on the record, and John Paul Jones contributes background vocals on the track as well.

The lyrics make reference to the reaffirming experience of playing to adoring audiences. The lyrics also refer to "the girl who won my heart, she is only three years old." Plant's daughter was three years old at the time the record came out. When the band toured Plant later changed the lyric in the song that said "she is only three years old" to "four years old," to reflect his daughter's age at the time of the performance.

Physical Graffiti

Physical Graffiti was the first multi-disc Zeppelin album and it was the first record of the band's out on their own Swan Song label. The Swan Song logo of the winged man was inspired by William Rimmer's *Evening, or the Fall of the Day* painting, the original of which hangs in the Boston Museum of Fine Arts. Page says he came up with the label's name during the recording sessions for the album. "I had a long acoustic guitar instrumental with just sparse vocal sections. The song was about 20 minutes long and the vocal was about six minutes, and the whole thing was quite epic really. Almost semi-classical, I suppose, and there

JIMMY PAGE,
RIVERFRONT
COLISEUM,
CINCINNATI,
APRIL 19, 1977

was no title for it. Someone shouted out 'What's it going to be called?' and I shouted out 'Swan Song,' and the whole thing stopped and we said what a great name for the LP. All the vibes started and suddenly it was out of the LP and on to the record label. I think Swan Song is a good name for a record label, because if you don't have success on Swan Song, well then, you shouldn't have signed up with them."

Peter Grant described the origin of the name of the label and in doing so shed some insight into Page's technique in the studio. "Whenever Led Zeppelin would get together to record a new album, Jimmy had this piece of music that there were no lyrics to. He'd always wheel it out and bang it out at first rehearsals, saying, 'Why can't we do something like this?' Actually he wasn't quite sure what to do with it himself. Finally, somebody said, 'Oh, Christ, come on, Page, that sounds like your swan song.' "

The album's title was another Page contribution. "It came out in the usual panic of trying to find a title for an album," he said. "I came up with that title because of the whole thing of graffiti on the album cover and it being a physical statement rather than a written one, because I feel that an awful lot of physical energy is used in producing an album."

The front of the album cover features a tenement in New York City. The elaborate sleeve shows a variety of images through the windows of the building. The original prototype for the jacket had the title written on the sleeve in red and white print and the inner sleeve pictures were different. Included in the many images on the inner sleeve as it was used are pictures of Aleister Crowley, Lee Harvey Oswald, and two series of photographs of the band in drag, from a wild night in New Orleans, and from a time the group dressed up like geisha girls while in Japan.

Recording for the new material on *Physical Graffiti* began in December 1973 and work on the record stretched out through July 1974. Recording took place in numerous locations, including Headley Grange with Ronnie Lane's Mobile Studio and at Olympic Studios in London. Mixing was done at Olympic Studios in London and Electric Lady in New York.

Physical Graffiti was released in the United States on February 24, 1975, and in the United Kingdom on February 25, 1975.

Custard Pie: This song represented a jam in the studio. The blues artist Sonny Terry had also recorded a song titled "Custard Pie," and that tune and Bukka White's "Shake 'Em on Down," served as lyrics for this song.

The Rover: Recorded at the same time as "D'yer Mak'er" for the fifth album. The band never played a full version of this song live, though pieces of it were worked into other songs and solos, notably "Sick Again."

In My Time of Dying: Inspired by a song from Blind Willie Johnson called "Jesus, Make Up My Dying Bed" originally recorded in 1927. Zeppelin's version featured almost identical lyrics to a version covered by Bob Dylan in the early 1960s. This song was recorded live in the studio with only minor overdubbing. A close listen to the track will reveal John Bonham coughing and then saying, "That's going to be the one, isn't it?" as the track fades. Also influenced by another version of the same song recorded by a Canadian band called Fear Itself, featuring singer/guitarist Ellen McIlwaine.

Robert Plant said that when he had his near-fatal car crash in Rhodos, this was the song that flashed before his eyes. "When I finally crawled out of the car, rolling around in the dust, I was scared to death I was going to get bitten by a scorpion just to finish the whole thing off. I rolled over in terrible pain and anguish, looked around me and said, 'Why the hell did I sing that song?' That's the one thing I shall never do again—not until the very end." Don't look for this song to crop up in the sets on any future reunion tour.

Houses of the Holy: Originally recorded for the fifth album and used as the title for that record, the track itself did not appear until years later. This tune was never performed live by Zeppelin.

Trampled Under Foot: Plant named this song in 1983 as one of his favorite Zeppelin tunes. "The more impromptu numbers are the ones that really

PLANT AND
PAGE, MADISON
SQUARE GAR-
DEN, NEW YORK
CITY, FEBRUARY
21, 1975

come to mind, rather than the time-consuming things that were worked out and constructed." Despite Plant's comments, a rehearsal tape exists with more a dozen different takes of this song.

Plant once introduced this song in concert by saying it was about the parts of a motor car. Then he pointed to a young woman in the front and said, "but it's really about young ladies like you, my dear." This tune was another example of Page's use of backward echo.

Robert Johnson's song "Terraplane Blues," also a song about a car, served as inspiration for this tune. At a show at Earl's Court in London, Plant made reference to Johnson's composition, at which point John Bonham accused Plant of borrowing the lyrics.

"Trampled Under Foot," backed with "Black Country Woman," was released as a single in the United States in March 1975, and the single hit number 38 on the *Billboard* charts.

Kashmir: Page was playing a Danelectro guitar on this song. The original demo for the song featured just Page and Bonham on drums. In a 1977 interview Plant described the genesis of the song and what it meant to him: "The rhythm came from Bonzo. The sort of striding majestic element really came from Jimmy and my leaning toward the East. I wrote the lyrics after driving into the Sahara Desert because I knew that I was on my way to the Spanish Sahara and there was the war between Morocco and the Spanish. I kept bumping down a dusty desert track and there was nobody for miles except, occasionally, a guy on a camel, waving his hand in the most nonchalant Arabic way. And I thought, 'Well, this is great but one day . . . Kashmir.' And the sun was beating down upon my face. Kashmir is my last resort. I think, if I truly deserve it one day, I should go there and stay there for quite a while. Or if I really need it at any point, it should be my haven, my Shangri-la."

In a 1988 interview Plant described it as "the definitive Led Zeppelin song." He said: "It's the quest, the travels and exploration that Page and I went on to far climes well off the beaten track. Of course, we only touched the surface. We weren't

anthropologists. But we were allowed, because we were musicians, to be invited in societies that people don't normally witness. It was quite a remarkable time, to open your eyes and see how Berber tribesmen lived in the northern Sahara. My interpretations lyrically are not that fantastic; they never have been. But that's what it was like for me then. That, really, to me is the Zeppelin feel."

Page also cites "Kashmir" as one of the highlights of the band's career. "There have been several musical milestones along the way and 'Kashmir' is definitely one of them."

"Kashmir" was also one of the few Zeppelin songs that the band considered redoing after they had released it on record. Sheet music was recently auctioned off by an art house of a score to "Kashmir," with John Paul Jones handwriting on it. The score was marked "Olympic Studios, November 10, 1976" and seems to indicate that the band was considering performing the song with strings, either in concert or in the recording studio. The score, put together by Jones but drawn up by someone named "Chris," has parts for viola, cello, trumpet and trombones, instruments not usually found in Led Zeppelin songs. The liner notes for the boxed set say the original title of the tune was "Driving to Kashmir."

In the Light: John Paul Jones was the chief composer of "In the Light." Jones says he played a EMS VCS3 synthesizer on this track. "It wasn't sophisticated enough to really sound like a synthesizer," he said, "and you really had to be on the ball because it was murder to keep in tune." Jones says he had too many problems with the synthesizer to take it on the road which is why the track never was performed live: "Robert was always saying, 'We've got to do "In the Light" onstage,' and I'd say, 'No way, or I'll have to contend with synthesizers as well.' " The song was originally titled "Take Me Home," and featured different lyrics.

Bron-Yr-Aur: Recorded for the third record, and not to be confused with "Bron-Y-Aur Stomp" from that record. The name means "Golden Breast" in Welsh. Live acoustic versions

of this song were performed as early as 1970, six years before the release of this track on record.

Down by the Seaside: Originally recorded for the fourth album, this song was never performed live. In 1980, looking back on the album, Plant said the track was one that at first was considered below standard. "Some of the best tracks on *Physical Graffiti* were considered at one time to be 'below standard' and we never put them out. When *Physical Graffiti* came along, we said, 'Well, what about "Down by the Seaside"?' And everybody laughed and said, 'Oh, you can't do that!' It was a good song, but at the time, the mood wasn't right."

Ten Years Gone: Originally planned as an instrumental, this song was about Plant's first love. "I was working my ass off before joining Zeppelin," he said, " and a lady I dearly loved said, 'Right, it's me or your fans.' Not that I had fans. But I said, 'I can't stop, I've got to keep going.' She's quite content these days, I imagine. She's got a washing machine that works by itself and a little sports car. We wouldn't have anything to say anymore. I could probably relate to her, but she couldn't relate to me. I'd be smiling too much. Ten years gone, I'm afraid."

Page's guitar riffs on this song were ones he'd been working on for a number of years. Page says that as many as 14 guitar tracks were used here, all overdubbed in harmony, and it can be thought to represent one of Page's first experiments with a guitar wall of sound.

Night Flight: Recorded originally for the fourth record, this tune listed John Paul Jones first in the credits. It was never performed live though it was played at a rehearsal in Minneapolis in 1975, indicating that the band had considered using it in their sets.

The Wanton Song: Plant says this is another of his favorite Zeppelin tracks. It is another tune that utilizes backward echo techniques. This track was composed in the studio. This song was played infrequently at the beginning of the 1975 tour and was never performed thereafter.

Boogie With Stu: Recorded for the fourth album, this track features Ian Stewart, the Rolling Stones's unofficial keyboard player. The original

title of this song, according to interviews the band did prior to the release of the fourth record, was "Sloppy Drunk." Plant said, "There's 'Sloppy Drunk' on which I play guitar and Jimmy plays mandolin. You can imagine it being played as people dive round the maypole." The album cover credits the song as being by the four members of Zeppelin, Stewart, and "Mrs. Valens," a reference to Richie Valens, the early rocker who had big hits with "La Bamba" and "Donna." The band later said they had, given Valens's mother part of the songwriting credit so that she would be sure to get some of the royalties from the song. The lyrics to the tune are essentially exactly the same as Valens's "Ooh My Head."

Black Country Woman: This song was recorded at the same time as "D'yer Mak'er" for the fifth album. It was recorded outside, in the garden at Stargroves, and an airplane can be heard going over in the beginning of the track. A close listen to the track will also reveal someone saying, "can't keep this airplane on," to which Plant says, "nah, leave it, yeah." It originally had a subtitle of "Never Ending Doubting Woman Blues," referring to a line in the original lyric that was cut off the final version: "yer never-ending nagging doubting woman blues."

Sick Again: Written about the L.A. groupie scene, this song did not endear Robert Plant to any of his old girlfriends. Playing the song in Chicago, Plant dedicated it to what he called "the L.A. queens." Page described the L.A. scene as an "incredible groupie feud which was getting done to razor blade sandwiches. The competition thing out there is incredible and you've got to keep out of the middle of it or else it'll get to you too. There's a new song we've done called 'Sick Again' that about sums it up." Plant said the song was "about ourselves and what we see in Los Angeles, but it's a pity you can't hear the lyrics properly live."

Presence

Recorded in just 18 days, soon after Robert Plant's near-fatal car accident, this record represented Led Zeppelin's most intense studio experience. At this point no one in the band knew if they would ever tour again as the extent of Plant's injuries were still unknown. Unlike previous albums, where the group had experimented with material in concert prior to taking it into the recording studio, this record was created in the studio: not a single track had been played live prior to the sessions. The band rehearsed first in Malibu near Los Angeles, then moved on to S.I.R. Studios in Hollywood for more formal rehearsals, and then finally left the U.S. and recorded the record in Munich.

Jimmy Page also calls this the band's "guitar album" because his instrument dominates much of the sound. And though Page served as producer of all of Zeppelin's albums, this record taxed his skills as a producer more than any other the group had ever recorded.

"I did 18-hour sessions," he says, "and 20-hour sessions to complete it. We overran our time allotment at the studio and Mick Jagger was coming in afterwards with the Stones, and I asked him if we could just have a couple of extra days to finish up. He said, 'Sure.' Anyway, the day we finished it, the Stones came in and asked how we'd gotten on. I said, 'Alright, I've finished thanks to the two extra days you gave us.' They said, 'The tracks?' And I said, 'No, the whole thing,' and they couldn't believe it. They knew how much we had left to do before those two days, and couldn't imagine how we'd completed the whole thing."

Page says the focus on the electric guitar, with the lack of any ballads, was in response to the band's mood: "It was just a reflection of the total anxiety and emotion at the period of time during which it was recorded. It's true that there are no acoustic songs, no mellowness or contrasts or changes to other instruments."

For Plant the record was a catharsis of sorts. "Presence was our phoenix," he said. "When you sit in a wheelchair and sing the whole album, the very fact that you've sung it is fantastic. We got it together in such a short time under such odds and not knowing what the outcome was going to be—not of the album but of the future of the band."

The album cover is one of the weirdest post-modern graphic pieces in the Zeppelin collection. The Hipgnosis design studio came up with "the object," though Page came up with the name for the record. Early press reports called the record "Obelisk."

Page says the object represents "ambiguity." "The way the cover came about," he adds, "was that after we'd returned from recording, we realized that the only feasible thing to do was to take a picture of the studio and its chaos, but we needed something better than that. So we contacted Hipgnosis and explained to the chap there, Po (Aubrey Powell), what had been going on. He returned and said that the thing that had always struck him about Led Zeppelin was a power, a force, an alchemical quality which was indefinable, which I guess he was relating to the magnitude of the band. He came up with this idea of interpreting this through an object which could be related to any object in a community that everyone was perfectly at home with." A "presence" is also a discrete tone control on some guitar amplifiers, separate from the bass and treble controls.

Recording took place at Musicland Studios in Munich in 18 days during November and December 1975. Mixing was done by Keith Harwood at Musicland Studios in December.

Presence was released in the United States on March 31, 1976, and in the United Kingdom on April 6, 1976.

Achilles Last Stand: In 1977 Plant said, "The whole point of 'Achilles' is that, though the story builds, it's centered around one spot on the top of the high Atlas Mountains. One tiny little spot on the side of a track 10,000 feet up, looking down over half of Southern Morocco.

"I fell over when I was singing it in the studio and was rushed to the hospital. They thought that I had fucked up my leg for good. So I spent two weeks yet again with it up in the air. I still hadn't walked—which is after four months without walking and I'd put all my weight on it—went down, bang. Pagey virtually carried me to the hospital. And when it got to a point where I could lower it again off the bed without touching the ground, I was wheeled to the studio while the others were asleep and did the whole vocal track all over again from start to finish. I said, 'Right from the top. I'm going to do it again and I'm going to call it that.' " Later Plant summed up the song by saying it was "about travels and dreams, and wishes and positivism."

Page said this was one of the few Zeppelin songs that he completely worked through in his home studio before recording the song with the band. He also said it had more guitar overdubs than most of his material: "There must be, say, half a dozen going at once. I knew that every guitar overdub had to be very important, very strong within itself to sort of identify each section. 'Achilles' changed immensely in the studio."

For Your Life: Plant described the song as "a sarcastic dig at one person in particular that I know, who was a really good person but got swallowed up with the whole quagmire of the downhill slide, the L.A. syndrome. You know the sort of thing. 'Hung on the balance of a crystal pane through your nose.' " Plant was then asked if he saw much of this activity: "Yeah, but when it affects people who I love then I sort of snap back at them—'Don't you understand that you are now immortalized? The parody of it all is there for you to behold.' These aren't people in the immediate surroundings but they're people who come and go, who we know, usually of the opposite sex. People get carried along with the whole momentum and the adrenaline of a rock 'n' roll band. We're in one that's been going for nine years, because we can still shake it better than anyone else. Then when you leave people behind in a situation you say, 'Bye, see you next time' and they sort of slide into the L.A. syndrome, and New York. You come back, and they don't look as well as they should do, you know, the smile has changed a bit. And 'For Your Life' is sort of waving your finger and saying, 'Now you watch it.' " Plant makes references in the lyrics to cocaine, the drug that dominated the L.A. scene in the late 1970s.

Led Zeppelin rehearsed this song with the intention of playing it live, but the song

JIMMY PAGE,
CHICAGO
STADIUM,
APRIL 7, 1977

was never performed live.

Royal Orleans: Named after a hotel in the French Quarter of New Orleans, located at 621 St. Louis Street. Page said this song, like "Achilles Last Stand," changed dramatically in the studio when he added massive overdubs. The song reportedly was a document of a particularly wild night in the French Quarter, a place where the band always seemed to get in trouble. Lyrics refer to John Cameron, who was a session player back when Page and John Paul Jones were doing sessions in London in the mid '60s, though it has been suggested the song is in fact about a night when Jones got drunk.

Nobody's Fault But Mine: Page described the beginning of this song as having "an Eastern sound" and said it was done by "three overtracked guitars, two in unison, and one in octave, and then they were phased. It's the phasing and then the octave guitar as well—doing it an octave above. When they're all mixed together, it comes out as sounding

quite odd." This tune along with "In My Time of Dying," were greatly inspired by Blind Willie Johnson, who was a major influence on the band in their formative years.

Candy Store Rock: This was another tune that was composed live in the studio. The lyrics were a takeoff on a couple of Elvis's songs. The tune was rehearsed for the 1977 tour but was never played in concert.

"Candy Store Rock," backed with "Royal Orleans," was released as a single in the United States in May 1976, though the single did not break the *Billboard* top 40.

Hots On for Nowhere: Also composed live in the studio. Plant said this track, and "Tea for One," were about hurt: "'Presence' isn't a precis on aspects of life in general, but aspects of hurt. That's what songs like 'Tea for One' and 'Hots On for Nowhere' are all about." The guitar riff on this tune bears a striking similarity to one Page had crafted earlier on the Screaming Lord Sutch song "Union Jack Car."

Tea for One: This song feels like a remake of

JIMMY PAGE,
NASSAU COLISE-
UM, UNIONDALE,
N.Y., FEBRUARY
13, 1975

the band's earlier "Since I've Been Loving You" and Page said that for that reason he approached the guitar solo with anxiety.

Plant said the lyrics referred to feeling homesick for England and his family while on tour in America. He said he came up with the idea for the song while sipping tea at the Plaza Hotel in New York City, a hotel where the band frequently stayed.

The Soundtrack from the Film *The Song Remains the Same*

Neither the live soundtrack album nor the film *The Song Remains the Same* is thought of by band members, their following, or critics as the group's high point. The filming had been wrought with problems over the years and the original director was fired when his vision differed from the band's. Peter Clifton was brought in to finish the project and the footage was edited swiftly for quick release. Everyone involved admitted that the movie would never have been released in this form if Robert Plant hadn't been in a car accident that made him unavailable for a tour.

JIMMY PAGE
AND ROBERT
PLANT, TOUR
REHEARSAL,
MINNEAPOLIS,
JANUARY 17,
1975

Most of the footage used in the film is from three nights at Madison Square Garden in 1973. Other footage was shot in Baltimore and in Pittsburgh and the movie begins with the band landing in their jet at the Pittsburgh airport. The group then gets in a limo, heads through a tunnel, and ends up in New York City, one of the stranger edits in rock 'n' roll moviemaking. Sloppy editing is also to blame for the fact that during the first song both Page and Jones are shown wearing two different sets of clothes, indicating that footage from different nights was mixed together for the final film cut.

The opening sequence showing gangsters features Peter Grant, the band's manager, and Richard Cole, the road manager. Some have suggested it was only appropriate that Cole played the role of a hit man in the movie since his allegations about the band's offstage antics provide the bulk of the material in Stephen Davis's book *Hammer of the Gods*.

No one involved with this project was completely satisfied with the results, most notably Jimmy Page. Even while doing press for the movie, he talked about how his idea for a live album would eventually come to pass and about the flaws of the film. "Well, that's just one of those unfortunate things," he said. "Because if you start picking that apart, well, first and foremost it's a soundtrack album and such simply has to be available. As for an actual live album, well, my idea, prior to Robert's accident, which dictated virtually everything we've done since, was to do a chronological affair with tracks dating back to 1970 with 'Communication Breakdown,' say, and going through the various incarnations right up to tracks we'll be doing on the next tour for 'Presence.' It will be great."

Page also specifically cited mistakes in his playing that can be seen in the movie and heard on the soundtrack album. "It wasn't the best performance, it was just the one that happened to have celluloid with it. And there are loads of howling guitar mistakes on it. Normally, one would be inclined to cut them out, but you can't when it's a soundtrack. It's an honest album in its own way, but a chronological live album is something I've always fancied."

Page had an even harder time supporting the film itself. "There's a lot of points to be weighed up. It's a musical, yes, but it's also a documentary. It's all pretty honest I think."

When asked by interviewers if the concert chosen was one of their best nights, Page was even more defensive. "Oh, forget about it as a film of the tour. As regards the gig, well, it's not a terribly good night and it's not terribly bad. Certainly not a magic one, but not tragic." Page said Bonham's sequence is his personal favorite.

One of Page's problems with the first director on the project, Joe Massot, was the director's failure to see the band as more than the Page and Plant show. "The cameramen were very Robert-Jimmy, Jimmy-Robert, and with the three cameramen on the job,

there was certainly a lack of distance shots. Listen, there's no point us making excuses. The facts are there to be understood. It's not a great film, just a reasonably honest statement of where we were at that particular time. . . . In a nutshell, the film sums up an era when the band finished its sets with 'Whole Lotta Love.' That doesn't mean anything now, does it?"

Plant felt strongly enough about his fantasy segment that he said it summed up the questing part of his life. Peter Grant took a much different perspective on the film, calling it "the most expensive home movie ever made."

The actual soundtrack album does differ slightly from the music used in the movie itself. "Celebration Day" appears on the soundtrack album but is not featured in the film. The film contains performances of "Black Dog" and "Since I've Been Loving You," which are not included on the soundtrack album.

When the movie was originally released on video the copy of the movie suffered from sound problems. The movie itself was released to theaters in four-track stereo which created almost a quadrophonic effect during some of the songs. The first video release took the soundtrack from only two of those tracks, meaning that much of the music was left out. Further releases of the video corrected the problem.

The Soundtrack From The Song Remains the Same was released in the United States on October 14, 1976, and in the United Kingdom on October 22, 1976.

In Through the Out Door

Many critics and fans saw *In Through the Out Door* as Led Zeppelin's response to punk rock, the aggressive, bare-bones music that transformed rock in the late 1970s. Zeppelin's response, both musically and graphically, was to come up with an album that was classy, modernized their sound, and did not pander to popular sentiment.

Jimmy Page named the record, and was most likely inspired by the French artist Marcel Duchamp's 1927 work "Door: 11 Rue, Lurrey," which

is also thought to be the inspiration for the elaborate cover design. The Duchamp work features a door that can be seen as both open and closed depending on your perspective. Another Duchamp piece from 1918 may also have provided inspiration in that the title seems to sum up well what the *In Through the Out Door* cover does: it is called "To Be Looked At (From the Other Side of the Glass), With One Eye, Close to, for Almost an Hour."

The visual design of *In Through the Out Door* created by Hipgnosis, qualifies as one of the most detailed and well-thought-out record jacket designs ever. The album cover was photographed at Shepperton Studios in London and a special reconstruction of the barroom scene was built for the photo session (ironically, Shepperton Studios would be rented by Robert Plant three years later to rehearse for his first solo tour, the first major live venture of any of the members after the band split).

Though the bar scene itself was created in a London studio, the bar was modeled after a New Orleans club that was a favorite with the band. The Absinthe Bar, located on Bourbon Street in the heart of the French Quarter, was the inspiration as it was a frequent hang out of the band when they were in town. Jimmy Page jammed here one night with Mason Ruffner and an autographed picture of Page hangs on the wall. Page also met his wife in the bar.

The album was issued with six completely different covers, all in plain brown paper bags (Zeppelin again buckled under to record company pressure and allowed their logo to be printed on the outside of the brown paper bags). Each cover design features a different photograph of the same scene in a bar: a man sits at the bar lighting a match while the bartender polishes a glass. The six different pictures are six different perspectives on the scene taken from within the same room.

JIMMY PAGE, NASSAU COLISEUM, UNIONDALE, N.Y., FEBRUARY 13, 1975

The photograph itself is reproduced in black and white with a sepia-tone print. Each cover, though, has a brush stroke superimposed over the photo and everything that appears within that brush stroke is reproduced in hand-tinted full color. Each different version of the cover has a different letter from "a" to "f" after the catalog number of the record. The model in the picture is not Jimmy Page, as some early rumors had it.

Tracks for the record were originally worked out by Page at his home studio. To record the album the band flew to Stockholm to use the Swedish band Abba's Polar Studio. "Abba were very kind," Plant explained, "and they said, 'Why don't you come over and have a look at the studios,' because they reckoned it was really hot. It's sort of a weird place to go, Sweden. I mean, if you've got any choice at all I think you might choose other alternatives. Like L.A.'s got a pretty good conductive mood for making raunchy records, although everybody seems to come out of there halfway on their knees by the end of studio time. But to trek to Sweden, in the middle of winter, a studio had to be good. And it was: it was sensational and had just the amount of live sound we like."

Recording of the album began in December 1978 and continued through February 1979. Mixing took place at Plumpton Studios and the Sol Studio, both studios essentially run by Jimmy Page.

In Through the Out Door was released simultaneously in the United States and the United Kingdom August 15, 1979.

In the Evening: This song and "Carouselambra" started out as demos done just with keyboards and drums. "The guitar was added, as it were," says John Paul Jones. "That's mainly because Bonzo and I were at the rehearsal first." Plant's review of the song was that it's "a great one, a real stomper. Again, he's using a lot of keyboards and strings and things like that."

Page said Jones used a Yamaha GX-1 on this track and that he himself used a bow on his guitar and a "Gizmotron." "I wanted people to say 'What the hell is that?' That's what I was going for."

South Bound Saurez: The name of this song has been misspelled ever since the release of the record. The correct title, as indicated by a Swan Song press release prior to the release of the record, is "South Bound Suarez," with "Suarez" being a Spanish word meaning "party," or "gather-

ing," similar to the French "soiree." Early reviews of the record from the advance tapes correctly spell the title but after the release of the record the incorrect spelling has become the standard. In an interview around the time of the release Plant muttered that the label couldn't even get the spelling of the song right.

Plant said the song reminded him of "about five o'clock in the morning in New Orleans, wishing you'd got the strength you had at nine a.m. It's a little bit more belting, something that people could immediately go, ah, that's a little bit like 'Custard Pie.' " This is one of only two songs in the entire Zeppelin catalog that Jimmy Page did not get any writing credit for.

Fool in the Rain: Three or four different versions of this song were recorded in the studio, though none was dramatically different from the version used on the album. Plant said this track was "most unusual for us, because I don't think we would have played it had the situation been different. With the World Cup in Argentina in 1978, and a lot of this South American thing going around, and any time you watch any soccer on the television, there's always this South American rhythm going on. It's not an attempt to be Carlos Santana."

"Fool in the Rain," backed with "Hot Dog," was released as a single in the United States in December 1979. The single went as high as number 21 on the *Billboard* charts, the highest such position for a Zeppelin song in seven years.

Hot Dog: Zeppelin filmed a promotional video for this song, using a live performance from Knebworth, though few people ever saw it because at the time there was nothing like MTV. The video was sent out to a number of record stores which were allowed to play the clip in their store but the video itself eventually had to be returned to the label which makes this a valuable collectible. Plant calls the song a tribute to hillbilly music. " 'Hot Dog' owes everything to the state of Texas," he said, "and to the state of mind of some of the people in Texas."

Carouselambra: Page said he used a "Gizmotron" on this song to help roll the strings. "It got slammed in the British press," Plant told an American journalist in 1979, "for being once again that tired old mystical feel. But it is in fact an extended piece with John Paul Jones dictating the movement, with a lyrical content that leans back towards the 'Battle of Evermore.' It's got nothing to do with that at all, though, it's just a shroud for something that I was relating to at the present. It's another one of those mystical hidden things where one day the person it was written about will go, 'My God, was it really like that?' "

All My Love: Robert Plant has said very little about this song. His son Karac had been killed one year earlier, and this track may be the singer's tribute to him. The performance is one of the most emotional Plant ever did and though the song was recorded several times in the studio, the track on the album represents the first vocal cut. Credited to "Plant/Jones," this is the only other Zeppelin song that Page did not get writing credit on.

I'm Gonna Crawl: On early pressings of this album the song was credited to "Page/Grant," indicating that Peter Grant and Jimmy Page wrote the song. This was a strange pressing error and the song was later correctly credited to "Page/Plant." Plant, who indeed co-wrote the song with Page, said that the tune had "nothing to do with carpet burns." He said the song was his tribute to Otis Redding and Wilson Pickett. "The first thing that Wilson Pickett ever did," he said, "was 'It's Too Late,' and all those great slow R&B things. I wanted to do something a little bit like that, but a little more tongue in cheek. The lyrics are a bit mundane, cheesy, but it's a great atmosphere. The only thing missing is the horn section, because Jonesy couldn't learn to play horns in time."

Coda

Coda is an assemblage of outtakes and previously unreleased songs put together after Led Zeppelin disbanded in the aftermath of John Bonham's death. The cover of this album is another Hipgnosis project and this time the design is rather straightforward. What fans have debated for years is the exact nature and meaning of the picture of the irrigation circles of crops on the back cover. The commonly held theory is that the ten crop circles represent the total of ten albums (including *Coda*) that Led Zeppelin released. Page mixed all these tracks himself at the Sol Studio in Berkshire.

Coda was released simultaneously in the United States and the United Kingdom November 19, 1982.

We're Gonna Groove: With this album the band seemed to take a different slant on crediting other songwriters. This tune co-credited Ben E. King, who had previously written the hit "Stand By Me," a tune Zeppelin played in concert once. Page uses a "sub octivider" on this track. This cut was recorded on June 25, 1969, at Morgan Studios in London.

Poor Tom: Originally considered for the third record, this was one of the songs written around the campfire at Bron-Yr-Aur. This version was recorded at Olympic Studios in London on June 5, 1970.

I Can't Quit You Baby: This is the second time the band recorded this song by Willie Dixon, and this cut is even heavier than Zeppelin's cover of the song on the first album. This version of the cut was recorded live during a soundcheck for the Royal Albert Hall show in London on September 1, 1970.

Walter's Walk: This song was never performed live but it was created during the middle of "Dazed and Confused" onstage in 1971 and 1972. The version used here was from a session at Stargroves with the Rolling Stones's Mobile Studio on May 15, 1972.

Ozone Baby: This song grew out of blues jams dating back to 1975 on "Dazed and Confused." Page again uses a "sub octivider." This version was recorded during the *In Through the Out Door* sessions on November 14, 1978, at Polar Studios.

Darlene: This song was an outtake from *In Through the Out Door*. It was recorded on November 16, 1978 at Polar Studios in Stockholm.

Bonzo's Montreux: This song was recorded after *Presence* and may have been considered for *In Through the Our Door*. The cut was recorded on September 12, 1976, at Mountain Studios in Montreux, Switzerland by Page and Bonham together.

Wearing and Tearing: Page says this song was originally recorded for *Presence* but that "as you can imagine, the song really couldn't fit on the album. That was done as a sort of really energetic punk-type thing." It was recorded on November 21, 1978, at Polar Studios in Stockholm.

The song was originally planned to be released as a single that would be available only at the band's 1979 Knebworth concerts. As they frequently did, the band ran into problems getting the records pressed and packaged in time and the single was never made. The first time the song was ever played live by the band was at the 1990 Knebworth Festival where Plant and Page reunited and played the tune.

Plant later described what the group had hoped to achieve with the song: "We wanted to put it out on a different label under the name of a different artist alongside the Damned and the Sex Pistols because it was so vicious and so emphatically fresh. And if you hadn't known it was us, it could have been anybody at all who was young and virile and all the things that we were then not supposed to be." It was to be the band's true swan song.

Led Zeppelin

The Led Zeppelin boxed set came about when Atlantic Records started to notice how well boxed retrospectives released on CD were selling. The Zeppelin catalog as pressed on CD was notorious for its inferior sound quality and for mastering problems like songs getting cut off too early, tremendous hiss, and inferior tapes.

Atlantic approached Page with the idea of a boxed retrospective collection and Page agreed. He approached the other remaining band members and asked them to compile lists of what they most wanted on the set and Page went from there. Page explained his impetus to *Musician's* Matt Resnikoff: "During the years of Zeppelin I went through the whole mastering process, right through to checking the white labels on the discs and cassettes. But when Atlantic put out the catalog on CD, I wasn't brought in at all. In fact, it was only when somebody told me the CDs were out that I was aware

that they had happened. I knew, right from the kickoff, that a far better job could have been done. I heard some horror stories of what happened at the time, because now everybody is trying to pass the buck. They hadn't put any effort into it at all. They'd just run the tapes and that was it, no EQing. I was keen to get a better sound quality for the CDs. It wasn't too difficult, I can assure you."

Page then went and tracked down as many of the original master recordings as possible, he told *Musician*. "Wherever possible, I went right back to the studio masters. Unfortunately, some of them have disappeared along the way. I must say about 80 percent of it is the original ones. However, where we couldn't find them we had to go to pre-production EQ copies and that's where the problems appeared. It was quite satisfying that the original tapes held up pretty well."

Tracking down some of the tapes proved to be a problem itself. "They were all over the place really, and it was a treasure hunt trying to find them all," Page said. "I had some in my own possession but then, other ones that were supposed to be in security archives, some were there and some weren't. The ones that I handled personally were where they ought to be."

In the process of remastering the tapes, Page was also presented with an opportunity to reorganize the songs for the four-CD collection. "By nature of the fact that it was a four-CD package it allowed me to represent them in a new form, so it became like the old picture within a new frame. It sheds new light on everything, I think. The hardest part was getting the running order, interlacing the tracks and all."

The boxed set included three songs that had been previously unreleased, two of them live tracks and the third a combination of two previously released songs, "Bonzo's Montreux" and "Moby Dick," that Page pieced together in the studio. "We didn't have any golden nuggets, so to speak," Page said addressing the controversial point of the lack of unreleased cuts on the box. "Everything that was left over since *In Through the Out Door* and after we'd lost John, that was completed with vocals or maybe needed to be remixed or whatever, had come out

KNEBWORTH

FESTIVAL,

AUGUST 4, 1979

on the *Coda* album."

The boxed set was designed by Richard Hutchison, and while the package is not as elaborate as some of the past Zeppelin projects, it too features some mysteries. The image on the front of the box, credited to "Mission Control, Bristol England," is of some of the strange circles that have appeared in crops in the English countryside. These crop circles gained international attention in the summer of 1990, when they began springing up overnight in previously normal fields. The crop circles sent a virtual army of researchers, scientists, journalists and various investigators to the cornfields of southern England in an attempt to determine the cause of these strange markings. The patterns developed in crops more than 400 times in the summer of 1990. The markings almost always spring up overnight and sometimes eyewitnesses reported they were accompanied by "warbling sounds and a moving orange light."

The image portrayed on the boxed set is one of the largest and most intricate of the crop markings found in a field near Wiltshire. Theories on the cause of the markings run from the scientific approach that they've been caused by wind shears and electrically charged weather conditions, to the wilder explanations that they've been caused by extraterrestrial visitors. To date, no scientific explanation has been commonly accepted. "I've been studying these circles for five years now," said Archie Roy, a researcher from the the University of Glasgow told one magazine reporter, "and I don't believe we have any real idea of what they are or what causes them."

The front cover of the box has four numbers, each positioned in a corner, 54, 69, 79, 00. Though the band has yet to comment on what they represent most fans conclude that 54 is for the 54 tracks included on the box, 69 and 79 represent the decade's worth of studio recordings that is included on the box, and the 00 refers to the infinity symbol—yet another mystical reference in the body of the band's work. The number 54 springs up again in the boxed set in that the booklet inside contains 54 pictures of the band, and finally the list price for the set was $54.98, which was the explanation for the numbers accepted by most record stores. The photo that is on the back cover of the booklet in the boxed set also appears on the inner sleeve to *Coda*, though on the boxed set booklet the photo has been flopped. Promotional posters called the set "The Definitive Collection."

The covers to the individual CDs, or album sleeves, with the boxed set are not of the group's album covers but instead are new images created just for the boxed set. Each of the four CDs features a different photo or graphic, and hidden within the image is one of the four band members' symbols. The first CD cover shows a feather in a circle (Plant's symbol); the second cover shows a sundial (Page's symbol Zoso is hidden in the shadow); the third cover features a rock (Bonham's three circles are etched in the rock); and the fourth cover shows a picture of a delta (and waterways in the swamp create John Paul Jones's complicated symbol).

There is at least one error in the booklet that

comes with the boxed set concerning a recording date. "I Can't Quit You Baby" is listed in the booklet as being from the soundcheck at the Royal Albert Hall show from September 1, 1970. The actual date of the show was January 9, 1970, and the error is probably accounted for by the difference between the English style of listing dates as numbers with the month second, and the American style of listing the month first (the English tour listing probably said "9/1/70" which actually means January 9, 1970 the date the Albert Hall show took place). Finally, the title for this song is different on the boxed set than on the first album: It originally was listed on the band's debut as "I Can't Quit You," but on the boxed set, and on the *Coda* album it has become "I Can't Quit You Baby." The text of the booklet also listed the date of the band's Live Aid reunion as July 13th, 1987 when the show took place on July 13, 1985. "Babe I'm Gonna Leave You" on the boxed set also has a different credit from the first record. On the first album it was credited as a traditional song, but on the set "Anne Bredon" has been added to the names of the band members.

Led Zeppelin was released in the United States on October 23, 1990, and in the United Kingdom on October 29, 1990. A two-CD compilation from the set titled *Remasters* was released in the United Kingdom on October 15, 1990.

Travelling Riverside Blues: A promotional CD single was issued of this track, the first Zeppelin promo CD. Page told *Musician* that part of the reason he included it was that during his solo *Outrider* tour the track kept getting radio airplay. "Everyone thought it was an outtake from the second album. Could've been, but it wasn't. It was just a radio broadcast, recorded live in the studio. That particular one didn't have an audience. I was given the opportunity to make overdubs on it, and unfortunately the engineer sort of whacks the fader right up for the guitar intro solo part, and that's a bit disturbing, but as a historical piece there seems to be a lot of interest in it, so we decided to put that on."

Plant seemed more excited about the inclusion of "Travelling Riverside Blues" on the set than any other band member. He said the song was about

"when a man gets personal and wants to have his fun. When I was a kid, I used to go to all the folk clubs and listen to people singing unaccompanied vocal work, rather in the lines of sort of English folk songs, the unaccompanied coal miner from Durham wailing away about the blokes making all the money and he's not getting any. Then you had the Woody Guthrie element. . . . On June 20, 1937, in Dallas, 'Travelling Riverside Blues' was first recorded on Columbia. And it says, 'If a man gets personal and wants to have his fun, best come back to Friar's Point mama and barrel house all night long.' Now the idea of that seemed much better than chartered accountancy. The idea of some troubadour going up and down the Mississippi River, getting off at the landing and playing and really having a good time, and being not so much a highwayman. It's not even the bard that goes from court to court and sings the praises of the king and then moves on safely. It's just the idea of this guy getting away with it. Robert Johnson didn't get away with it forever—he was murdered."

"Travelling Riverside Blues" was recorded for "John Peel's Top Gear" radio show on the BBC on June 23, 1969.

White Summer/Black Mountain Side: Page said this track is "from a live broadcast, in front of an audience, but you don't really get to hear any of the audience. They're not rustling candy papers and things." It was recorded and broadcast live on June 27, 1969, at London's Playhouse Theatre for the BBC's "Playhouse Theatre Over Radio One."

Moby Dick/Bonzo's Montreux: Page explained the reason for including these two tracks to *Musician*: "Everyone agreed on what they basically wanted. There was certainly 'Moby Dick' and 'Bonzo's Montreux,' and I didn't want to leave one out, so I had this sort of brain wave that it could possibly be done. I didn't have any proper recording equipment at home, but armed with a metronome I checked out the two things and the tempos sounded pretty similar. I just thought it would work."

—Charles R. Cross

JOHN PAUL JONES, CHICAGO, JANUARY 1975

Part Five

TRAIN
KEPT
A
ROLLIN'

TRAIN KEPT A ROLLIN'

Performances 1968 - 1990

The news that Chicago fans of Led Zeppelin had waited years to hear arrived on September 25, 1980. A full page advertisement in the *Chicago Tribune* announcing mail-order ticket sales for Led Zeppelin in concert at Chicago Stadium for four nights in November. After three years of waiting, Led Zeppelin was returning to the United States for a full-scale tour, called by the Swan Song press release, "Led Zeppelin, The 1980s, Part One." Chicago was the first U.S. city to make the announcement of tickets going on sale.

Surely thousands of fans were on their way to the bank to obtain money orders, were filling out the order form, or had already dropped their envelope in the mailbox before they heard the bad news, the heartbreaking news that John Henry Bonham was dead. There would be no shows at Chicago Stadium, no North American tour, there would in fact be no more Led Zeppelin. Euphoria became bitter sadness in a matter of hours. And though their music would live on, as alive with each listen as it was the day it was recorded, Led Zeppelin's live legacy became sealed with the cancelation of the 1980 North American tour.

Bonzo played his last Led Zeppelin show at the Eissporthalle in Berlin, Germany, on July 7, 1980. And though there have been a handful of "reunion" dates between the surviving members since, July 7, 1980 marked the last of some 400 dates that Led Zeppelin played since their first gig in Copenhagen in September 1968. In that time, Led Zeppelin toured North America 11 times, the United Kingdom at least five times (with many off-tour appearances), Europe many times, Japan twice, as well as one tour of Australia and New Zealand. And it was those tours and shows, more than their records, that made Led Zeppelin the most popular band in the world for a decade and, some would argue, long after. It was the repeated visits to Boston, Los Angeles, London, Osaka, and Montreux that built up a fan base without the aid of Top 40 singles. Led Zeppelin will be remembered for their records, but the concerts may be their legacy.

Those shows in the "houses of the holy," as the band called the huge halls in which they played, presented a different Led Zeppelin than the one found on vinyl. A song like "Dazed and Confused," which lasts a brief six minutes on record, would stretch into a half hour odyssey behind the bow of Jimmy Page. Robert Plant could take the five-minute "Whole Lotta Love" and turn it into a 25-minute history of rock 'n' roll that on any given night could include lyrics or even complete versions of songs like Roy Orbison's "Only the Lonely," Elvis Presley's "Baby I Don't Care" or "Let's Have a Party." John Paul Jones would build sweeping classical melodies into a 15-minute version of "No Quarter" or John Bonham would turn the quick hitting "Moby Dick" into a 20-minute percussion orgy. And the people would cheer for more.

Perhaps the greatest thing about Led Zeppelin in concert was that the shows were always evolving. Not only would sets change tour to tour and night to night, but even the versions of the songs themselves could change dramatically. A song like "Achilles Last Stand" might be mournful one night, aggressive the next, and jubilant the third. Different textures and moods were woven into the songs every night, depending on the mood of the band.

Zeppelin created legions of fans through relentless touring in their first five years. It seems unthinkable now, in today's competitive concert marketplace, for a band to hit the same area four different times in a single year, but Zeppelin did it in many American cities in 1969. What might be feared as overexposure had no such effect, for each time Zeppelin returned to a market, they played to more and more people in larger and larger venues. Word spread quickly, even without radio airplay, and the records sold at a phenomenal clip. Led Zeppelin was a personal secret for millions of fans simultaneously, who all thought they had discovered something unique.

Led Zeppelin reinvented rock 'n' roll concerts, playing three hours when the standard was less than half that, using immense P.A. systems that allowed them to be heard from any seat in an arena, becoming the first band to use giant video screens as early as 1975. As immense as their popularity continues to be, they were simply without equal in the decade of the seventies. Announcements of tours in

JIMMY PAGE DURING THE BOW SOLO ON THE 1975 U.S. TOUR

1975 and 1977 were met with outright hysteria, and how could you blame their fans? Led Zeppelin concerts were rock 'n' roll at its very best: loud, long, and passionate.

What follows is a chronology of Led Zeppelin's career, including every date Led Zeppelin is known to have performed. The listing has been pieced together from newspaper reviews, published band itineraries, tapes, tour books, ticket stubs, and fan recollections. With dates stretching back over 22 years, complete information on every specific show is simply no longer available, but the list, though not perfect, presents the most complete picture yet offered of Led Zeppelin's in-concert history. Set lists are given for every different tour and for notable shows. Specific show details are also included where available and pertinent, as are rehearsal sessions, recording sessions, and important nonconcert dates in the band's history, such as album release dates. Every effort has been made to verify these dates, and any speculation regarding dates has been clearly noted. Many previously published lists of Zeppelin tour dates repeat errors about the band's early history. The band was infamous for canceling shows and entire tours, and this list only includes shows that were known to have taken place (dates for shows that were canceled are noted as such).

Compiling a set list for any Led Zeppelin concert is not unlike putting together a jigsaw puzzle. The band threw so many snippets of songs, both their own numbers and other artists' tunes, into their performances that determining what part of the song is "Whole Lotta Love" and what is "The Crunge" is subjective. (The band began playing parts of "The Crunge" during "Whole Lotta Love" as early as 1971, and varying lengths of it, both instrumental and vocal, would appear within the song over the next two tours, without ever playing the song by itself, distinctly. The band did this sort of onstage experimentation frequently.) At times the group would throw an entire song into the middle of another song, while on other occasions they would use ten seconds of a guitar riff from a popular song of the day. A classic example of this improvisational style would be from Osaka, Japan, on September 29, 1971, when during the middle of "Whole Lotta Love" the group played bits and pieces of "Boogie Mama," "I Gotta Know," "Twist and Shout," "Fortune Teller," "Good Times Bad Times," "You Shook Me," and even a line or two from "Smoke Gets in Your Eyes." The more notable inclusions within medleys of this sort are noted in parentheses in the list that follows. Encores are delineated from the rest of the set by a double slash.

When the four members of the band first sat together in a rented rehearsal studio on Gerrard Street, near London's Chinatown, the magic began. The group played a number made classic by the Yardbirds called "Train Kept a Rollin'." The band members individually used the same adjectives to describe the sound and the feel they created together: "stunning," "wonderful," "exhilarating," "magic." The group used this same number to start the shows on their first and second tours and then didn't play the song again until the 1980 tour of Europe. At

their last show in Berlin on July 7, 1980—less than three months before the untimely death of drummer John Bonham—they kicked off their concert with the thunder of Bonham's bass drum and performed an outstanding version of "Train Kept a Rollin'," and though the group would soon no longer be, the song remained the same.

8/68 London, England

The Yardbirds, featuring Jimmy Page on guitar, play their last show in July and officially break-up. Page wants to continue on and decides to form a new band himself, retaining the assistance of then Yardbirds manager Peter Grant. A noted session player, Page looks to other such musicians as potential band members. First to join is bass and keyboard player John Paul Jones, who had worked with Page before in the studio. Jones himself had never been in a permanent band, but was well known for his work with other artists, including Donovan.

As for a singer, Page's first choice is Terry Reid, former lead singer for Peter Jay and the Jaywalkers, but Reid, who has a solo deal already in the works, turns him down. He does recommend a blues singer from Birmingham, Robert Plant. Page goes to hear Plant with his current band Hobbstweedle, and is impressed enough to later comment that he was surprised a singer of Robert's caliber had not yet been discovered. Plant agrees to join the band, and suggests his friend John Bonham, who he had played with a year earlier in the Band of Joy, as the drummer. Bonham was already gaining a reputation in the business, and had offers from Joe Cocker and Chris Farlowe, but he chooses to join Plant.

The new band is formed and after little more than a week's rehearsal, the group travels to Scandinavia for their first tour.

9/14/68 Copenhagen, Denmark

First show ever by the members of the group that would come to be known as Led Zeppelin. For the first shows of their career, the band is billed for contractual reasons as "The New Yardbirds." Jimmy Page, who had retained the Yardbirds name following the last Yardbirds gig on July 7, 1968, was fulfilling a Scandinavian Yardbirds tour that had been booked months earlier. Earliest sets include "Communication Breakdown," "Dazed and Confused" (a song done by the Yardbirds on their last tour), "Babe I'm Gonna Leave You," "How Many More Times," and "White Summer/Black Mountain Side." Page also says that Elmer Gantry's "Flames" was played on the first Scandinavian tour, and was considered, though not recorded for *Led Zeppelin I*. The Yardbirds' "For Your Love" was often the encore song during Zeppelin's first few tours.

9/20/68 Stockholm, Sweden

More than 20 minutes of the show are later broadcast on Swedish radio, including "I Can't Quit You," "I've Got to Move" (introduced as "a thing by Otis Rush"), "Dazed and Confused," and "How Many More Times."

Other cities visited during the Scandinavian tour are Gothenburg and Malmo, Sweden, and probably Oslo and one other city in Norway. The trial run is a success and the band returns to England.

It is during the break after the Scandinavian dates that the band

FOLLOWING PAGES: INDIANAPOLIS, IND., JANUARY 25, 1975

members, now calling themselves Led Zeppelin, enter Olympic Studios, London, to record their first album. In little more than 30 hours, *Led Zeppelin I* is completed. It will be released in America in January and in April in the U.K. The name Led Zeppelin is suggested by Keith Moon, though John Entwistle of the Who, claims it was he, not Keith, who came up with the name and suggested it to his then chauffeur Richard Cole, who soon after went to work for Jimmy Page and Peter Grant.

10/15/68 Surrey, England, Surrey University
The band is billed for the first time as Led Zeppelin.

10/18/68 London, England, The Marquee
The band is again billed as "The New Yardbirds" for this show and, for the last time, the following night. Despite the fact that Led Zeppelin has no album available yet, or any song on the radio, a crowd of more than 1,200 shows up for the performance, the biggest crowd at the Marquee in over two years.

10/19/68 Liverpool, England, Liverpool University

11/9/68 London, England, The Roundhouse
On a bill with John Lee Hooker, the band is listed as "Yardbirds, now known as Led Zeppelin," with the latter getting the larger billing.

11/16/68 Manchester, England, College of Science and Technology
The band appears for a fee of £225.

11/23/68 Sheffield, England, Sheffield University
By the end of November, manager Peter Grant concludes the negotiations that sign Led Zeppelin to Atlantic Records, with a reported advance of $200,000, one of the largest sums ever given to a new band. Dusty Springfield, for whom Jones had done a great deal of session work, is instrumental in influencing Atlantic to sign Page's new band. Once inking the deal, Zeppelin is promptly booked for a U.S. tour, opening for other Atco/Atlantic groups Vanilla Fudge and Iron Butterfly.

12/10/68 London, England, The Marquee
Billed this night as "Led Zeppelin (nee the Yardbirds)."

12/16/68 Bath, England, The Bath Pavilion

12/19/68 Exeter, England, City Hall

12/20/68 London, England, Fishmongers' Hall
FIRST U.S. TOUR

12/26/68 Denver, Colo., Auditorium Arena
Zeppelin begin their first U.S. tour, as opening act for fellow Atco/Atlantic artists Vanilla Fudge, who top the Denver bill along with Spirit. Zeppelin is not even listed in advertisements for the show, though a reviewer in the *Rocky Mountain News* the following day does comment on "the Led Zeppelin" (sic), calling them "blues oriented," and taking special note of Jimmy Page, who was "exceptionally fine, and used a violin bow on his guitar strings to good effect." He was not as impressed with John Bonham, whose drum solo he described as "uneventful, unsuitable, uninventive."

Over the next 12 months, Led Zeppelin will tour the U.S. four times, hitting markets like New York City as often as once every two or three months. Perhaps no other band ever stormed the U.S. in the manner Led Zeppelin did in 1969.

12/27/68 Seattle, Wash., Seattle Center Arena

12/30/68 Spokane, Wash., Gonzaga University
First known set list from the U.S., as Zeppelin opens for Iron Butterfly. Plant speaks about the cold weather outside, telling the crowd that the equipment had to be warmed up for three hours with gas stoves. "How Many More Times" becomes an ever-changing medley song for the band to include parts of other songs, usually covers. In Spokane it includes snatches of "The Hunter" and "Rosie" as it will during most shows over the next year. "Pat's Delight" is the name given to what will eventually become "Moby Dick." Named for Bonham's wife, the drum solo is a response to the drum portion of "In-A-Gadda-Da-Vida," which was a hit at the time. Train Kept a Rollin'/I Can't Quit You/As Long as I Have You/Dazed and Confused/White Summer/How Many More Times/Pat's Delight.

12/31/68 Portland, Ore.
Following this show, Zeppelin begin to drive back to Seattle to catch a flight to Los Angeles, driving through a snowstorm so powerful that a state patrolman pulls them off the road and tells them to stop driving. But Peter Grant is determined to make it through and forges on despite Richard Cole, the band's road manager and driver, almost sending the car over an embankment. Arriving in Seattle four hours and much panic later, they realize the reason the airport is so deserted is that it is New Year's Eve. Drinks are suggested, but Robert Plant and John Bonham are both only 20 years old and are denied entrance to the bar.

1/2–5/69 Los Angeles, Calif., Whiskey A Go Go
First headlining shows with Alice Cooper.

1/9–12/69 San Francisco, Calif., The Fillmore West
Zeppelin and Taj Mahal support Country Joe and the Fish. Zeppelin plays two sets each night and the show includes "As Long as I Have You," a long jam which contains part of a song called "Fresh Garbage" that will eventually evolve into "Whole Lotta Love." The medley will remain an important part of any Zeppelin show for most of the band's career as a vehicle for improvisation on their own material and the inclusion of cover songs by others. A version of "You Shook Me" from the first night is later broadcast on San Francisco FM station KSAN, and the set closes with the Yardbirds' "For Your Love." Partial set list from 1/10: Train Kept a Rollin'/I Can't Quit You/As Long as I Have You (including "Fresh Garbage")/Dazed and Confused/How Many More Times//White Summer/Black Mountain Side/Killing Floor/You Shook Me/Pat's Delight/Babe I'm Gonna Leave You/Communication Breakdown//For Your Love.

1/13/69 San Diego, Calif., Fox Theatre

1/17-18/69 Detroit, Mich., Grande Ballroom
The band is unceremoniously billed as "Led Zeptlin" (sic). Supported the first night by Linn County and Lawrence Blues Band, and by Target the second night.

1/22/69 Miami, Fla., The Image Club
Assumed date for the Miami show. A few days of rest and relaxation for the band, after some unbearable weather two weeks earlier on the West Coast. Plant tells the crowd, "We've been here four days so it's nice to be able to get down and play again." "As Long as I Have You" includes "Mockingbird." *Led Zeppelin I*, is released in the U.S., though it won't be released in England for nearly four months.

1/23/69 Boston, Mass., Boston Tea Party
The Boston set again includes "Killing Floor." Zeppelin will

visit the Tea Party often during their first few tours and it becomes a favorite venue, because of the tremendous crowd response. In interviews the band often talks about the reaction they received in Boston and how much they looked forward to returning.

1/29/69 Philadelphia, Pa., Electric Factory
1/31/69 New York, N.Y., The Fillmore East
Opening again for Iron Butterfly, sharing the slot with gospel group Porter's Popular Preachers. This is one of the first audiences the band plays to that has had a chance to hear the first album, which has just been released in America. Two sets each night, similar to those played at the Fillmore West dates. These two New York appearances attract a great deal of attention and afford Atlantic Records its first chance to showcase their recent signees.

2/1/69 New York, N.Y., The Fillmore East
Short set with "You Shook Me" as the encore.

2/2/69 Toronto, Ontario, The Rockpile
In Ritchie Yorke's review the next day he erroneously describes the band, saying, "Bonham is not Jack Bruce, but he's

on the right road, Jones is a fine drummer with precision timing." Despite his mistake he becomes one of the band's favorite journalists, and later writes one of the first Led Zeppelin biographies.

2/7–8/69 Chicago, Ill., The Kinetic Playground
First U.S. tour ends with two appearances on a bill with Vanilla Fudge and Jethro Tull.

Other cities likely visited on the first tour are Atlanta, Baltimore, Pittsburgh, and Cleveland. The band returns to England for more club dates, but will return to the U.S. in less than two months for another tour which will feature them as headliners on most nights.

3/1/69 Plymouth, England
3/7/69 Hornsey, London, England, Northern Wood Tavern
Other shows in March include the Crawdaddy Club in Richmond and a date in Cardiff, where the band is refused admission for not wearing neckties.

3/13/69 Copenhagen, Denmark, Gladsaxe
Zeppelin play two shows here in one day, including a staged performance that is filmed and later broadcast by Danish Television. Though never officially released, the black-and-white program was rebroadcast by the BBC in its entirety in 1989. It

represents the earliest known Led Zeppelin video footage and because of its quality it is the most sought-after video. In 1990 the program is released as a bootleg video, by far the best of what little Zeppelin video there is.

3/14/69 Stockholm, Sweden, Koncerthuset

3/21/69 London, England, BBC Studios

Led Zeppelin appear on the BBC's "How Late It Is" television program, their only U.K. TV appearance, as last-minute replacements for the Flying Burrito Brothers. They perform "Communication Breakdown," though their first album still is yet to be released in the U.K..

3/22/69 Birmingham, England, Stepmother's

3/24/69 London, England, Cook's Ferry Inn

3/25/69 Staines, England

"Dazed and Confused" is filmed for the movie "Supershow." Apart from *The Song Remains the Same*, the song is the only live Zeppelin footage available officially on home video.

3/28/69 London, England, The Marquee

Playing with Eyes of Blue. A press release regarding this show describes Zeppelin as "the most talked about (and raved about) British group of the moment."

3/30/69 Potters Bar, England, Farx

4/1/69 West Hampstead, England, Klooks Kleek

On this date *Led Zeppelin I* is finally released in the U.K..

4/5/69 London, England, The Roundhouse

4/8/69 Welwyn, Garden City, England, The Cherry Tree

4/12/69 Tolworth, England, Toby Jug

4/14/69 Stoke-on-Trent, England

4/17/69 Sunderland, England

SECOND U.S. TOUR

Recording for *Led Zeppelin II* was squeezed in between dates on the second U.S. tour, including studio time in Vancouver, Los Angeles, and New York City.

4/18/69 New York City, N.Y., NYU Jazz Festival

Zeppelin starts their second U.S. tour on a bill with Errol Garner and Dave Brubeck.

4/24/69 San Francisco, Calif., The Fillmore West

Their set has changed only slightly from the first tour, still including the embryonic versions of both "Moby Dick" and now "Whole Lotta Love." Sharing the bill in San Francisco are fellow Atlantic recording artists Brian Auger and Julie Driscoll.

4/25–26/69 San Francisco, Calif., The Winterland

4/27/69 San Francisco, Calif., The Fillmore West

Two sets on April 27, including Train Kept a Rollin'/I Can't Quit You/As Long as I Have You (including "Fresh Garbage" and "Shake")/You Shook Me/How Many More Times/White Summer/Killing Floor/Babe I'm Gonna Leave You/Moby Dick/Dazed and Confused//Communication Breakdown.

5/1/69 Irvine, Calif., Crawford Hall, U.C. Irvine

5/2–3/69 Pasadena, Calif., The Rose Palace

While Led Zeppelin are in the Los Angeles area, they continue studio work on the second album. Notable cuts laid down in California include "Moby Dick," "What Is and What Should Never Be," "Whole Lotta Love," and the vocals to "The Lemon Song," recorded at Mirror Sound in Los Angeles.

5/4/69 San Bernardino, Calif.

5/9/69 Portland, Ore.

5/10/69 Vancouver, British Columbia, PNE Agrodome

Supported by Bob Buckley and Spring for a very strange bill.

5/11/69 Seattle, Wash., Greenlake Aqua Theatre

Zep shares the bill with Three Dog Night, who a *Seattle Times* reviewer claims "stole the show."

5/13/69 Honolulu, Hi., Honolulu International Center

Led Zeppelin plays their first show ever on the island and spend a few days off on the beaches. The midtour stopover in Hawaii will become a regular fixture on future Zeppelin tours. They become one of the few bands to include the island on most tours.

5/16/69 Detroit, Mich., Grande Ballroom

Two shows in one night.

5/17/69 Athens, Ohio, Ohio University

5/18/69 Minneapolis, Minn., Guthrie Memorial Theater

At a meeting Monday morning following the show, the band, who don't have to appear in Chicago until the weekend and have had a bad experience so far in Minneapolis, decide to leave for New York City, where they do interviews by day and record by night.

5/23–24/69 Chicago, Ill., The Kinetic Playground

5/25/69 Columbia, Md., Merriweather Post Pavilion

Led Zeppelin share the bill with Uncle Dirty and their only known appearance with the Who, a band that at the time was more popular than Led Zeppelin.

5/28–29/69 Boston, Mass., Boston Tea Party

The second night is reportedly one of the longest shows in the band's history. John Paul Jones says the set went without a break for over three hours, and encores were Beatles and Stones covers, including "I Saw Her Standing There" and "Please Please Me," after the band had exhausted their own catalog.

5/30–31/69 New York, N.Y., The Fillmore East

Zeppelin's second U.S. tour closes in New York City, where Zeppelin share a bill with Woody Herman and Delaney & Bonnie. Two sets each night. The second U.S. tour may also have included dates in Philadelphia and Pittsburgh.

6/13/69 Birmingham, England, Town Hall

A review in *New Musical Express* of this show describes the interplay of Plant and Page onstage this way: "The two have a novel way of singing and playing together—Robert utters a few words, usually gibberish, and Jimmy has to repeat them as nearly as possible on his guitar. It's startling the way he manages."

6/15/69 Manchester, England, Free Trade Hall

6/16/69 London, England, Aeolian Hall Studio

Appearance on the "Dave Symonds Show," the first of a handful of BBC appearances this month. Zeppelin perform "The Girl I Love," "Communication Breakdown," and "Something Else." Zeppelin's arrangement of "The Girl I Love" is remarkably similar to their own "Moby Dick," which at this point in time is unreleased.

6/20/69 Newcastle, England, City Hall

6/21/69 Bristol, England, Colston Hall

6/23/69 London, England, BBC Studios

The band records a John Peel session,

SNAPSHOTS FROM THE ACOUSTIC SET, U.S. TOUR, FALL, 1970

a regular weekly program on the BBC hosted by Peel, where rock artists come in and perform live in the studio for broadcast. What Is and What Should Never Be/Communication Breakdown/Travelling Riverside Blues/Whole Lotta Love. It is this version of "Travelling Riverside Blues" that later appears on the Led Zeppelin boxed set in 1990. Other songs are recorded during 1969 that will be included in future Top Gear broadcasts, including "You Shook Me," and "I Can't Quit You."

6/26/69 Portsmouth, England, Guild Hall

6/27/69 London, England, Playhouse Theatre

Aired on the BBC Radio One "Playhouse Theatre Over Radio One" program. The nearly one-hour program includes a short interview with Plant and Page, along with seven live songs: Communication Breakdown/I Can't Quit You/Dazed and Confused/White Summer/Black Mountain Side/You Shook Me/How Many More Times. It is this version of "White Summer/Black Mountain Side," that is contained on the Zeppelin boxed set. Zeppelin are the first band to be given a full one-hour live concert program by the BBC.

6/28/69 Bath, England, The Pavilion

Bath Blues Festival appearance.

6/29/69 London, England, Royal Albert Hall

Led Zeppelin's first appearance at the famed hall. In early interviews, Jimmy Page has said that he doesn't think a rock show could work at Royal Albert Hall. After concluding the regular set and an encore, the crowd is still screaming for more. Zeppelin returns to the stage only to find their power has been turned off. Unheeded, Plant shouts, "Put the power on," picks up a harmonica, and wails until the power returns, at which time the band kicks into their final encore of the night, "Long Tall Sally."

THIRD U.S. TOUR

7/5/69 Atlanta, Ga., Atlanta Pop Festival

Third U.S. tour begins, with *Led Zeppelin II* not yet released. A piece of "Tobacco Road" is played within the "How Many More Times" medley.

7/6/69 Newport, R.I., Festival Field, Newport Jazz Festival

Appearing in the "Schlitz Mixed Bag" lineup with Herbie Hancock, Big Joe Turner, and the Buddy Rich Orchestra, among others. Zeppelin doesn't actually take the stage until 1:00 A.M. the morning of July 7. This show may have been followed by three dates in Florida.

7/11/69 Baltimore, Md., Baltimore Jazz Festival

Continued festival appearances that place Zeppelin onstage with some of their blues and jazz idols.

7/12/69 Philadelphia, Pa., The Spectrum

Headlining the Spectrum Pop Festival on a bill with Johnny Winter, Al Kooper, Jethro Tull and Buddy Guy.

7/13/69 New York, N.Y., The Singer Bowl

Zeppelin join in for a huge jam at a five-band show headlined by the Jeff Beck Group with Rod Stewart on vocals. Also joining in on "Jailhouse Rock" are members of Vanilla Fudge, Jethro Tull, and Ten Years After. Zeppelin's own tour continues on in the Midwest and Northeast with shows at the music halls in Cleveland and Cincinnati, and Pittsburgh.

7/18–19/69 Chicago, Ill., The Kinetic Playground

Supported by Savoy Brown and Litter.

7/20/69 Detroit, Mich.

Likely an outdoor venue appearance in a summer series.

7/21/69 New York, N.Y., Central Park

Two shows on a sold-out bill with B. B. King as part of the Schaefer Music Festival. "How Many More Times" includes part of "The Woody Woodpecker Theme" and Buffalo Springfield's "For What It's Worth."

7/25/69 West Allis, Wisc., Exhibition Hall, State Fair Grounds

One has to wonder just how a state fair crowd reacted to the sounds and haircuts of the four musicians playing in front of them. Set opens with "Train Kept a Rollin'" and includes "I Can't Quit You," "Dazed and Confused," "White Summer," "How Many More Times" (including snatches of "See My Baby," "The Hunter," "The Lemon Song," and "Everybody Needs Somebody"). "Communication Breakdown" closes the show.

7/26/69 Vancouver, British Columbia, PNE Agrodome

Capacity crowd of 4,000. A review in the *Vancouver Sun* describes the power of Led Zeppelin resulting from the "genius of guitarist Jimmy Page, whose baby face belies his musical message, that of jarring and unnerving the listeners with a fortissimo yowl that never lets up, never allows time for recovery."

7/27/69 Woodinville, Wash., Gold Creek Park, Seattle Pop Festival

The only time Led Zeppelin ever share a bill with the Doors. Plant is less than impressed with Morrison, stating later in an interview: "He was screwed up. He was giving the impression he was into really deep things. . . . You can get into a trip of your own that you don't realize what's going on in the outside world. Morrison went onstage and said, 'Fuck you all,' which didn't really do anything except make a few girls scream. . . . It was really sickening to watch. . . . There were one or two people there crying, 'You're God, you're king,' and I was thinking, 'Why?' "

7/30/69 Portland, Ore.

7/31/69 Eugene, Ore.

8/1/69 Santa Barbara, Calif., Fairgrounds Arena

8/3/69 Houston, Tex., Houston Music Hall

8/4/69 Dallas, Tex., State Fair Coliseum

8/6/69 Sacramento, Calif., Memorial Auditorium

8/7/69 Berkeley, Calif., Community Theatre

8/8/69 San Bernardino, Calif., Swing Auditorium

8/9/69 Anaheim, Calif., Anaheim Convention Center

On a bill with Jethro Tull, one band the members of Zeppelin were never fond of. John Paul Jones told *Guitar World*, "Ian (Anderson) is a pain in the ass. We toured with 'Jethro Dull' once and I think he probably spoke three words to Jimmy or I at any one time. . . . (Page) had a title for a live album when Jethro was playing in Los Angeles: *Bore 'Em at The Forum*."

8/10/69 San Diego, Calif., Sports Arena

Again sharing a bill with Jethro Tull. Zeppelin play two encores which a reviewer the next day said, "cost the promoter an additional couple grand," as the band ran well over their allotted time.

8/13/69 Phoenix, Ariz.

ROBERT PLANT, MADISON SQUARE GARDEN, SEPTEMBER 19, 1970

8/17/69 Wallingford, Conn., Oakdale Musical Theatre
Zeppelin perform in this small Connecticut city, the weekend of the Woodstock festival. Some reports say Led Zeppelin was on the original bill for the Woodstock festival, but pulled out for unknown reasons.

8/18/69 Toronto, Ontario, The Rockpile
Zeppelin are scheduled to play two shows, but cut the first short when it's discovered that the promoter doesn't have enough money to pay the band their full appearance fee. Nonetheless, the band are in good spirits for the second show, as evidenced by Plant's introductions of the band: "I'd like to take this time to introduce Led Zeppelin to you. On bass guitar and Hammond organ, 'King' John Paul Jones. On drums and lead guitar (laughs) . . . on drums John Henry Bonham. On lead guitar, as many chicks as he can find . . . Jimmy Page." At this point Bonham leans in to say, "And the old one, from the labor club, Robert Plant." As they return to the stage for their encore, Plant tells the crowd, "We'd like to do one more for you. It's an old thing by Bing Crosby. It's called 'Communication Breakdown.' " Late set: Train Kept a Rollin'/I Can't Quit You/Dazed and Confused/White Summer/Black Mountain Side/You Shook Me/How Many More Times (including "Over Under Sideways Down," "Travelling Mama," and "Hideaway")//Communication Breakdown. Other Midwest dates likely follow this show in Indianapolis and St. Louis.

8/24/69 Jacksonville, Fla., Veterans Memorial Coliseum
Dates in other Florida cities are likely following this show.

8/30/69 Forest Hills, N.Y., The Pavilion, Singer Bowl Music Festival
A very important show in the early development of the band as they drew a sell-out crowd of 10,000 to the Pavilion, while an estimated 3,000 listen from outside.

8/31/69 Dallas, Tex., Motor Speedway, Texas International Pop Festival
The mostly festival tour of the U.S. ends as a complete success, with Led Zeppelin playing to their largest crowds so far. If that isn't enough, advance orders for *Led Zeppelin II* exceeded half a million copies. Upon returning to England, the band earns their first vacation time, although it is short, as *Led Zeppelin II* must be completed before the band begins their unprecedented fourth tour of America in October. Jimmy vacations in Morocco before returning to Olympic Studios to complete the record.

10/10/69 Paris, France, Olympia
Zeppelin also play a few dates in Germany this month.

10/12/69 London, England, Lyceum Ballroom
Show opens with a snatch of "Good Times Bad Times" before the band cranks into "Communication Breakdown," an introduction that will continue in use on the next U.S. tour. "Heartbreaker" and "What Is and What Should Never Be," from the just completed *Led Zeppelin II*, are added. Partial set list: Good Times Bad Times intro/Communication Breakdown/I Can't Quit You/Heartbreaker/You Shook Me/What Is and What Should Never Be/Dazed and Confused/How Many More Times (including "Eyesight to the Blind" and

a rare "Let That Boy Boogie").

FOURTH U.S. TOUR
10/17/69 New York, N.Y., Carnegie Hall
Led Zeppelin becomes one the first rock bands since the Beatles to play the famed Carnegie Hall, though one of the Carnegie board members is uneasy about letting Zeppelin's type of music in after reading a review of a show which quoted from "The Lemon Song." The band is originally asked to make a one-off appearance at Carnegie Hall. As long as they are returning to America, the band decides to do a short trek across the country for their fourth U.S. tour in less than a year. Two shows on one day, with the second set beginning promptly at 8:30 P.M. with "Communication Breakdown," and ending with a cover of Eddie Cochran's "Summertime Blues."

These shows are very important to the band and to John Bonham in particular, whose performance is inspired by appearing on the same stage formerly occupied by two of his drum heroes. Bonham tells the rest of the band as they take the stage, "This is it lads. Gene Krupa and Buddy Rich, they've all played here, so I'd better be good tonight." *Led Zeppelin II* is also released this month and will eventually reach number one, displacing the Beatles' *Abbey Road*. Enthusiasm for the band is high at Atlantic Records, where at a reception before the shows an employee is quoted as saying, "Led Zeppelin and the

Times/Communication Breakdown/I Can't Quit You/Heartbreaker/Dazed and Confused/White Summer/Black Mountain Side/How Many More Times medley/Moby Dick.

10/31/69 Providence, R.I., Rhode Island Auditorium
11/1/69 Syracuse, N.Y., War Memorial Auditorium
11/2/69 Toronto, Ontario, O'Keefe Centre

Two shows in one night at the same venue. A review the next day said, "the complete 100 minute performances were rather staggering," though the reviewer did note, "a couple of songs from the 2nd album were not as well received as old familiar songs like 'Dazed and Confused,' 'How Many More Times' and 'Communication Breakdown.' "

11/4/69 Kitchener, Ontario, Memorial Auditorium

Page's amplifier blows out and Bonham isn't feeling well, cutting the set to less than an hour. A newspaper review indicates a final Canadian date on the tour in the 19,000 seat PNE Coliseum in Vancouver within a week of this show.

11/5/69 Kansas City, Kan., Memorial Hall

Two shows in one night.

11/6–8/69 San Francisco, Calif., Winterland

Zeppelin share the bill with opening acts Isaac Hayes and Roland Kirk. "How Many More Times" includes "C'mon Everybody" and "Something Else." The U.S. tour ends and the band returns to England. Recording of *Led Zeppelin III* commences following this gig. Early tracks laid down include a powerful, unreleased electric version of "Bron-Yr-Aur," renamed on its bootleg release as "Jennings Farm Blues," and an early version of "Hats Off to (Roy) Harper," which is musically not unlike the released version, but replaces the finished lyrics with an improvisational vocal by Robert Plant singing lines and phrases from whatever blues song comes to mind.

Though working, the band will spend Christmas at home, after spending Christmas in America the year before. John Bonham has brought a Christmas gift with him from the States for his young son Jason, aged three. "I've bought him a great set of miniature drums. It's an absolutely perfect replica, down to the bass drum pedal and hi-hat. Even I can play them."

1/7/70 Birmingham, England, Town Hall
1/8/70 Bristol, England, Colston Hall

Set now includes "Thank You" and "Since I've Been Loving You."

1/9/70 London, England, Royal Albert Hall

Another triumphant appearance at Albert Hall. The over two-hour set garners rave reviews from most in the British music press and the show keeps getting longer. Says Page, "We'd actually finished 'How Many More Times' and were going into 'The Lemon Song,' but the audience was still clapping so we just went into another riff and carried on for a further ten minutes." The show is filmed and recorded by the BBC, and eventually a portion of the audio recording is broadcast on a syndicated U.S. radio special. That segment includes a very lyrically different "Bring It on Home," "Whole Lotta Love," Eddie Cochran's "C'mon Everybody," and "How Many More Times" medley. In later years, this show is frequently mentioned by Page as one of the shows that would be a source for a retrospective live album.

The filmed portion of the show is

Who are the two biggest acts in America. It's like the Monkees never existed." This would be Zeppelin's last North American tour to include small venues.

10/18/69 Detroit, Mich., Olympia Stadium

Zeppelin share a the bill with MC5, Lee Michaels and Grand Funk Railroad.

10/19/69 Chicago, Ill., The Kinetic Playground

Two shows in one night, on a bill with Santana

10/20/69 Cleveland, Ohio, Music Hall
10/21/69 Philadelphia, Pa., Electric Factory
10/22/69 *Led Zeppelin II* is released in the U.S..
10/26/69 Boston, Mass., Boston Garden

Other midwestern and northeastern cities are played this month, including St. Louis and likely a few other markets. Zeppelin are paid $45,000 for this gig.

10/30/69 Buffalo, N.Y., Kleinhans Music Hall

Supported by the James Gang, featuring Joe Walsh. The *Buffalo Evening News* described Zeppelin's sound as "a tin bucket spiralling down a wall and caught by a string at the very last instant, leaving a maelstrom of whirling, concordial sounds. Jimmy Page catches the bucket with the strings of his guitar and the sound discharged belongs to Led Zeppelin." A partial set list, similar to the summer tour shows: Good Times Bad

never officially released, but does come out on a bootleg video in 1989. Included in the video portion are "We're Gonna Groove," "I Can't Quit You," "White Summer/Black Mountain Side," "Whole Lotta Love," "Communication Breakdown," "C'mon Everybody," and a rock 'n' roll medley that includes "Long Tall Sally," "On Down the Line," and "Whole Lotta Shakin' Going On." It is one of the few Zeppelin performances, official or unofficial, ever captured on film or video.

1/13/70 Portsmouth, England, Guild Hall
1/15/70 Newcastle, England, City Hall
1/16/70 Sheffield, England, City Hall
1/24/70 Leeds, England, Town Hall

The final stop of the tour in Edinburgh on 2/7 is canceled when Robert Plant suffers minor injuries in an auto accident. He recovers in time for the start of the European tour.

2/23/70 Helsinki, Finland, Koncerthuset

"How Many More Times" includes a piece of "Be Bop a Lula."

2/25/70 Gothenburg, Sweden, Gothenburg Cirkus
2/26/70 Stockholm, Sweden
2/28/70 Copenhagen, Denmark

Led Zeppelin temporarily bill themselves as "The Nobs" in response to a threat from Eva von Zeppelin, the widow of Count Ferdinand von Zeppelin, a German general who was the namesake of the dirigible. Eva was enraged that the band was using and tarnishing her family name. The band uses the name "The Nobs," as an adaptation of the name of Swiss promoter Claude Knobs. This show was promoted by Fritz Rau, but his name didn't carry the same humor value. It isn't known whether the band alters their name temporarily as a bit of humor to spite von Zeppelin or in response to a serious legal threat. On future tours of Scandinavia and Germany, Led Zeppelin would use their own name.

Other German cities, as well as Brussels, Amsterdam, and

Rotterdam are probably played on this 1970 European tour.

3/7/70 Geneva, Switzerland, Victoria Concert Hall
3/8/70 Munich, Germany, Circus Kroner
3/9/70 Vienna, Austria, Konzerthaus
3/10/70 Frankfurt, Germany, Festhalle
3/11/70 Dusseldorf, Germany
3/12/70 Hamburg, Germany, Musikhalle
3/14/70 Montreux, Switzerland, Jazz and Blues Festival

Dynamic set to close the European tour at the Montreux Jazz and Blues Festival. "We're Gonna Groove," which won't be released until 1982's *Coda*, opens the show. Zeppelin continues to use this cut as an opener until midyear, when it's replaced by "Immigrant Song." We're Gonna Groove/I Can't Quit You/White Summer/Black Mountain Side/Dazed and Confused/Heartbreaker/Since I've Been Loving You/Thank You/What Is and What Should Never Be/Moby Dick/How Many More Times medley/Whole Lotta Love.

FIFTH U.S. TOUR

3/21/70 Vancouver, British Columbia, PNE Coliseum

Zeppelin's fifth U.S. tour will play almost exclusively venues of 10,000 seats or more. A portion of this show is broadcast on a local FM station and is later pressed as one of the earliest known Zeppelin bootleg LPs titled *Pb*. "Communication Breakdown" is played as a medley and includes parts of "Ramble On." Broadcast songs: Heartbreaker/Thank You/What Is and What Should Never Be/Communication Breakdown/Since I've Been Loving You/Whole Lotta Love.

3/22/70 Seattle, Wash., Seattle Center Arena
3/23/70 Portland, Ore., Memorial Coliseum
3/25/70 Denver, Colo., Denver Coliseum

Zeppelin's fifth U.S. tour sets remain similar to those on the just-completed European tour. Plant reminisces about the band's very first U.S. show performed here 18 months earlier. The "How Many More Times" medley includes bits of "Ramble On," "Rosie," "The Hunter," "Boogie Children," and "The Lemon Song." We're Gonna Groove/I Can't Quit You/Dazed and Confused/Heartbreaker/ Since I've Been Loving You/Thank You/Moby Dick/How Many More Times medley//Whole Lotta Love.

3/26/70 San Diego, Calif., Sports Arena
3/27/70 Los Angeles, Calif., The Forum

"How Many More Times" includes "Boogie Mama" and "I'm a Man."

3/28/70 Dallas, Tex., Memorial Auditorium

Set includes "White Summer/Black Mountain Side" and "Bring It on

Home," in a particularly powerful performance.

3/29/70 Houston, Tex., Hofheinz Pavilion
3/30/70 Boston, Mass., Boston Garden
3/31/70 Philadelphia, Pa., The Spectrum
4/2/70 Detroit, Mich., Cobo Hall
4/3/70 Pittsburgh, Pa., Syria Mosque
4/5/70 Baltimore, Md., Civic Centre

"How Many More Times" includes "That's Alright Mama" and "Honey Bee."

4/6/70 Memphis, Tenn., Ellis Auditorium
4/7/70 Raleigh, N.C., Dorten Auditorium

Set includes "Bring It on Home."

4/8/70 Atlanta, Ga., Municipal Auditorium
4/9/70 Tampa, Fla., Curtis Hickson Hall

"Moby Dick" now runs some 25 minutes, coming just before a long "How Many More Times" medley that includes pieces of "Steal Away," "Boogie Mama," and "The Lemon Song." "Thank You" is now preceded by a bit of John Paul Jones's organ improvisation. We're Gonna Groove/Dazed and Confused/Heartbreaker/Bring It on Home/White Summer/Black Mountain Side/Since I've Been Loving You/Thank You/What Is and What Should Never Be/Whole Lotta Love/Moby Dick/How Many More Times medley.

4/11/70 St. Louis, Mo., Missouri Arena
4/12/70 Chicago, Ill., Chicago Amphitheater
4/13/70 Montreal, Quebec, Forum de Montreal

Zeppelin become the first band to ever sell-out the Montreal Forum, but despite this, reviewer Juan Rodriguez of the *Montreal Star*, under the innocent headline "Sell-out crowd greets Led Zeppelin, event of the year," turns in what has to be one of the worst reviews the band ever received: "These are the salad days for hype and Led Zeppelin is the most hyped group of all. Their one overriding gimmick is the loudness of their music (if it could be called that): everything is built around this element. Make enough noise and fans cease to listen; they are mesmerized into a dumb stupor and will accept anything.

"To say that Led Zeppelin is an awful group is merely an understatement. 'Heavy' is the Zeppelin schtick. The volume is turned up high and each note sounds like an avalanche. False meaning is thus attached to each sound; listeners are conned into the belief that because Zeppelin is ridiculously loud, then they must necessarily play important music. Nothing could be further from the truth. The group is ridiculously monotonous. There is a patent lack of rhythm in Zeppelin's noise. . . . No need to worry about mistakes either, because no one knows the difference, including the musicians (a charitable word). Imagination is wholly absent from Zeppelin's performance. . . . None of it is coherent. None of it shows any character. None of it resembles anything of the human spirit that a performer would normally want to express.

"If Led Zeppelin is heavy hype then singer Robert Plant must be the biggest shuck of all. . . . He is without talent as a singer or performer. He waves his arms uselessly, he clutches his microphone predictably. He cannot dance and his moves are graceless and tasteless. . . . As a singer, Plant comes on as if he is being tortured by a band of nasties and ordered to sing. He sounds hung up but that is his only dimension, because screeching is the only way of conveying truth. Consequently he is utterly false. . . . Listening to Page was for me, about as satisfying as watching a television picture signal."

4/14/70 Ottawa, Ontario, Ottawa Civic Centre
4/15/70 Winnipeg, Ontario
4/17/70 Salt Lake City, Utah, Salt Palace
4/18/70 Phoenix, Ariz., Arizona Coliseum

Plant collapses onstage in exhaustion, ending the show prematurely.

4/19/70 Las Vegas, Nev., Convention Center Rotunda

This final scheduled date of the tour is canceled by Plant's physical condition and a protest mounted by fans against the local promoter's ticket prices for their Las Vegas appearance, denying the band their wish to catch Tom Jones's show at the International Hotel. Zeppelin's fifth U.S. tour ends as a success, though crowd control problems plagued the tour in Pittsburgh, Vancouver, and Boston.

With the tour over, the band returns to England. Looking for a place to relax, Plant and Page travel to Bron-Yr-Aur cottage near the Snowdonia mountains in Wales. Though they have gone to the cottage primarily for vacation and not expressly to write songs, they have brought along guitars and a good deal of writing does take place. A recording, commonly referred to as the "Campfire Sessions," documents Plant and Page both playing acoustic guitar, with Plant occasionally singing or adding harmonica. A number of unfinished instrumentals are played, and though they are all in formative stages, strains of what would become "Dancing Days," "Over the Hills and Far Away," and "Stairway to Heaven" can be heard within these instrumental workouts. A few more finished numbers are also worked out, namely "Gallows Pole" and "Down by the Seaside."

During this break between tours, Page also takes time to appear on television on the BBC's "Julie Felix Show," where he performs "White Summer/Black Mountain Side."

5/19/70 Hampshire, England, Headley Grange
Led Zeppelin enters the studio to begin rehearsing and recording their third album during the last two weeks of May and the beginning of June. Rehearsal tapes reveal early versions of "That's the Way," with different lyrics and "Friends," sung with the words to "Bring It on Home." Also worked out are "Poor Tom," which won't be released until its appearance on *Coda* in 1982, "Immigrant Song," played at a much slower pace and including musical pieces of "Out on the Tiles," "Bron-Yr-Aur," which will show up on *Physical Graffiti* five years later and, "Hey Hey What Can I Do," with slightly different lyrics. According to press reports some seventeen tracks are eventually recorded for *Led Zeppelin III* and Jimmy Page completes the mixes in New York City, just prior to the start of the American tour in August, though credits on the album state that it was mixed at Island Studios in London.

6/22/70 Reykjavik, Iceland
6/28/70 Shepton Mallet, England, Bath and West Showground

Headlining the Bath Festival of Blues and Progressive Music 1970, on a bill that includes Jefferson Airplane, Frank Zappa and the Mothers, Santana, and the Byrds. Zeppelin's biggest gig to date, in front of over 150,000 people, and a show many consider to be one of their finest ever. Material from the third album, which won't be released until October, is previewed here, including "That's the Way," which is introduced as "The Boy Next Door." At the end of the show, Plant tells the crowd that they turned down two shows (and nearly a quarter million dollars) in America to play the Bath Festival, though they were paid $60,000, their largest British appearance fee to date. Immigrant Song/Dazed and Confused/Bring It on Home/Since I've Been Loving You/Thank You/That's the Way/What Is and What Should Never Be/Moby Dick/How Many More Times (including "Johnny B. Goode," "Long Tall Sally," "Long Distance Call")/ Whole Lotta Love/Communication Breakdown/ Long Tall Sally.

7/9/70 Cologne, Germany, Sporthalle A small crowd of 4,000 greets the band at the first show of a short German tour. A thousand fans outside demand free admission, and smash windows when they aren't given it.

7/10/70 Essen, Germany, Grugahalle
7/11/70 Frankfurt, Germany, Festhalle
The set includes Page's new acoustic composition "Bron-Yr-Aur," which will be

included on tours until its release on *Physical Graffiti* in 1975. Longtime supporter and *Melody Maker* reporter Chris Welch joins the band on timbales during "Whole Lotta Love."

7/12/70 West Berlin, Germany, Deutschlandhalle

"Whole Lotta Love" includes "I'm a Man," "Hoochie Cootchie Man" and "Long Distance Call."

SIXTH U.S. TOUR

Details on this tour are very unclear, though based on press reports it would appear that the first week of the tour, which was set to open in Cincinnati on August 5, and continue through Quebec, Charlotte, Atlanta, and New Orleans never happened. Press reports from the week August 3 say the band wasn't flying out of England until Sunday, August 9. The answer to the disparity may be contained in a New York press report which says that some dates on the tour were canceled because of the death of John Paul Jones's father. This allowed Page extra time to complete the mixing of *Led Zeppelin III*. Those first dates of the tour were the likely victims of that cancelation.

Following Hampton, the tour likely hit other eastern cities like Boston and Chicago. An advertisement for "Strawberry Fields," an "international carnival of sound and freedom" in Canada appeared in *Rolling Stone* with Led Zeppelin billed for the weekend of August 7-9, but this too appears to have never happened.

8/10/70 Hampton, Va., Hampton Roads Coliseum

Opening night of the delayed tour: Immigrant Song/Heartbreaker/Dazed and Confused/Bring It on Home/That's the Way/Bron-Yr-Aur/Since I've Been Loving You/Thank You/What Is and What Should Never Be/Moby Dick/Whole Lotta Love (including "Moving On")//Communication Breakdown (including "Good Times Bad Times").

8/15/70 New Haven, Conn., Yale Bowl

Similar, though shorter set than Bath, 6/28. "Whole Lotta Love" is preceded by a long medley that includes "Boogie Mama," "Shake," "Move on Down the Line," "Honey Bee," and "The Lemon Song." Encore is a medley of "Communication Breakdown" and "Good Times Bad Times." Immigrant Song/Heartbreaker/Dazed and Confused/Bring It on Home/Since I've Been Loving You/What Is and What Should Never Be/Moby Dick/Whole Lotta Love medley//Communication Breakdown (including "Good Times Bad Times").

8/18/70 Albuquerque, New Mex.

8/19/70 San Antonio, Tex., Municipal Auditorium

8/20/70 Fort Worth, Tex., Tarrant County Convention Center

8/21/70 Tulsa, Okla.

"That's the Way" returns to the set, as does "Bron-Yr-Aur." The "How Many More Times" medley has now been dropped, and in its place is a 26-minute "Whole Lotta Love" medley that includes parts of "Baby Please Don't Go," "That's Alright," "My Baby Left Me," and "Boogie Children." Show closes with "Communication Breakdown." The Tulsa show is followed by dates in Winnipeg and Detroit at the end of August.

9/1/70 Seattle, Wash., Seattle Center Coliseum

9/2/70 Oakland, Calif., Coliseum Arena

9/3/70 San Diego, Calif., Sports Arena

9/4/70 Los Angeles, Calif., The Forum

Source show for the first two widely circulated Zeppelin bootlegs *Live at the Los Angeles Forum* and *Live on Blueberry Hill*. Another show often mentioned by fans as one of the band's best. Two-hour set includes "Bron-Yr-Aur," and a 16-minute "Whole Lotta Love" medley, including "Let That Boy Boogie." Outstanding encore begins with a version of "Communication Breakdown," that includes "Good Times Bad Times," "For What It's Worth" and the Beatles' "I Saw Her Standing There." The second encore is a rare early version of "Out on the Tiles" and the night ends with an outstanding rendition of Fats Domino's "Blueberry Hill."

9/6/70 Honolulu, Hi., Honolulu International Center

Zeppelin play one night, but plans for two weeks of vacation in the Hawaiian sun are abandoned as make-up dates for the canceled first week must be played.

9/9/70 Boston, Mass., Boston Garden

The beginning of Zeppelin's problems in Boston, which had been one of the first cities to support the band, but would be passed over on later tours. The band was scheduled to appear at the Boston College Eagle Rock Festival outdoors in August, but that event was canceled due to "political pressure" from city officials. To make up the shows, Zeppelin agreed to return to Boston and play two shows in one day on September 9. With only 1,200 tickets sold for the early show, a decision was made to cancel it and play only one evening performance, and according to press reports, the promoter and the college ended up losing over $20,000, while Zeppelin walked away with over $60,000 for the one show. This unfortunate circumstance soured much of the local rock press against the band, and reviews of the show were merciless. "Whole Lotta Love" includes "For What It's Worth" and "Ramble On."

9/14/70 Rochester, N.Y. Memorial Auditorium

9/19/70 New York, N.Y., Madison Square Garden

The band plays two shows, one afternoon, one evening. "Communication Breakdown" includes a bit of the Guess Who's "American Woman." First appearance at this venue which Zeppelin will return to during every future visit to the U.S. Mixing for *Led Zeppelin III* was completed just prior to the tour and the record will finally be released in October. A date at the Pennsylvania Fairgrounds, in Allentown, the following day is canceled.

10/5/70

Led Zeppelin III is released in the U.S. Critics who put down the hard-rocking sound of the first two albums, now complain that Led Zeppelin has gone soft. Fans too are surprised by the heavily acoustic sound of the album, and the band spends much of their interview time justifying the change in sound on *Led Zeppelin III*.

10/21/70

Led Zeppelin III is released in the U.K.

1/71 Hampshire, England, Headley Grange

Rehearsals for the fourth album. Tapes from the sessions reveal the building process of the writing of "Stairway to

FOLLOWING

PAGES: THE

FORUM,

LOS ANGELES,

MARCH 24,

1975

Heaven," worked on in three distinct parts on just acoustic guitar and organ, then a full version with vocals added, and finally an over eight-minute version that adds drums and electric guitar. "Black Dog" is worked on at length, as is an unnamed acoustic instrumental. Early versions of "No Quarter" and "The Ocean" are also rehearsed, though they will be recorded later for inclusion on *Houses of the Holy*.

3/5/71 Belfast, Ireland, Ulster Hall
Led Zeppelin embark on a small club tour, playing the same venues they visited during their first U.K. tour, for the same fee, in an effort to get closer to their fans. Unlike the coliseums and arenas just played in America, some of which seat as many as 18,000 people, most of the crowds on this tour are less than 2,000.

3/6/71 Dublin, Ireland, Boxing Stadium
On this U.K. tour, Zeppelin debuts material that will be included on the fourth album, including a song Plant introduces as "a bit of an epic," "Stairway to Heaven." Atlantic executive Phil Carson, a close friend and supporter of the band who joins them onstage on many occasions over the years, joins them on bass during "Rock and Roll." Immigrant Song/Heartbreaker/Since I've Been Loving You/Black Dog/Stairway to Heaven/Dazed and Confused/Going to California/Bring It on Home/Moby Dick/Whole Lotta Love (including "Suzie Q" and "Honey Bee")//Communication Breakdown/Rock and Roll.

3/9/71 Leeds, England, Leeds University
Set includes "You Shook Me."

3/10/71 Canterbury, England, University of Kent
3/11/71 Southampton, England, Southampton University
3/13/71 Bath, England, Bath Pavilion
3/14/71 Hanley, England, Hanley Place
3/16/71 Liverpool, England, Liverpool University
Date canceled and made up in May.

3/18/71 Newcastle, England, Mayfair Ballroom
3/19/71 Manchester, England, Manchester University
3/20/71 Birmingham, England, Stepmother's
"Stairway to Heaven" is dedicated to Roy Harper, who is in the hospital. "Dazed and Confused" contains a long section of "The Crunge," as it often will during the next few years.

3/21/71 Nottingham, England, Nottingham Rowing Club
3/23/71 London, England, The Marquee
3/25/71 London, England, Paris Theatre
Broadcast on the John Peel's Radio One Sunday Show on the BBC April 4, and rebroadcast many times after in both the U.K. and U.S. The Paris Theatre was the BBC's own studio theater used for both music and dramatic performances and Zeppelin played here to a few hundred select fans. A truly majestic performance, including some striking acoustic work from Page and Jones. This is easily the most bootlegged of all Zeppelin performances, and one of the best. Immigrant Song/Heartbreaker/Since I've Been Loving You/Black Dog/Dazed and Confused/Stairway to Heaven/Going to California/That's the Way/What Is and What Should Never Be/Whole Lotta Love (including "That's Alright Mama," "Fixing to Die," "Mess of Blues" and "Honey Bee.")//Communication Breakdown/Thank You.

ROBERT PLANT ON THE 1977 U.S. TOUR

5/10/71 Liverpool, England, Liverpool University
Makeup date for show canceled in March. Following this date, Zeppelin will not play again until mid-June when they do a short European tour through Scandinavia, Germany, and finally, Italy.

7/5/71 Milan, Italy, Vigorelli Velodrome
Zeppelin's only Italian date is marred by the worst riots of their career, as police and security personnel use large quantities of tear gas to maintain crowd control. A bottle is thrown just after the band goes into "Whole Lotta Love" to end the show, and the police attack the crowd with more tear gas, forcing the band to leave the stage through a cloud of gas. Some roadies have to be carried off on stretchers, while a crowd of over 10,000 tries to escape the stadium. Remaining dates in the country are canceled, and Zeppelin would never return again to play in Italy.

7/21/71 Copenhagen, Denmark, KB-Hallen
An amazing set to end the European tour includes the only known performances of "Four Sticks" and "Gallows Pole." Plant tells the crowd that "Four Sticks" is something they've never done before and that it "hasn't got a title yet." Brilliant end of the set includes a long "Whole Lotta Love" medley, "Communication Breakdown" with a long bass solo, "Misty Mountain Hop," and "Rock and Roll," introduced as "It's Been a Long Time."

8/7–8/71 Montreux, Switzerland, The Casino
SEVENTH U.S. TOUR
8/19/71 Vancouver, British Columbia, Pacific Coliseum
8/20/71 Seattle, Wash., Seattle Center Coliseum
8/21–22/71 Los Angeles, Calif., The Forum
Another outstanding set of shows in what has to be Zeppelin's favorite American city. It is at these shows that Page remembers the band receiving a standing ovation for "Stairway to Heaven," even though the crowd had never heard the song before, as the fourth album wouldn't be released for another three months. First night includes "Rock and Roll." A brief cover of the Ventures, "Walk, Don't Run" is used to open the show. 8/22 set: Walk, Don't Run/Immigrant Song/Heartbreaker/Since I've Been Loving You/Black Dog/Dazed and Confused/Stairway to Heaven/Celebration Day/That's the Way/What Is and What Should Never Be/Moby Dick/Whole Lotta Love (including "Take It Easy Baby," "You Shook Me," and "Minnesota Blues")/Communication Breakdown (including "I Had a Dream Last Night")/Thank You.

8/23/71 Fort Worth, Tex., Tarrant County Convention Center
8/24/71 Dallas, Tex., Memorial Auditorium
8/25/71 Houston, Tex., Hofheinz Pavilion
8/26/71 San Antonio, Tex., Municipal Auditorium
8/27/71 Oklahoma City, Okla.
8/28/71 St. Louis, Mo., Missouri Arena
8/29/71 New Orleans, La., Municipal Auditorium
8/31/71 Orlando, Fla., Civic Auditorium
9/1/71 Miami, Fla., Jai Alai Fronton
9/3/71 New York, N.Y., Madison Square Garden
Show closes with "Rock and Roll."
9/4/71 Toronto, Ontario, Maple Leaf Gardens
9/5/71 Chicago, Ill., Chicago Amphitheater

9/7/71 Boston, Mass., Boston Garden
9/9/71 Hampton, Va., Hampton Roads Coliseum
9/10/71 Syracuse, N.Y., War Memorial Auditorium
9/11/71 Rochester, N.Y., Memorial Auditorium
9/13–14/71 Berkeley, Calif., Community Theater
Second set includes "Going to California." Bootleg copies of this show are often misidentified as being from the L.A. Forum. Second night, "Heartbreaker" includes Paul Simon's "59th Street Bridge Song."
9/16–17/71 Honolulu, Hi., Honolulu Intl. Center
9/23–24/71 Tokyo, Japan, Budokan Hall
First ever shows in Japan. Every night during "Whole Lotta Love" the band include any of a few dozen rock 'n' roll oldies, and usually "How Many More Times," "You Shook Me," and "Good Times Bad Times." Experimentation in the medley probably peaks at these shows, as the band recognize they can do no wrong and search for familiar tunes to an audience that speaks a different language. 9/24 set: Immigrant Song/Heartbreaker/Since I've Been Loving You/Black Dog/Dazed and Confused/Stairway to Heaven/Celebration Day/That's the Way/Going to California/Tangerine/What Is and What Should Never Be/Moby Dick/Whole Lotta Love (including "Boogie Mama," Bo Diddley's "I'm a Man," Buddy Holly's "Rave On," and "Hello Mary Lou")//Thank You/Communication Breakdown.
9/27/71 Hiroshima, Japan, Hiroshima Public Gymnasium
Benefit concert for victims of the atomic bomb blast in 1945, this is one of the few charity shows Zeppelin will ever play. Same set as 9/24, but without "Tangerine" and "Thank You." "Whole Lotta Love" includes snatches of "Boogie Mama" and "Be Bop a Lula."
9/28–29/71 Osaka, Japan, Osaka Festival Hall
On the 28th "Tangerine" returns to the set the first night and the medley includes "High Heeled Sneakers," "Bachelor Boy," and "Maybelline," while the acoustic set contains brief renditions of "Down by the Riverside," and an acapella attempt at "We Shall Overcome." Zeppelin also uses snatches of "Please Please Me" and "From Me to You" to introduce "Celebration Day." Final night of the Japanese tour is the longest of the five, highlighted again by an incredible medley including "I Gotta Know," "Twist and Shout," "Fortune Teller," and a brief version of "Smoke Gets in Your Eyes." Only performance on this tour of "Rock and Roll," which will open every show on the 1972 Japanese tour. The band receives enormous press coverage in Japan, and the shows are successful, prompting immediate plans for a return trip in 1972. Immigrant Song/Heartbreaker/Since I've Been Loving You/Black Dog/Dazed and Confused/Stairway to Heaven/Celebration Day/That's the Way/Going to California/Tangerine/Friends/What Is and What Should Never Be/Moby Dick/Whole Lotta Love medley//Communication Breakdown/Thank You/Rock and Roll.
11/8/71
Led Zeppelin IV is released without an official title in the United States. The album sleeve itself carries neither the album name nor the band's name. It becomes the biggest selling album ever, largely on the basis of the song "Stairway to Heaven."
11/11/71 Newcastle, England, City Hall
11/12/71 Sunderland, England, Locarno

11/13/71 Dundee, Scotland, Caird Hall
11/16/71 Ipswich, England, St. Mathew's Baths
11/17/71 Birmingham, England, Kinetic Circus
11/18/71 Sheffield, England, Sheffield University
11/19/71
Led Zeppelin IV is released in the U.K.
11/20–21/71 London, England, Wembley Empire Pool
Zeppelin are supported at these dates not only by fellow bands Stone the Crows (featuring Maggie Bell who would later sign with Zeppelin's label Swan Song) and Bronco, but jugglers, trapeze artists, and performing pigs to give the shows circus feel at this Electric Magic Festival appearance.
11/24/71 Manchester, England, Free Trade Hall
Set includes "Bron-Y-Aur Stomp."
11/25/71 Leicester, England, University of Leicester
11/29/71 Liverpool, England, Liverpool Stadium
11/30/71 Manchester, England, Kings Hall Belle Vue
12/2/71 Bournemouth, England, Royal Ballrooms
"I Can't Quit You" is included in the "Whole Lotta Love" medley, on the closing night of the U.K. tour.
2/16/72 Perth, Australia, Subiaco Oval
Following vacation time in Bombay and a stop in Singapore, where the band had planned a show, but were denied admittance into the country because of their long hair, Led Zeppelin go down under. The first show of the Australian tour suffers from crowd control problems when hundreds of fans climb fences or, in some cases, use wire cutters to get through fences into the show. Police respond in a somewhat brutal manner, raising the indignation of the mayor and the members of the band.
2/19/72 Adelaide, Australia, Memorial Drive
First outdoor afternoon gig in two years, since playing pop festivals two years earlier.
2/20/72 Melbourne, Australia, Kooyong Tennis Courts
Plant is not feeling well, though he tells the crowd that the doctor told him that Tom Jones had been worse during his trip down under.
2/23/72 Auckland, New Zealand, Western Spring Stadium
Led Zeppelin play to 25,000 fans, a huge crowd considering the size of both the city and country.
2/24/72 Brisbane, Australia, Festival Hall
2/27/72 Sydney, Australia, Showgrounds
Australian tour ends and Plant and Page return to England via Bombay. While there, they do some experimental recording with the Bombay Symphony Orchestra, recording versions of "Friends" and "Four Sticks." After that, they return to England, where in May they begin work on the fifth album at Olympic Studios, which has just been equipped with a state-of-the-art 16-track recording system. Journalist Ritchie Yorke is invited to visit the studio, where he reports hearing two of the new songs, "Dancing Days" and a song he calls "Slush," which would later be renamed "The Song Remains the Same." Plant is not present at some of the sessions as his son Karac has just been born.

JIMMY PAGE,

EIGHTH U.S. TOUR
6/6/72 Detroit, Mich., Cobo Hall
6/7/72 Montreal, Quebec, Forum de Montreal

CHICAGO

STADIUM,

APRIL 7, 1977

6/9/72 Charlotte, N.C., Memorial Coliseum
Led Zeppelin's seventh U.S. tour begins without any new songs in the set, but some are added quickly in the next two weeks. Zeppelin's sets are now stretching over two and a half hours. Returning for the encore, Plant tells the crowd, "We were on our way to the airport and we couldn't do it." Immigrant Song/Heartbreaker/Celebration Day/Black Dog/Since I've Been Loving You/Stairway to Heaven/Tangerine/Dazed and Confused/That's the Way/Bron-Y-Aur Stomp/What Is and What Should Never Be/Moby Dick/Whole Lotta Love medley/Rock and Roll//Communication Breakdown.

6/10/72 Buffalo, N.Y., Memorial Auditorium
6/11/72 Baltimore, Md., Civic Center
Set closes with "Communication Breakdown."

6/13/72 Philadelphia, Pa., The Spectrum
6/14–15/72 Uniondale, N.Y., Nassau Coliseum
The advertisement for these shows states emphatically, "Very few groups can create vibrations like Led Zeppelin. They've captured it on records, and in concert, they bring the art of audience involvement to new heights. It's been a year since they've been in the states. Don't miss their only New York concert." Second night encore includes "Thank You," "Bring It on Home," "Rock and Roll," and "Communication Breakdown."

6/17/72 Portland, Ore., Memorial Coliseum
6/18–19/72 Seattle, Wash., Seattle Center Coliseum
A Vancouver date is scrapped when fans scuffle and vandalize while waiting for tickets, sending many of them to Seattle. Second night set is considered one of Zeppelin's finest ever, including the only known complete version of "Black Country Woman." This is the first known show to contain "Dancing Days," "The Ocean," and "Over the Hills and Far Away." "Dancing Days" is played twice in fact, closing the show as the last song of a nearly 45 minute encore. Jones's organ solo before "Thank You," includes bits of "Amazing Grace" and "Everyday People." Immigrant Song/Heartbreaker/Black Dog/The Ocean/Since I've Been Loving You/Stairway to Heaven/Going to California/Black Country Woman/That's the Way/Tangerine/Bron-Y-Aur Stomp/Dazed and Confused/What Is and What Should Never Be/Dancing Days/Moby Dick/Whole Lotta Love (including "Boogie Children" and "Let's Have a Party")//Hello Mary Lou/Only the Lonely/Heartbreak Hotel/Going Down Slow/Rock and Roll/Louie Louie/Thank You/Money/ Over the Hills and Far Away/Dancing Days.

6/21/72 Denver, Colo., Denver Coliseum
6/22/72 San Bernardino, Calif., Swing Auditorium
6/25/72 Los Angeles, Calif., The Forum
Another triumphant appearance at the L.A. Forum, and another brilliant set as Zeppelin further integrate material from the forthcoming *Houses of the Holy* LP into the set. "Over the Hills and Far Away" now moves to the first half of the show where it will remain in future sets. "Whole Lotta Love," contains several long bits of "Let That Boy Boogie," "Let's Have a Party," "Heartbreak Hotel," "Slow Down," and "Going Down Slow." "Dazed and Confused" includes a brief bit of "The Crunge" with vocals.

CONTACT SHEET FROM THE AMBASSADOR EAST HOTEL, CHICAGO, JANUARY 20, 1975

"Louie Louie" and "Everyday People" lead into "Thank You," and the set closes with a long "Bring It on Home."

6/27/72 Long Beach, Calif., Long Beach Arena
6/28/72 San Diego, Calif., Sports Arena
6/29/72 Phoenix, Ariz., Memorial Coliseum
6/30/72 Houston, Tex., Hofheinz Pavilion
7/1/72 Dallas, Tex., Memorial Auditorium
7/2/72 St. Louis, Mo., Missouri Arena
7/3/72 Baton Rouge, La., L.S.U. Assembly Center
7/6/72 Orlando, Fla., Coliseum
7/7/72 Jacksonville, Fla., The Coliseum
7/8/72 Atlanta, Ga., Municipal Auditorium
7/9/72 Charlotte, N.C., Memorial Coliseum
7/10/72 Louisville, Ky.
7/11/72 Cincinnati, Ohio, Coliseum
7/13/72 Philadelphia, Pa., The Spectrum
7/17/72 Boston, Mass., Boston Garden
7/19/72 Chicago, Ill., Chicago Amphitheater
7/20/72 Pittsburgh, Pa., Civic Arena
7/21-22/72 New York, N.Y., Madison Square Garden
10/2-3/72 Tokyo, Japan, Budokan Hall

Zeppelin returns to Japan, turning in two 15-song sets in Tokyo. Opening night includes "My Baby Left Me," "The Lemon Song," "I Can't Quit You," and "Boogie Mama" in the "Whole Lotta Love" medley, and a three-song encore of "Heartbreaker," "Immigrant Song," and "Communication Breakdown." Also unusually, "The Song Remains the Same" is introduced as "Zep," though the second night it will be introduced as "Overture." 10/3 set: Rock and Roll/Black Dog/Over the Hills and Far Away/Misty Mountain Hop/Since I've Been Loving You/Dancing Days/Bron-Y-Aur Stomp/The Song Remains the Same/The Rain Song/Dazed and Confused/Stairway to Heaven/Whole Lotta Love medley (including "Boogie Mama," "Let's Have a Party," and "You Shook Me")//The Ocean/Immigrant Song/Communication Breakdown.

10/4/72 Osaka, Japan, Osaka Festival Hall

Same set as previous night, omitting "Communication Breakdown" so the Japanese audience could go home early.

10/5/72 Nagoya, Japan, Nagoya Public Hall

Same set, with "Immigrant Song" as the only encore, and again "The Song Remains the Same" is introduced as "Overture." During his organ improvisation before "Thank You," John Paul Jones plays a piece of the traditional Japanese song "Sakura Sakura." "Whole Lotta Love" medley includes "That's Alright Mama."

10/9/72 Osaka, Japan, Festival Hall

"Moby Dick" replaces "Stairway to Heaven." Outstanding "Whole Lotta Love" medley including "Lawdy Miss Clawdy," "Heartbreak Hotel," "Wear My Ring Around Your Neck," and "Going Down Slow," followed by a wonderful encore that ends with Ben E. King's "Stand by Me."

10/10/72 Kyoto, Japan, Kyoto Citizen's Hall

Final show in Japan is a short 11-song set. "Stairway" returns. Medley again includes "Going Down Slow" and "Boogie Mama."

10/27-28/72 Montreux, Switzerland, The Casino
11/30/72 Newcastle, England, City Hall
12/1/72 Newcastle, England, City Hall
12/3-4/72 Glasgow, Scotland, Greens Playhouse
12/7-8/72 Manchester, England, Hard Rock
12/11-12/72 Cardiff, Wales, Capitol
12/16-17/72 Birmingham, England, The Odeon
12/20/72 Brighton, England, The Brighton Dome

The evening's encores include a set of Christmas songs.

12/22-23/72 London, England, The Alexandra Palace

Zeppelin's biggest shows to date indoors in London, capping a brilliant year that sees them conquer England, Europe, Australia, Japan, and the United States. Extra long "Whole Lotta Love" medley includes "Somebody to Love," "Boogie Children," "Let's Have a Party," "Heartbreak Hotel," "I Can't Quit You," and "Going Down Slow." This set list would remain fairly constant for the rest of the U.K. and European dates before the 1973 American tour. 12/23 set: Rock and Roll/Over the Hills and Far Away/Black Dog/Misty Mountain Hop/Since I've Been Loving You/Dancing Days/Bron-Y-Aur Stomp/The Song Remains the Same/The Rain Song/Dazed and Confused/Stairway to Heaven//Whole Lotta Love medley/Immigrant Song/Heartbreaker.

1/2/73 Sheffield, England, City Hall

Shows in Preston and Bradford are postponed until the end of the month as Plant contracts the flu. The new album, *Houses of the Holy* is expected this month, but problems with the color printing of the sleeve delay it until March. Encores includes "Heartbreak Hotel" and "I Can't Quit You."

1/7/73 Oxford, England, New Theatre

In introducing "Dancing Days," Plant says "This is a ditty off the new album that's due out anytime between now and August. I've been taking lessons in learning how to sing in American, which has really come to my aid." Rock and Roll/Over the Hills and Far Away/Black Dog/Misty Mountain Hop/Since I've Been Loving You/Dancing Days/Bron-Y-Aur Stomp/The Song Remains the Same/Dazed and Confused/Stairway to Heaven//Whole Lotta Love/Heartbreaker.

1/14/73 Liverpool, England, The Empire

1/15/73 Stoke, England, Trentham Gardens

Plant introduces "Misty Mountain Hop," saying, "This is a song about what happens if you walk through a park and there's a load of hippies sitting in a circle." Partial set list: Rock and Roll/Over the Hills and Far Away/Black Dog/Misty Mountain Hop/Since I've Been Loving You/Dancing Days/Bron-Y-Aur Stomp/The Song Remains the Same/The Rain Song/Dazed and Confused/Stairway to Heaven//Whole Lotta Love (including "Somebody to Love").

1/16/73 Aberystwyth, England, King's Hall

1/18/73 Bradford, England, St. George's Hall

Small crowd of less than 1000. It can be argued that Led Zeppelin's soundchecks were something more than their concert performances. Without the crowds, Led Zeppelin show their more humorous side and perform some favorite songs, including rock 'n' roll classics, which for Robert Plant usually meant any number of songs from the Elvis Presley catalog. Plant was an enormous fan of Elvis, and he rarely skipped an opportunity to sing one of the King's songs, as evidenced by his Honeydripper and Skinnydipper performances of the early 1980s, and his released versions of "Little Sister," with Rockpile on the *Concerts for the People of Kampuchea* charity LP, and "Let's Have a Party," on the 1990 Presley cover song compilation *Last Temptation of Elvis*. Page was only too happy to oblige, playing licks by one of his own idols, Presley's frequent guitarist Scottie Moore. This night's soundcheck includes "Baby I Don't Care," "Blue Suede Shoes," and "Let's Have a Party." Long version of "Whole Lotta Love" in the evening encore includes "Blue Suede Shoes," "You Shook Me" and "Shape I'm In."

1/20-21//73 Southampton, England, Gaumont Theatre

Soundcheck on the 20th includes rousing Plant-led versions of "Treat Me Like a Fool," "Frankfurt Special," and a wonderful cover of the Elvis hit "King Creole."

1/25/73 Aberdeen, Scotland, Music Hall

1/27/73 Dundee, Scotland, Caird Hall

"Whole Lotta Love" includes "Baby I Don't Care," and ends with "Communication Breakdown."

ROBERT PLANT,

THE MYRIAD,

OKLAHOMA CITY,

APRIL 3, 1977

1/28/73 Edinburgh, Scotland, King's Theatre

Two and a half hour show in front of 1,472 closes with "Heartbreaker" and "Thank You."

1/30/73 Preston, England, Guild Hall

3/3/73 Copenhagen, Denmark

3/4/73 Gothenburg, Sweden

3/6-7/73 Stockholm, Sweden, Tennish Allen

Two song encore of "Heartbreaker" and "The Ocean."

3/10/73 Oslo, Norway

3/13/73 Frankfurt, Germany, Festhalle

3/14/73 Nuremburg, Germany, Messehalle

3/16/73 Vienna, Austria, Stadthalle

3/17/73 Munich, Germany, Olympiahalle

3/19/73 Berlin, Germany, Deutschlandhalle

3/21/73 Hamburg, Germany, Musikhalle

Plant introduces "Misty Mountain Hop," saying, "This is a song about when people come to take you away for smoking hashish." "Whole Lotta Love" medley includes a short piece of "Cold Sweat."

3/22/73 Essen, Germany, Grugahalle

"Whole Lotta Love" medley includes "Somebody to Love," "Let That Boy Boogie," "Baby I Don't Care," "I Can't Quit You," and "The Lemon Song."

3/24/73 Offenburg, Germany, Orthenau-halle

"Whole Lotta Love" medley includes "The Lemon Song," "Baby I Don't Care," and "Let's Have a Party."

3/26/73 Lyon, France

3/27/73 Nantes, France

Riots at this show and the previous night in Lyon cause cancelation of shows scheduled for 3/29 at Marseilles and 3/31 at Lille.

3/28/73 Nancy, France

3/28/73

Led Zeppelin's fifth album, *Houses of the Holy*, is released in the U.S. The album had been released in the U.K. a week earlier.

4/1-2/73 Paris, France, Palais des Sports
NINTH U.S. TOUR

5/4/73 Atlanta, Ga., Braves Stadium

Zeppelin's first American stadium date draws nearly 50,000, giving irrefutable evidence by the first show of the tour that Zeppelin is the biggest band in America and the world.

5/5/73 Tampa, Fla., Tampa Stadium

1973 American tour is Zeppelin's biggest to date, opening in two open-air sports stadiums, including this show in front of 55,000 people, the biggest crowd ever to see a single band, breaking the record set by the Beatles at Shea Stadium in 1965. Billed as "An event. The supershow of the year!" Rock and Roll/Celebration Day/Black Dog/Over the Hills and Far Away/Misty Mountain Hop/Since I've Been Loving You/No Quarter/The Song Remains the Same/The Rain Song/Dazed and Confused/Stairway to Heaven/Moby Dick/Heartbreaker/Whole Lotta Love medley//The Ocean/Communication Breakdown.

5/6/73 St. Petersburg, Fla., Bayfront Civic Center Auditorium

5/7/73 Jacksonville, Fla., The Coliseum

5/10/73 Tuscaloosa, Ala., University of Alabama

5/11/73 St. Louis, Mo., Missouri Arena

5/13/73 Mobile, Ala., Municipal Auditorium

5/14/73 New Orleans, La., Municipal Auditorium

Houses of the Holy hits number one in America. Atlantic Records

throws a major party in New Orleans on 5/15 to celebrate.

5/16/73 Houston, Tex., Hofheinz Pavilion

5/18/73 Dallas, Tex., Memorial Auditorium

5/19/73 Fort Worth, Tex., Tarrant County Convention Center

5/22/73 San Antonio, Tex., Municipal Auditorium

5/23/73 Albuquerque, N. Mex., Univ. of New Mexico

5/25/73 Denver, Colo., Coliseum

5/26/73 Salt Lake City, Utah, Salt Palace

5/28/73 San Diego, Calif., Sports Arena

5/31/73 Los Angeles, Calif., The Forum

The first L.A. date, scheduled for the previous day 5/30, is postponed until 6/3, as Page sprains his finger.

6/2/73 San Francisco, Calif., Kezar Stadium

Afternoon show in front of more than 49,000 fans. Show is opened by longtime friend of the band, Roy Harper. The press reports after the show that patients at the University of California Medical Center some three blocks away complained they couldn't nap.

6/3/73 Los Angeles, Calif., The Forum

"Whole Lotta Love" medley includes "Going Down," "I'm a Man," "The Hunter," and "Let That Boy Boogie."

7/6-7/73 Chicago, Ill., Chicago Stadium

First night is the standard '73 tour set, following a few weeks off in Hawaii, but the pre-show soundcheck is something special, beginning with three songs by Chuck Berry, "School Day," "Nadine," and "Reelin' and Rockin'." Also included in the set are "Move On Down the Line," "Love You Like a Hurricane," "Come On," "Peter Gunn Theme," "Dynamite," "Shakin' All Over," "Hungry for Love," and "I'll Never Get Over You." The recording of this material is often credited to the 1975 tour dress rehearsal in Minneapolis.

7/8/73 Indianapolis, Ind., Market Square Arena

7/9/73 St. Paul, Minn., Civic Centre

7/10/73 Milwaukee, Wisc., The Arena

The *Milwaukee Journal* the following morning: "Led Zeppelin was as true to its music as it was last time around. . . . But Led Zep never forgot what it was there for—to play the sometimes sweet, sometimes sour hard rock that has kept it on top while others have come and gone."

7/11/73 Cleveland, Ohio, Richfield Coliseum

7/12-13/73 Detroit, Mich., Cobo Hall

First night "Whole Lotta Love" medley includes "Going Down."

7/15/73 Buffalo, N.Y., War Memorial Auditorium

An ecstatic, if verbose, description of the show appeared in the next morning's *Buffalo Evening News* under the headline, "Led Zeppelin kneads crowd to Silly Putty": "Led Zeppelin doesn't give concerts; they perform physical transformations. . . . The sheer enormity of the sound did it, an enormity that resonates into your paleolithic pity, the cry of the dinosaur summoning out that primitive quickening in the face of monstrosity. . . . Two hours and 50 minutes of massive sensory massage."

BEFORE THE SHOW, OAKLAND STADIUM, JULY 23, 1977

7/17/73 Seattle, Wash., Seattle Center Coliseum

A reviewer in the *Seattle Post Intelligencer* concludes that Zeppelin's music is, "obviously intended to heighten or prolong a drug experience, or may be a drug experience itself," which eventually produces, "a sense of spiritualism that works on the same principle as a church choral service."

7/18/73 Vancouver, British Columbia, PNE Coliseum

7/19/73 Philadelphia, Pa., The Spectrum

7/21/73 Providence, R.I., Civic Center

7/23/73 Baltimore, Md., Civic Center

7/24/73 Pittsburgh, Pa., Three Rivers Stadium

Film footage is shot for inclusion in *The Song Remains the Same.*

7/25/73 Boston, Mass., Boston Garden

7/27-29/73 New York, N.Y., Madison Square Garden

A triumphant three night stand at Madison Square Garden. The first night is used extensively as the main source of concert footage in *The Song Remains the Same* film, though all three nights are filmed at least in part. The success of the tour is muted by the discovery of more than $200,000 missing from Zeppelin's deposit box in the Drake Hotel safe.

1/74 Hampshire, England, Headley Grange

Rehearsal and recording commence at Headley Grange for Led Zeppelin's sixth album. Later overdubs and mixdowns will take place at Olympic Studios. Known tapes of the rehearsals reveal an early version of "Trampled Under Foot," with very different lyrics and music, also an early version of what would become "In the Light," with lyrics that imply the early title was "Take Me Home," one take of which includes piano. Also worked on the rehearsal tapes are "The Wanton Song," "Sick Again," an acoustic version of "The Rover" and "In My Time of Dying." Despite recording, 1974 is Zeppelin's first full year off from touring since their inception.

2/14/74 London, England, Rainbow Theatre

Page, Plant, and Bonham join Roy Harper.

5/10/74 Los Angeles, CA, Hotel Bel Air

Led Zeppelin and Atlantic throw a party to announce the formation of Led Zeppelin's own label, Swan Song, to be distributed by Atlantic. The label will not only be home to future Zeppelin albums, but the work of other artists including Bad Company and Dave Edmunds.

7/20/74 Hertfordshire, England, Knebworth Festival

Led Zeppelin has been negotiating to be the festival headliner, but despite early press reports to the contrary, the talks fall through and Zeppelin do not perform.

9/4/74 New York, N.Y., Central Park

Page joins Bad Company at the Schaefer Music Festival.

10/31/74 Chislehurst, England, Chislehurst Caves

Party to announce the formation of the Swan Song label in the U.K., includes naked women climbing out of coffins, sacrificial altars and other appropriate cave-dweller fixtures. In November, rehearsals begin for Led Zeppelin's tenth U.S. tour, and their biggest to date.

12/19/74 London, England, Rainbow Theatre

Jimmy Page and John Paul Jones guest with Bad Company.

1/11/75 Rotterdam, Holland, Ahoy Sportspaleis

1/12/75 Brussels, Belgium, Forest Nationale

Zeppelin warm-up for their tenth U.S. tour, trying out new material from the as-yet-unreleased *Physical Graffiti*. Set includes a rare performance of "When the Levee Breaks," which will continue into the first few dates of the upcoming American tour, and then disappear completely. Rock and Roll/Sick Again/Over the Hills and Far Away/When the Levee Breaks/The Song Remains the Same/The Rain Song/Kashmir / The Wanton Song/No Quarter/Trampled Under Foot/In My Time of Dying/Stairway to Heaven//Whole Lotta Love/ Black Dog.

1/17/75 Minneapolis, Minn., Met Center
Before beginning their tenth North American tour the following night, Zeppelin rehearse at the Met Center on the 17th, hamming it up for photographer Neal Preston.

TENTH U.S. TOUR

1/18/75 Minneapolis, Minn., Met Center
1/20–22/75 Chicago, Ill., Chicago Stadium
Zeppelin returns to America with their biggest tour yet, though at the start of the tour, Plant is hampered by the flu, and Page has broken a finger and is unable to play the solo on "Dazed and Confused." So for early dates on the tour, "Dazed" was replaced by bowed version "How Many More Times." Partial set list from 1/21: Rock and Roll/Sick Again/Over the Hills and Far Away/When the Levee Breaks/The Song Remains the Same/The Rain Song/Kashmir/The Wanton Song/How Many More Times/Stairway to Heaven/Trampled Under Foot/Moby Dick.

1/24/75 Cleveland, Ohio, Cleveland Coliseum
1/25/75 Indianapolis, Ind., Market Square Arena
A scheduled date in St. Louis on January 27 is postponed until February due to one of Robert Plant's frequent bouts with the flu, a doctor would occasionally tour with the group.

1/29/75 Greensboro, N.C., Coliseum
Plant has now recovered from the flu, but problems continue as the unruly crowd throws firecrackers and generally misbehaves. Fans outside without tickets are even worse, rioting with police. Rock and Roll/Sick Again/Over the Hills and Far Away/In My Time of Dying/The Song Remains the Same/The Rain Song/Kashmir/No Quarter/Trampled Under Foot/Moby Dick/How Many More Times/Stairway to Heaven//Whole Lotta Love/Black Dog/Communication Breakdown.

1/31/75 Detroit, Mich., Olympia Stadium
2/1–2/75 Pittsburgh, Pa., Civic Arena
2/3/75 New York, N.Y., Madison Square Garden
The first of six New York area dates

2/4/75 Uniondale, N.Y., Nassau Coliseum
Show was scheduled for Boston, but canceled because of crowd control problems during ticket sales. The cancelation prompts Zeppelin's office to issue the following statement: "In seven years of touring America, Led Zeppelin has never had a concert canceled, nor has there ever been a serious incident at one of their concerts. It is unfortunate that the officials in Boston have so little confidence in the young people of Boston—I do not think there would be any problems if the concert was held."

2/6/75 Montreal, Quebec, Forum de Montreal
"Dazed and Confused" returns to the set now that Jimmy's finger has healed sufficiently. Encore includes "Heartbreaker."

2/7/75 New York, N.Y., Madison Square Garden
2/8/75 Philadelphia, Pa., The Spectrum
2/10/75 Landover, Md., Capital Centre
2/12/75 New York, N.Y., Madison Square Garden

Final night in New York City is an outstanding show, with lots of talking to the audience by Robert Plant. "Dazed and Confused" includes "San Francisco," and a long bow passage, while "Heartbreaker" contains a snatch of "That's Alright Mama."

2/13–14/75 Uniondale, N.Y., Nassau Coliseum
2/16/75 St. Louis, Mo., Missouri Arena
Make-up show for canceled January date.

2/24/75
Led Zeppelin's sixth album, *Physical Graffiti*, is released in the U.S.

2/25/75
Physical Graffiti is released in the U.K.

2/27/75 Houston, Tex., Sam Houston Coliseum
2/28/75 Baton Rouge, La., L.S.U. Assembly Center
3/2/75 Bent Harbour, Tenn., University of Tennessee
3/3/75 Fort Worth, Tex., Tarrant County Convention Centre
3/4–5/75 Dallas, Tex., Memorial Auditorium
3/7/75 Austin, Tex., Frank Irwin Events Center
3/8/75 West Palm Beach, Fla., Raceway
Zeppelin is scheduled to headline the Florida Rock festival, but the show is canceled by speedway owner David Rupp, because of conflicts with the concert promoter. Danny Goldberg, vice-president of Swan Song issues the statement: "The group and their manager Peter Grant are very disappointed that they will be unable to play Florida on this tour due to circumstances utterly beyond their control. I know that they have a very special feeling for Florida, due in part to the fact that the biggest concert they ever played was in Tampa." A suggestion is made that Zeppelin play a benefit concert at the Orange Bowl on the same date, but no formal proposal is offered to the band, and Florida is passed over on the 1975 tour.

3/10/75 San Diego, Calif., Sports Arena
Plant admonishes the crowd to calm down a number of times throughout the evening. "Whole Lotta Love" includes "The Crunge," and the encore ends with "Black Dog," while the crowd builds to a frenzy, ignoring Plant's suggestions.

3/11–12/75 Long Beach, Calif., Long Beach Arena
The gray weather the first night prompts Plant to comment that they've come to here and found "English weather in L.A." Second night includes one of the only vocal versions of "The Crunge" in the middle of "Whole Lotta Love."

3/17/75 Seattle, Wash., Seattle Center Coliseum
3/19–20/75 Vancouver, British Columbia, PNE Coliseum
"Heartbreaker" closes the set the second night. Page's jamming this night and at recent shows, during "Whole Lotta Love," seems to be moving close to the riff that will eventually become "Ozone Baby."

3/21/75 Seattle, Wash., Seattle Center Coliseum
After turning in a 35-minute "Dazed and Confused" at the 3/17 Seattle show, Page turns in the longest known performance of "Dazed and Confused," dedicated to Jimi Hendrix, which clocks in at over 40 minutes and includes passages from Joni Mitchell's "Woodstock" and Buffalo Springfield's "For What It's Worth." Unusual set includes the surprise return of "Since I've

Been Loving You" to the set, "Trampled Under Foot," with parts of "Gallows Pole," and a long encore of "Whole Lotta Love," "Black Dog," "Communication Breakdown," and "Heartbreaker."

3/24–25/75 Los Angeles, Calif., The Forum

All three nights in Los Angeles, the band is introduced to the stage by X-rated film star Linda Lovelace. During this week, the five previous Led Zeppelin albums return to the *Billboard* LP chart, behind the number one album *Physical Graffiti*, making Zeppelin the first group in history with six albums on the chart at the same time. *Physical Graffiti* also becomes the fastest album in history to hit the top of the charts, doing so in only two weeks, a feat made even more remarkable by the fact that it is a double album, retailing for nearly twice the price of a standard LP.

3/27/75 Los Angeles, Calif., The Forum

Final show of the U.S. tour is a great performance by all four members, and even though the set list is the same as other shows, the show is a full four hours long, one of their longest ever. "In My Time of Dying" includes a piece of "You Shook Me."

5/17–18/75 London, England, Earls Court

The first two of five triumphant nights, playing to over 15,000 people per night. These shows were Zeppelin's first ever in England to use their full U.S. arena stage and sound system. Zeppelin also invested in a giant video screen to provide close-up views from every seat, the first such usage by any band. The original three-night engagement had to be expanded to five due to unprecedented ticket demand. Opening night set: Rock and Roll/Sick Again/Over the Hills and Far Away/In My Time of Dying (including "You Shook Me")/The Song Remains the Same/The Rain Song/Kashmir/No Quarter/Tangerine/Going to California/That's the Way/Bron-Y-Aur Stomp/Trampled Under Foot/Moby Dick/Dazed and Confused/Stairway to Heaven//Whole Lotta Love/Black Dog.

5/23–25/75 London, England, Earls Court

Shows on the 24th and 25th close with "Communication Breakdown," which includes some lyrics from "D'yer Mak'er." Final night also includes "Heartbreaker." After two months off following Earls Court, U.S. stadium dates are scheduled for August and September. These include dates in Oakland Stadium, August 23–24, the Rose Bowl in Pasadena, September 6, as well as shows in Kansas City, Louisville, New Orleans, Tempe, Denver, and Atlanta. This is to be followed by the group's third tour of Japan, some European dates and the first appearances in other cities of the Far East. Unfortunately, these plans are canceled when Robert Plant and his wife are injured in a serious automobile accident on the Greek island of Rhodos. As the band is on tax exile and can't return to England, Plant recuperates in Malibu, California.

After a few weeks the band arrives and does some rehearsing in Los Angeles, and once Plant has recovered enough to fly, the band reconvenes in Munich, Germany for the quick recording of the band's seventh album, *Presence*. Plans are again made for a large-venue tour that will begin in Europe in November, move to Japan in December, and to warm weather stadiums in the U.S. in January. Once again, a date is set for the Rose Bowl in Pasadena in January, but this tour too is can-celed. Led Zeppelin would not play a formal concert again for over two years.

10/10/75 St. Helier, Jersey (Channel Islands), Behan's Nightclub

Zeppelin make their first appearance since Plant's accident, backing house piano man Norman Hale, who had a big British hit in the early Sixties with his band the Tornadoes, in front of only 350 people. Robert doesn't participate until the end of the set, watching from a seat out front and eventually singing into a boom mike, while Page, Bonham, and Jones, play a 45 minute mixture of Zeppelin tunes and cover songs. Plant won't walk unaided until the first of the year in Paris, where he tosses off the line, "One small step for man, one giant leap for six nights at Madison Square Garden." The band is on these independently governed islands near France because of the low taxation rate and the English country lifestyle, something they miss as they remain away from Britain for tax purposes.

3/31/76

Led Zeppelin's seventh album *Presence* is released in the U.S.

4/6/76

Presence is released in the U.K.

5/23/76 Los Angeles, Calif., The Forum

Plant and Page join Bad Company. During his time off from the band, Page works on his soundtrack score to the film "Lucifer Rising," by Kenneth Anger.

9/25/76

John Peel hosts the last BBC Top Gear program and rebroadcasts "Travelling Riverside Blues" and "Whole Lotta Love" from the '69 Top Gear sessions.

10/14/76

Led Zeppelin's Soundtrack from the Film *The Song Remains the Same* is released in the U.S.

10/20/76 New York, N.Y., Cinema One

World premiere of Led Zeppelin's film, *The Song Remains the Same*. All four members are in attendance and grant some interviews.

10/22/76

The Soundtrack from the Film *The Song Remains the Same* is released in the U.K.

12/12/76 Montreux, Switzerland, Mountain Studios

Jimmy Page joins John Bonham at Mountain Studios to record Bonzo's drum orchestra piece "Bonzo's Montreux." The song is considered for inclusion on *In Through the Out Door*, but isn't released until the *Coda* LP in 1982. In 1990, Jimmy Page mixes this tune together with "Moby Dick" to create one song, and includes the combination on the 1990 boxed set anthology.

ELEVENTH U.S. TOUR

1977 North American Tour will be Zeppelin's biggest ever, with shows running consistently three hours and now highlighted by a short acoustic set, which sees the return of a few songs that haven't been played in many years. Gone from some early dates is "Moby Dick" and gone for good is "Dazed and Confused." Page instead takes a guitar solo each night before "Achilles Last Stand." The addition of this song, "Nobody's Fault But Mine," and others, makes the '77 tour set significantly different from the shows two years earlier. In the encores on the tour, "Whole Lotta Love" is used as a short introduction to "Rock and Roll."

4/1/77 Dallas, Tex., Memorial Auditorium
Led Zeppelin's '77 U.S. tour is originally scheduled for February, set to open in Fort Worth on the 27th, but Plant comes down with tonsillitis, and the tour is postponed a month and a half. Said Plant, after his first show nearly two years, "The whole show possessed an element of emotion that I've never known before. I could just as easily have knelt on the stage and cried. I was so happy. I don't think I've ever sung better in America."

4/3/77 Oklahoma City, Okla., The Myriad
"Going to California" is changed lyrically this night to become "Going to Oklahoma." The Song Remains the Same/Sick Again/Nobody's Fault But Mine/In My Time of Dying/Since I've Been Loving You/No Quarter/Ten Years Gone/The Battle of Evermore/Going to California/Black Country Woman/Bron-Y-Aur Stomp/White Summer/Black Mountain Side/Kashmir/Page solo/Achilles Last Stand/Stairway to Heaven//Rock and Roll/Trampled Under Foot.

4/6–7/77 Chicago, Ill., Chicago Stadium
In four nights, Zeppelin play to 76,000 people.

4/9–10/77 Chicago, Ill., Chicago Stadium
4/12/77 Minneapolis, Minn., Met Center
4/13/77 St. Paul, Minn., Civic Centre
4/15/77 St. Louis, Mo., Missouri Arena
4/17/77 Indianapolis, Ind., Market Square Arena

4/19–20/77 Cincinnati, Ohio, Riverfront Coliseum
4/23/77 Atlanta, Ga., The Omni
4/25/77 Louisville, Ky., Kentucky Fairgrounds and Exposition Center
4/27–28/77 Cleveland, Ohio, Richfield Coliseum
A soundboard tape of the first night becomes the source of one of the most famous Zeppelin bootlegs, *Destroyer*. Though most fans agree that the performance on the four-LP set was nothing exceptional, the tape is the first high quality recording of Zeppelin to surface since the FM broadcasts of '70 and '71. Ironically, the first pressings of the set credited the tape to Seattle, rather than Cleveland. The second night is booted as well, as *The Destroyer*, though from an audience tape. First night set: The Song Remains the Same/Sick Again/Nobody's Fault But Mine/In My Time of Dying (including "You Shook Me")/Since I've Been Loving You/No Quarter/Ten Years Gone/The Battle of Evermore/Going to California/Black Country Woman/Bron-Y-Aur Stomp/White Summer/Black Mountain Side/Kashmir/ Moby Dick/Page solo (including "The Star Spangled Banner")/Achilles Last Stand/Stairway to Heaven//Rock and Roll/Trampled Under Foot.

4/30/77 Detroit, Mich., Pontiac Silverdome
Zeppelin break their own single-artist concert attendance records, packing 76,229 people into the Silverdome. Following this show, Zeppelin take a two-week break and return to England.

5/18/77 Birmingham, Ala., Memorial Coliseum
5/19/77 Baton Rouge, La., L.S.U. Assembly Center

5/21/77 Houston, Tex., The Summit
Another marvelous review in the local press following the show: "In a nutshell, their music is still just what it's always been—tons of overamplified sound and fury, signifying nothing and completely lacking in subtlety (even including the acoustic set). I can only hope they stay away for at least another two years!"
5/22/77 Fort Worth, Tex., Tarrant County Convention Center
Page's guitar solo spot includes a snatch of "Dixie." "Whole Lotta Love" is added to the encore.
5/25–26/77 Landover, Md., Capital Centre
Combined attendance over the four nights of over 78,000.
5/28/77 Landover, Md., Capital Centre
Second-night version of "Moby Dick" includes part of "Out on the Tiles," which will pop up in the song over the remainder of the tour.
5/30/77 Landover, Md., Capital Centre

5/31/77 Greensboro, N.C., Greensboro Coliseum
6/3/77 Tampa, Fla., Stadium
Canceled after 20 minutes due to rain. The band hope to retake the stage after the rain stops, but while waiting, fans rush a barricade, injuring 41. As a result, a prearranged rain date the following day is canceled by local authorities, who ban Zeppelin from returning. The band want to schedule a new Tampa date for their fans' sake, but the authorities make the ban permanent. The band never returns to Tampa.
6/7–8/77 New York, N.Y., Madison Square Garden
Tickets to the Madison Square Garden shows are available through the usual outlets and through the "Tour '77 Contest." Scratch tickets were given out through record stores, and tickets reading "Tour '77" under the black scratch-off bar win two seats, which could be claimed at Atlantic's New York office.

PLANT AND PAGE, KEZAR STADIUM, SAN FRANCISCO, JUNE 2, 1973

Powerful *Times* critic John Rockwell, who had criticized Zeppelin's 1975 appearances, is much kinder this time around, describing the opening night set as a "reassertion of the band's pre-eminence in the fickle youth market. . . . a triumphant reassertion." Acoustic set includes a brief bit of "Rawhide."

6/10-11/77 New York, N.Y., Madison Square Garden
6/13-14/77 New York, N.Y., Madison Square Garden
6/19/77 San Diego, Calif., Sports Arena
Acoustic set includes brief rare version of "Mystery Train."

6/21-23/77 Los Angeles, Calif., The Forum
Over 120,000 see Zeppelin in Los Angeles over six nights. Robert Hilburn's review of the opening night in the *Los Angeles Times*, offers a piece of constructive criticism for the band: "If the show were edited down to two hours, the gap between critics' often cold view of Zeppelin and the fans' adoration would be lessened considerably. Besides the low yield of the solos, the long shows tend to point out the band's limitations as songwriters. The tunes, mostly, are exercises in style rather than substance. The band has little of the intriguing point of view or commentary of the Stones, the Who, Kinks or other more fully satisfying, classic English rock outfits from the '60s. But the best moments of Tuesday's show—which featured excellent lighting, sound, staging values—should keep Zeppelin fans enthralled and may even gain some respect for the band among the skeptical."

The 23rd is an outstanding show that becomes the source of another famous bootleg, *For Badge Holders Only*. Keith Moon guests in the drum seat for "Rock and Roll" and "Whole Lotta Love." The Song Remains the Same/Sick Again/Nobody's Fault But Mine/Over the Hills and Far Away/Since I've Been Loving You/No Quarter/Ten Years Gone/The Battle of Evermore/Going to California/Black Country Woman/Bron-Y-Aur Stomp (including "Dancing Days")/White Summer/Black Mountain Side/Kashmir/Trampled Under Foot/Moby Dick/Page solo (including "America")/Achilles Last Stand/Stairway to Heaven//Whole Lotta Love/Rock and Roll.

6/25-27/77 Los Angeles, Calif., The Forum
"In My Time of Dying" replaces "Over the Hills and Far Away" on the 25th, in a set that closes with "Communication Breakdown." Acoustic set for the final L.A. show on 6/27 includes "Hats Off to (Roy) Harper," and "Dancing Days."

7/17/77 Seattle, Wash., The Kingdome
Third leg of the tour begins in front of 65,000 fans.

7/20/77 Tempe, Ariz., A.S.U. Activities Center
7/23-24/77 Oakland, Calif., Oakland Stadium
Set dressing includes a model of the Stonehenge monument located behind the band, which would later inspire parody in the "rockumentary" film, *This Is Spinal Tap*. Final shows on U.S. soil are marred by the beating a security man receives by members of the Zeppelin entourage. Four (including Bonham and Peter Grant) are arrested and eventually fined. Promoter Bill Graham is outraged and vows to never promote Led Zeppelin again.

7/27/77 New Orleans, La., The Superdome
On the heels of the Oakland incident, the band travels to New Orleans, where what would be their largest American date ever, along with remaining tour dates in Chicago, Buffalo, Pittsburgh, and Philadelphia (in front of over 95,000 at JFK Stadium), is canceled when Robert is forced to return home where his son Karac has died suddenly of a stomach infection. The tragedy affects Plant deeply and the band ceases all activity for the better part of a year, prompting a new round of rumors that Led Zeppelin is breaking up.

5/78 Near Forest of Dean, England, Clearwell Castle
Zeppelin hold their first rehearsals since the end of the '77 tour. This appears to be a reacquainting session, as the band doesn't move to reenter the recording studio for another twelve months.

7/23-24/79 Copenhagen, Denmark, Falkonerteatret
Led Zeppelin return to the city of their inaugural live show for their first performances in exactly two years at a small theatre of only 2,000 seats. 7/23 set: The Song Remains the Same/Celebration Day/Black Dog/Nobody's Fault But Mine/Over the Hills and Far Away/Misty Mountain Hop/Since I've Been Loving You/No Quarter/Hot Dog/The Rain Song/White Summer/Black Mountain Side/Kashmir/Trampled Under Foot/Achilles Last Stand/In the Evening/Stairway to Heaven/Rock and Roll. Second-night is a marked improvement over a rusty opener, and the set includes "Ten Years Gone" and "Sick Again," while "Whole Lotta Love," replaces "Rock and Roll" in the encores.

8/4/79 Hertfordshire, England, Knebworth Festival
First U.K. appearance in four years, and though the critics are unkind, fans and band couldn't be happier. The entire show is videotaped, but remains unreleased in any format, with the exception of a little used promotional clip of "Hot Dog," until the band authorizes the release of videos for "Ten Years Gone" and "Kashmir" to MTV for inclusion on their Led Zeppelin weekend in 1990, the only live footage of Zeppelin shown to the public since the release *The Song Remains the Same*. The Song Remains the Same/Celebration Day/Black Dog/Nobody's Fault But Mine/Over the Hills and Far Away/Misty Mountain Hop/Since I've Been Loving You/No Quarter/Ten Years Gone/Hot Dog/The Rain Song/White Summer/Black Mountain Side/Kashmir/Trampled Under Foot/Sick Again/Achilles Last Stand/Dazed and Confused/In the Evening/Stairway to Heaven//Rock and Roll/Whole Lotta Love/Heartbreaker.

8/11/79 Hertfordshire, England, Knebworth Festival
"Ten Years Gone" and "Heartbreaker" are pulled from the set. "Let That Boy Boogie" is added to the end of "Whole Lotta Love," and the show closes with "Communication Breakdown." Following the show, the Honorable David Lytton Cobbold, who owned the festival grounds, was fined £150 for allowing Zeppelin to play past midnight.

8/15/79
Led Zeppelin's eighth studio album, *In Through the Out Door*, is released worldwide. Speculation runs rampant that the band will tour by year's end, but they won't return to the stage for ten months.

12/29/79 London, England, Hammersmith Odeon
Plant, Jones and Bonham join Paul McCartney's Rockestra at this benefit concert for the people of Kampuchea. Plant also joins Rockpile, singing "Little Sister."

6/17/80 Dortmund, Germany, Westfalenhalle
"Led Zeppelin Over Europe 1980," Zeppelin's first European tour since spring of 1973, begins in Dortmund with shows an-

nounced less than three weeks prior to opening night. The tour through five countries is something of a warm-up for a major tour of the U.S. expected in the fall. The set is shorter than previous tours, just over two and a half hours and void of the long solo pieces like "Dazed and Confused," "No Quarter," and "Moby Dick." In fact, the longest song of the set is now "Stairway to Heaven." Page's solo section has also been omitted from "Achilles Last Stand." All shows open with "Train Kept a Rollin'," a song which Zeppelin hasn't played since they used it to open shows on the their very first tour.

Sets on the tour vary little from night to night, though the encore does alternate occasionally between "Communication Breakdown" and "Whole Lotta Love." Three songs from the new album *In Through the Out Door* are included in the set. Opening-night set: Train Kept a Rollin'/Nobody's Fault But Mine/Black Dog/In the Evening/The Rain Song/Hot Dog/All My Love/Trampled Under Foot/Since I've Been Loving You/Achilles Last Stand/White Summer/Kashmir/Stairway to Heaven//Rock and Roll/Communication Breakdown.

6/18/80 Cologne, Germany, Sporthalle
6/20/80 Brussels, Belgium, Forest Nationale
6/21/80 Rotterdam, Holland, Ahoy Sportpaleis
6/23/80 Bremen, Germany, Stadthalle
6/24/80 Hanover, Germany, Messehalle
6/26/80 Vienna, Austria, Stadthalle
6/27/80 Nuremburg, Germany, Messezentrum Halle
Canceled after three songs, due to Bonzo's exhaustion.
6/29/80 Zurich, Switzerland, Hallenstadion
6/30/80 Frankfurt, Germany, Festhalle
7/2–3/80 Mannheim, Germany, Eisstadion
7/5/80 Munich, Germany, Olympiahalle
Joined onstage by Bad Company drummer Simon Kirke, who takes the drum stool for "Whole Lotta Love," which stretches into a more than 13-minute jam that includes several parts of "Let That Boy Boogie."
7/7/80 Berlin, Germany, Eissporthalle
Bonham's final show is the closing night of the European tour. Set ends with "Whole Lotta Love." The European tour has ended as a complete success and plans proceed to set up the North American tour.
9/5/80 New York, N.Y.
Official announcement is made that Led Zeppelin will tour America beginning in October. The tour is called on the press release "Led Zeppelin, The 1980s, Part One."
9/11/80 New York, N.Y.
The first leg of North American tour dates is announced. The first month of the tour is scheduled to run as follows: Oct. 17, Forum, Montreal, Quebec; Oct. 19–20 & 23, Capital Centre, Landover, Md.; Oct. 22 & Nov. 3–4, Spectrum, Philadelphia, Pa.; Oct. 26–27, Richfield Coliseum, Cleveland, Ohio; Oct. 29–30, Joe Louis Arena, Detroit, Mich.; Nov. 1, War Memorial Auditorium, Buffalo, N.Y.; Nov. 6–7, Civic Arena, Pittsburgh, Pa.; Nov 9, Civic Centre, St. Paul, Minn.; Nov. 10, 12–13 & 15, Chicago Stadium, Chicago, Ill.
9/25/80 London, England, Windsor
John Bonham is found dead at Jimmy Page's home 30 miles outside of London. His death is the result of a tremendous drinking bout the night before. He passed out and never woke

up, choking on his own vomit as he slept. An ad announcing tickets for the upcoming shows appears in the *Chicago Times* this morning, as well as the *Buffalo Evening News*.
12/4/80 London, England
Swan Song issues the following statement from the band: "The loss of our dear friend, and the deep sense of harmony felt by ourselves and our manager, have led us to decide that we could not continue as we were." Though the vagueness of the message causes speculation that the band would reform with new members, Led Zeppelin officially break-up.

The band members go their separate ways. Plant starts anew by singing cover songs, fronting his short lived bands The Honeydrippers and The Skinnydippers, before he issues his first solo album in 1982. Page's first work after the break-up is the soundtrack to the film "Death Wish II," and in 1984 forms a new band with former Bad Company lead singer Paul Rodgers called the Firm. John Paul Jones records a soundtrack album himself, and does some producing, though he is not as public as Plant and Page. Plant tours behind his own band in 1983, but refuses to play any Zeppelin material. Page joins him onstage in London on December 13, 1983, but no Zeppelin material is played.
11/19/82
Led Zeppelin's ninth and final album, *Coda*, is released in the U.S.
7/13/85 Philadelphia, Pa., JFK Stadium
Zeppelin returns at the Live Aid benefit concert. Plant, Page, and Jones are joined by Plant band member Paul Martinez on bass and drummers Tony Thompson (formerly of Chic and drummer on Bowie's Serious Moonlight tour) and Phil Collins. A hasty rehearsal is held the day before, and the performance, though rough, satisfies the crowd and fuels an enormous round of reunion rumors. Page's reaction to Live Aid was mixed, as was to be expected: "Live Aid felt like one hour's rehearsal which we all had after not having played together for seven years. But it was great to be part of it, really. At one point I was almost forgetting why I was really there. I was so worried about forgetting this chord and that chord because I hadn't played the numbers for years. But to be part of Live Aid was wonderful." Live Aid set: Rock and Roll/Whole Lotta Love/Stairway to Heaven.

Following the Live Aid appearance, rumors began anew that Led Zeppelin would reform with Tony Thompson on drums. Some rehearsals with the proposed line-up begin in early 1986, but Plant walks out of the sessions after a couple days.

In 1988, Jimmy Page leaves The Firm to do his own solo work. Plant forms a new band and, after having struggled for the previous two years, his solo career takes off behind his biggest hit to date *Now and Zen*. For his 1988 solo tour, Plant includes Zeppelin songs, stating that enough time and distance had passed for him to be comfortable with the material.
4/17/88 London, England, Hammersmith Odeon
Page joins Plant's band onstage for a mini-Zeppelin set that includes "Rock and Roll," "Misty Mountain Hop," and "Trampled Under Foot." The first Zeppelin reunion since Live Aid.

ROBERT PLANT
ON THE 1971
U.S. TOUR

PLANT AND
PAGE, BRUS-
SELS, BELGIUM,
JUNE 20, 1980

5/14/88 New York, N.Y., Madison Square Garden

A second and more formal reunion as the closing act of a massive show honoring the 40th anniversary of Atlantic Records. Plant and his band are already on the bill, but rumors that Led Zeppelin will perform run rampant. After hours of waiting, Plant, Page, Jones, and Bonham take the stage as Led Zeppelin. Only Bonham was Jason Bonham, John Bonham's son, who Page wanted to fill his father's drum seat for this performance. Page later commented on the night, "It was really Jason's night. The atmosphere was fabulous and I made a few mistakes, but that doesn't make any difference. The greatest tragedy that night was the television broadcast sound. . . . The keyboard sound never made it onto tape. I found that unforgivable." Kashmir/Heartbreaker/Whole Lotta Love/Misty Mountain Hop/Stairway to Heaven

The two years after the Atlantic reunion there are more rumors of a Led Zeppelin reunion. The thought of Jason Bonham taking his father's place seems only natural to many fans. This attention seems to cause Robert Plant to pull away from the band, and in promoting his *Manic Nirvana* LP, he makes many derogatory comments about Zeppelin songs during interviews and states that he is completely opposed to a reunion tour. Nonetheless, in August of 1990, Plant brings Page onstage at the Knebworth Festival in England for another mini-Zeppelin set that even includes "Wearing and Tearing," a song Zeppelin never played live and had intended to release as a single when they had played the Knebworth festival eleven years earlier. Further fueling the rumors, Plant, Page, and Jones, play a short Zeppelin set at Jason Bonham's wedding reception in the summer. The release of the Led Zeppelin boxed set anthology in October 1990 pushes rumors further and joint interviews in support of the boxed set garner publicity for the band.

In 1991 the stories remain the same, and the reunion rumors push on, saying that drummer Simon Kirke will join Led Zeppelin, or that Page is forming a new band with former Whitesnake lead singer and Plant soundalike David Coverdale. An unconfirmed report claims a January 1991 meeting of the surviving members of Led Zeppelin, held expressly to discuss reunion plans, led to a tentative agreement to tour between July and October of 1991, only to be vetoed by Robert Plant hours later, leaving fans in a most familiar place, still waiting, with fingers crossed.

JIMMY PAGE ON
THE 1980
EUROPEAN
TOUR, THE
BAND'S LAST
TOUR

RESOURCES

Celebration Day

The authors would appreciate updates on concert dates, set lists additions, and corrections to be included in any future editions of this work. Write us care of Backstreet Records, P.O. Box 51219, Department Z, Seattle, Wash. 98115-9966.

Led Zeppelin fans may want to consider checking out the numerous fanzines published about the band. *Zoso* is the premier U.S. fanzine and can be obtained by writing to 41 Sutter Street, Suite 1495, San Francisco, Calif. 94104. *Electric Magic* is a new and notable fanzine from Canada available from 186 Bordeaux Drive, Woodbridge, Ontario, Canada, L4L 8B6. *Oh Jimmy* is the leading Jimmy Page fanzine and it is published in both English and Italian. You can reach *Oh Jimmy* by writing Tim Tirelli, Via Pedretti, N. 12, 41015 Nonatola, Modena, Italy. Another U.S. fanzine is *The Ocean*, available by writing 46 Briarwood Dr., Westwood, Mass. 02090. *Proximity* was an important Zeppelin fanzine in the early 1980s and though it is no longer being published, back issues are available from Hugh Jones, Cellophane Square, 1315 NE 42nd Street, Seattle, Wash. 98105. Contributor Robert Godwin has published a complete collector's guide to official and unofficial Zeppelin releases along with a price guide to Zeppelin collectibles which can be obtained by writing Collector's Guide, P.O. Box 305, 688 Brant Street, Burlington, Ontario, Canada, L7R 3Y2. An excellent source of Zeppelin collectibles is Rick Barrett's *Led Zeppelin Catalog*. Write him at P.O. Box 66262, Houston, Tex. 77266-6262.

PHOTO CREDITS

In the Light

ACKNOWLEDGMENTS

Hats off to . . .

The authors would like to acknowledge the contribution and support of the numerous people who helped with this effort, who believed in Led Zeppelin when it wasn't hip, and whose assistance was integral to the creation of this book. Special thanks go to Robert Godwin, Hugh Jones, Bill Bratton, and Neal Preston who still today remember laughter. Essential help was also provided by Paul Newton, Kimberly Preston, Isgo Lepijian, Eileen Archer, Sam Rapallo of *Electric Magic*, Taylor of *Zoso*, Susan Hedrick and Tim Tirelli of *Oh Jimmy*, Bob Kaus of Atlantic Records, Howard Mylett, Jared Houser, Stan Gutoski, Mark Stricherz, Rick Barrett, Stuart Chaseman, Sean Green, Sean Connolly, Hiroshi Marutani, Robert Cornfield, Jesse Reyes, Mary Schuh, David Day, Michael Pietsch, Grant Alden, Jeff Gilbert, Aleister Crowley, Sean Hurley, Joe McMichaels, Laura Gold, Dave DiMartino, Jimmy Guterman, Ira Robbins, Dave Schulps, Jeff McCord, Art Chantry, Margie Harris, Robert Allen, Krista Hudson, Marc Eliot, Chris Charlesworth, Basil Hedrick, Phil Jump, Matt Jaffe, Michelle McMillian, Jeff Kleinsmith, Lara Williamson, Michael Manuel, Rick Sands, Dennis and Ilse Flannigan, R. Tagliabue, Herb Cross, Kevin Larson, Ian Whitley, Beth Roberts, Gillian Gaar, Chuck Erb, Ken McCabe, Bob Zimmerman, Steve Jump, the folks at TMQ, Western Type, Jenny Rose, Chuck at A&A, *The Rocket* Magazine, Harry Horman, Carl Miller, Claude Gassian, Chris Dreja, Herb Greene, Jim Marshall, London Features, Sue Schneider, Michael Zagaris, Chuck Boyd, Art Aubrey, B. Wentzell, Robert Ellis, Courtney Miller, Abby, Julie Welch, Pete Howard, Jeff Lorian, the staff of the Edgewater Hotel, and the many other fans, too numerous to list here. To all of you, we'll let the fifth track on the second Led Zeppelin album say it all, "Thank You."

PRESS RELEASE ATLANTIC RECORDS PUBLICITY

FOR IMMEDIATE RELEASE
FROM: BOB KAUS
DECEMBER 4, 1980

We wish it to be known that the loss of our dear friend and the deep respect we have for his family, together with the sense of undivided harmony felt by ourselves and our manager, have led us to decide that we could not continue as we were.

Led Zeppelin

ATLANTIC RECORDS 9229 SUNSET BLVD. LOS ANGELES, CA 90069